The
Wilmington
Ten

The Wilmington Ten

VIOLENCE, INJUSTICE, AND

THE RISE OF BLACK POLITICS

IN THE 1970S

Kenneth Robert Janken

The University of North Carolina Press   Chapel Hill

This book was published with the assistance of the Thornton H. Brooks Fund of the University of North Carolina Press

© 2015 Kenneth Robert Janken

Jacket illustration: Wilmington Ten press conference, *News and Observer*,
24 January 1978. Used by permission of the *News and Observer*.

Library of Congress Cataloging-in-Publication Data
Janken, Kenneth Robert, 1956– author.
The Wilmington Ten : violence, injustice, and the rise of black politics in the 1970s /
Kenneth Robert Janken.
    pages cm
Includes bibliographical references and index.
ISBN 978-1-4696-2483-9 (cloth : alk. paper) —
ISBN 978-1-4696-2484-6 (ebook)
1. Riots—North Carolina—Wilmington—History. 2. African Americans—
North Carolina—Wilmington—History. 3. Wilmington (N.C.)—Race relations.
4. Wilmington (N.C.)—History. I. Title.
F264.W7J36 2015
305.8009756'27—dc23
2015022646

Parts of several chapters appeared as "Remembering the Wilmington Ten:
African American Politics and Judicial Misconduct in the 1970s," *North Carolina
Historical Review* 92 (January 2015): 1–48.

For Pat

Contents

Illustrations and Maps

Introduction

Wilmington and the 1898 Mentality

The case of the Wilmington Ten amounts to one of the most egregious instances of injustice and political repression from the post–World War II black freedom struggle. It took legions of people working over the course of the 1970s to right the wrong. Like the political killings of George Jackson and Fred Hampton, the legal frame-up of Angela Davis, and the suppression of the Attica Prison rebellion, the Wilmington Ten was a high-profile attempt by federal and North Carolina authorities to stanch the increasingly radical African American freedom movement. The facts of the callous, corrupt, and abusive prosecution of the Wilmington Ten have lost none of their power to shock more than forty years after the fact, even given today's epidemic of prosecutorial misconduct. Less understood but just as important, the efforts to free the Wilmington Ten helped define an important moment in African American politics, in which an increasingly variegated movement coordinated its efforts under the leadership of a vital radical Left.

In the first week of February 1971, African American high school students in the newly desegregated school system in Wilmington, North Carolina, staged a school boycott to protest systematic mistreatment by the city's education authorities, teachers, police who were called to campus, and white adult thugs who harassed them on school grounds. The students issued a list of demands and established a boycott headquarters at a church in town.

As news of the boycott was disseminated through the local media, the homegrown paramilitary Rights of White People (ROWP) organization launched violent attacks on the church and the students gathered there. Enduring drive-by shootings and receiving no police protection, the boycotters and their supporters fought back, establishing an armed guard around the church's perimeter. Some supporters, to this day unknown, burned a number of nearby white-owned businesses, including a mom-and-pop store called Mike's Grocery close to the church. (In the chaos, other instances of arson apparently were committed by business owners eager to collect insurance money.) At the same time Mike's was going up in flames, police shot and killed a student leader who many claim was unarmed. The next morning, an armed white vigilante was shot and killed as he prepared to attack the church.

While city officials had greeted the massive violence against blacks with a yawning indifference, the death of a white provocateur-cum-terrorist stimulated a swift response. Wilmington's mayor finally declared a curfew and the governor mobilized the National Guard, which raided and took control of the boycott headquarters. The authorities' show of force reduced the level of violence in the city, but what calm did return felt sullen, as none of the black students' and parents' grievances had been addressed.

After the rebellion was suppressed, local white officials and the press called the police to task for not being aggressive enough against the boycott. One judge stated from the bench that he would have treated protesters as Lieutenant William Calley had treated the villagers of My Lai. The daily newspaper called protesters hoodlums. There were a few letters to the editor from sympathetic whites who counseled understanding, but the loudest voices issued full-throated howls for retribution.

A year later, in March 1972, smarting still from the uprising and wishing to exact payment for it, local and state authorities arrested seventeen persons on charges related to the week of violence—all of them involved with the protest, none from the ROWP. In September 1972, ten of them—the Wilmington Ten—were put on trial for burning Mike's and conspiring to shoot at the police and firefighters who responded to the blaze. (An eleventh person, George Kirby, was to have been tried with the others, but he jumped bail and the trial proceeded without him.) During the trial, the judge bulldozed the defense, and the prosecutor produced witnesses who he knew would implicate the Ten by lying. With the judge's active assent, the prosecutor illegally excluded most blacks from the jury. Given the legal machinations, after a few hours of deliberation the Wilmington Ten, not surprisingly, were convicted on all counts and sentenced to a total of more than 280 years in prison.

In short order a widespread and worldwide campaign arose to free them. Powered by the grassroots organizing of black nationalist organizations, it came to include adherents of other political ideologies, elected officials, elite public opinion makers, foreign governments, and Amnesty International, which designated the Wilmington Ten prisoners of conscience. In December 1980, faced with both a mobilized domestic and international public outcry and overwhelming evidence of judicial and prosecutorial misconduct, a federal appellate court overturned the convictions.

The case of the Wilmington Ten—Ben Chavis, Reginald Epps, Jerry Jacobs, James McKoy Wayne Moore, Marvin Patrick, Ann Shepard,[1] Connie Tindall, Willie Earl Vereen, and Joe Wright—was outrageous, but in its repression and resistance it was not singular. In Wilmington, the Port City, the modern traditions of spasms of violence, repression, and racial progress had been braided together since the late nineteenth century. And in the modern black freedom struggle of the 1960s and 1970s, the doggedness with which the authorities persecuted the Wilmington Ten was replicated in other places in cases with numbers attached: the Panther Twenty-One, the Charlotte Three, the Ayden Eleven, the Greensboro/ Communist Workers Party Five.

TWENTIETH-CENTURY WILMINGTON, along with the entire state of North Carolina, was shaped by the disciplinary tool of blunt force in response to the economic, political, and social vitality exhibited by African Americans after Emancipation. Violence, the memory of violence, and the continuing threat of violence kept the black population in check. William Chafe's foundational *Civilities and Civil Rights: Greensboro, North Carolina, and the Black Struggle for Freedom* and contributors to David Cecelski and Timothy Tyson's *Democracy Betrayed: The Wilmington Race Riot of 1898 and Its Legacy* clearly analyze the racial paternalism and codes of manners and deference that fixed the narrow confines within which blacks' grievances would be adjudicated. Greensboro's economic and political elites generally confronted the challenge to their rule by utilizing non-brutal methods. During times of outward calm (but subterranean black community dissatisfaction with the segregated status quo), the elites' private philanthropy, such as rehabilitating segregated recreational facilities, created relations of obligation and dependence. Such patron-client ties stifled the creation of a black politics that presented African Americans as full and equal citizens rather than as wards. In the same vein, during times of outward conflict such as sit-ins or other mass protests, the elites and their political representatives insisted on cooling-off periods and cessation of unruly activity before they would agree to negotiations leading to limited and gradual reforms. And, of course, behind their insistence on civil, polite, and orderly dialogue in venues physically removed from mass gatherings lay the ever-present possibility of jail and official or officially sanctioned violence.[2]

The 1880s and 1890s witnessed a remarkable degree of social mobility for emancipated African Americans and their children, who also mounted a surprising challenge to the developing Jim Crow order. As historian Glenda Gilmore convincingly argues in *Gender and Jim Crow*, the first generation of African Americans to grow up in North Carolina after the Civil War achieved a stunning degree of education and developed a high level of communal life, including the growth of denominational networks and publications and the establishment of colleges, normal institutes, and business enterprises. Wilmington's black population was especially prosperous, boasted a large amount of real property, and held stakes in important parts of the economy of what was then the state's largest city. Black Republicans—practically all were Republicans in the late nineteenth century—developed political alliances with disaffected white Democrats-cum-Populists to press for the democratization of state and local politics. Turning back more than a decade of Democratic domination in the post-Reconstruction era, in the 1890s African American politicians ascended to a variety of positions in the state, including judgeships, magistrates, and justices of the peace. In Wilmington, the majority of elected officials were black, as this biracial Fusion movement gained strength.[3]

African Americans' social mobility and political agency, which were manifest in other southern states to some degree as well, were direct challenges that invited forceful responses from the so-called New South industrial, agricultural, and merchant elite. Mississippi began the process of disfranchisement of African Americans in 1890 when it rewrote its constitution. The *Plessy v. Ferguson* decision in 1896 codified the logic of racial subordination as constitutional law. In North Carolina the merchant, industrial, and agricultural elites, alarmed at the headway made by the biracial Fusion movement, mapped an agitational campaign against so-called Negro Rule. Unfortunately, the mass of white workers and small farmers who were learning to cooperate with their black counterparts had not had the time to unlearn their Pavlovian response to the calumny of sexually predatory black men. White women and men were drawn into a white supremacy campaign that included the formation of armed bands to force African Americans from public life. The culmination of the demagoguery was the Wilmington race riot of 1898.

As election season geared up in the summer and fall of 1898, North Carolina's civic elite orchestrated circuit-riding speakers and the placement of articles and editorials in newspapers across the state that threatened blacks and pressed whites to take control—through the ballot or by force or both. In Wilmington, which had an active, alert, and involved black electorate, white vigilantes, forerunners of the ROWP organization of the 1970s, blocked African Americans from voting on Election Day and threatened those who persisted in trying to cast a ballot. Two days later, unwilling to wait for the legal date to assume the offices they had stolen,

Wilmington's scions like Hugh MacRae and ex-Confederate officer Alfred Waddell violently overthrew the local government.

As recorded in the state-sanctioned and exhaustively researched *1898 Wilmington Race Riot Report*, written by LaRae Umfleet to commemorate the riot's centennial, dozens and perhaps hundreds of African Americans were slaughtered. The violence gutted the material basis of black advancement. White elites illegally appropriated black-owned property and forced hundreds of blacks into exile. Until then the Port City's population had been majority black, but afterward, the 1900 census showed, whites outnumbered blacks. With the coup d'état and the subsequent disfranchisement of African Americans, blacks' political institutions were disorganized, as the Republican Party adopted lily-whitism. The GOP purged blacks from its ranks, with the conceit that doing so would keep it competitive in state elections, but to little avail as North Carolina joined its southern neighbors in a white supremacist, Democratic one-party dictatorship.[4] The riot and disfranchisement were the coup de grâce to African American political hopes in the state and much of the South for the next half century. By the time of the Atlanta race riot of 1906, organized black political resistance was impuissant. (The Republican Party did not become competitive again until the mid-1960s, when it welcomed into its ranks the flood of white Democrats opposed to such major pieces of legislation as the Civil Rights Act of 1964 and the Voting Rights Act of 1965. But the legacy of Democratic dominance gripped the state's politics so strongly that it was not until 2012 that the GOP gained control of both houses of the state legislature, with the added bonus of also winning the governorship for the first time in twenty years.)

Not just in the short term but well into the twentieth century, 1898 was an ideological impediment to Wilmington's black communities. Bertha Todd, a prominent black Wilmingtonian and educational administrator who moved to the city in the 1950s and was the students' respected adversary in the February 1971 school boycott, diagnosed the chronic layers of reticence, caution, fear, and conservatism that stifled African American political expression in Wilmington as the "1898 mentality." Anthropologist June Nash studied the lingering effects of the riot on those who lived through the violence and on their children and grandchildren. In "The Cost of Violence," she argues that the African American elites who remained in the city survived by linking themselves tightly to the white elites of Wilmington and convincing themselves that the riot was the work of the mob while suppressing the knowledge that the white elites had organized that mob. Concentrating on self-improvement and uplifting less fortunate African Americans, they both lived dignified lives and stayed in their assigned subordinate places. Black workers, who made up the majority of the community, simply learned to keep their heads down and not talk about the racial violence. Members of what Nash called the "riot generation" lived a life of defeatism, a frame of mind that lasted into the 1960s. Leslie Hossfeld, in *Narrative, Political Unconscious and Racial Violence in Wilmington, North Carolina*, found that the Wilmington riot of 1898 lived in African Americans' memories and suffocated most impulses to engage in avenues of social or political change.

White boosters of Wilmington worked through the two world wars and into the second half of the twentieth century to increase the city's economic fortunes and attract new industry. They alternately buried the memory of the 1898 riot—destabilizing violence was bad for business—and made oblique references to it as a warning to blacks, and especially black workers, to stay in their place. Similar findings of the Jim Crow order's strategy in North Carolina of the iron fist and the velvet glove, of violence and paternalism, are confirmed by several of the *Democracy Betrayed* contributors' essays. It was the school boycott of February 1971 and the subsequent uprising in Wilmington that publicly snapped black Wilmingtonians' political somnolence and fear.[5]

AT ITS CORE, this book attempts to answer a series of simple questions. How did a school boycott lead to what amounted to a week-long uprising? Why did North Carolina and the federal government punish the Wilmington Ten, and why was the new assertiveness of African Americans so fearsome in Wilmington, eastern North Carolina, and the Tar Heel state more broadly? How did African American organizations with disparate political agendas coalesce around freeing the Wilmington Ten, and how was the movement connected to the new black politics of the 1970s that was coming into its own? And how did African American political action intersect with the United States' domestic and international Cold War policy, to the benefit of the cause of freeing the Ten?

Chapter 1 narrates and contextualizes the Wilmington school boycott and subsequent uprising. The students' dissatisfaction with the formally unitary school system in New Hanover County presents an apparent conundrum that the chapter seeks to resolve: Why did black students in a southern city toward the end of the civil rights movement whose principal aim was inclusion protest the integration of the school system? And it explores whether the boycott and attending advocacy of self-defense broke faith with the past history of civil rights activity. The chapter concludes that the contradiction is more apparent than real. Contrary to national lore, whose stamina in the face of decades of mounting research is stunning, there was no clean separation between advocates of nonviolence and advocates of "armed self-reliance," a handy phrase coined by Robert F. Williams of Monroe, North Carolina, and brought to public attention again by Timothy Tyson in his *Radio Free Dixie: Robert F. Williams and the Roots of Black Power*. Rather, there was substantial interchange between proponents of both approaches. Scholars of the black freedom struggle have benefited from David Levering Lewis's 1969 insight in his *King: A Biography* that the power of nonviolence in the Birmingham campaign derived in no small part from the authorities' fear of violence from the rank and file who were beyond Martin Luther King's direct control. By the late 1960s the philosophical debate about nonviolence had diminished in relevance as people in local struggles sought out strategies and tactics that were situationally appropriate and not necessarily ideologically pure.[6]

Likewise, the separation-integration duality is more porous than the national civil rights movement story allows. It is significant that Gregory Congregational Church, which was the boycott headquarters, was part of the multiracial United Church of Christ and had a white pastor. Though not the norm, it was certainly not unheard of for militant black nationalist movements to acquire white allies and participants. Patrick Jones's study of the Black Power movement in Milwaukee, *The Selma of the North*, recovers the central role of a white Catholic priest in promoting the civil rights insurgency. Peniel Joseph's *Stokely: A Life* reveals that even as his rhetoric and public image became more strident and anti-white, Stokely Carmichael maintained fruitful, respectful, and complex relationships with the nonviolent Martin Luther King and Bayard Rustin and a variety of white leftists. Likewise, the Black Panther Party welcomed principled alliances with white radicals, as Joshua Bloom and Waldo Martin detail in *Black against Empire*. The mass demand for the dismantling of the segregated order was not a demand for token inclusion but for full inclusion on terms of equality. In his history of the desegregation of the public schools in Charlotte, North Carolina, *The Long Dream Deferred*, Frye Gaillard records the observations of the Reverend Darius Swann, whose name graces the landmark Supreme Court decision that mandated extensive busing for desegregation purposes. Swann had unique credentials for pursuing his case. Prior to his moving to Charlotte, the Presbyterian minister had in the 1950s been a missionary in India. He not only imbibed Gandhism in its heyday but also experienced a society that was not riven by color prejudice, and he could imagine an order in which his claims on society would not be restricted on account of his race. But, he reflected, his vision would not be met simply by the presence of black children in any number in previously all-white schools. The measure was whether those children would be valued and whether their distinctness would be considered an asset in the common project of building a new society. African Americans rejected the idea that leaving schools that doubled as community institutions; enduring hostile white students, teachers, and administrators; and being excluded from the life of the institution was an acceptable price to pay to sit next to a white child. Historian David Cecelski, in *Along Freedom Road*, chronicled a year-long boycott of Hyde County, North Carolina, schools in 1968 by black parents and students whose alternative was to suffer the ordeal of desegregation; after more than two years of paying the price, black students in Wilmington decided that the terms of the bargain to integrate the schools had to be renegotiated and walked out.[7]

Philosophical debates over nonviolence and separatism did not propel the movement in Wilmington and North Carolina, though those debates did occur. Rather, as chapter 2 argues, what stimulated the growth of the movement was the appearance of organizations dedicated to breaking through the suffocating restrictions of paternalism that the white elite of North Carolina and elsewhere deployed to manage the change in the racial order that they knew they would not be able to stop. The chapter follows three organizations in North Carolina as they promoted their variants of Black Power and struggled to break the gradualist consensus on race liberation: the United Church of Christ's Commission for Racial Justice, the Wilmington Movement organized by the North Carolina chapter of the Southern Christian Leadership Conference, and the Student (later Youth) Organization for Black Unity. What William Chafe identifies as the progressive mystique and Matthew Countryman, in his study of civil rights and Black Power in Philadelphia, *Up South*, calls civil rights liberalism channeled protest into matrixes of negotiations and conversations whose rules were set by the ruling powers. Organizations that relied on tactics of disruptions such as sit-ins and boycotts were disempowered once they were corralled into respectful spaces that emphasized polite manners. In Wilmington, that forum was the state-sanctioned Good Neighbor Council, later renamed the Human Relations Commission, an organization that self-consciously included members of the Ku Klux Klan and the ROWP. The outer limits of change were what the white power structure was willing to accept. In Wilmington, as in other places where this method of management was employed, there was a lot of talk but little action.[8]

The challenge was fabricating a way to break through both the rabid opposition of white supremacist organizations like the ROWP and the persiflage of racial moderates and gradualists, such as those who staffed the Good Neighbor Council. Clearly bombastic Black Power rhetoric was part of the three organizations' plans—emboldening blacks and scaring whites could shake things up and alter the balance of power. But for the most part the members of the three organizations who led and participated in the struggle in North Carolina were not revolutionary poseurs. Certainly, they grappled with and espoused different theories of liberation, but as the Maoists back in that time said, it was imperative to shoot the arrow at the target. That is, their theories of social change had to be tested in practice, and it was through that process that the organizations made gains. And it is of more than passing interest that the composition of the Black Power trend in North Carolina did not eclipse religious activists but rather incorporated black Christian nationalists and found ways to develop united fronts with a range of political actors of different persuasions without sacrificing principles.

Chapters 3, 4, and 5 closely examine the frame-up and trial of the Wilmington Ten, the legal appeal of their convictions, and the development of a nationwide and international movement to free them. The particulars of the harassment of Ben Chavis, the especially odious actions of the prosecution in soliciting perjured testimony and illegally excluding blacks from the jury, and the active assistance of the North Carolina judiciary in all aspects of the legal charade are situated in the context of a nefarious federal government plan to spy on, disrupt, and destroy the Black Freedom Movement known as COINTELPRO and the companion strategy of repression through the legal system. The skill and brilliance of the legal team were essential to the eventual overturning of the convictions of the Wilmington Ten in 1980. Just as important to the freedom of the Ten— more important, if one takes into account the development of sustained political power—was the extrajudicial pressure brought to bear on the case. The multiyear campaign to free the Wilmington Ten that was carried out by religious and secular black nationalists, the Communist-affiliated National Alliance against Racist and Political Repression, Amnesty International, and the Workers Viewpoint Organization of the Maoist New Communist movement was sophisticated in a number of ways. In North Carolina, which was the point of emphasis for the Commission for Racial Justice, the case of the Ten was linked with a multitude of other local issues, such as police brutality and discrimination in the criminal justice system; the Wilmington Ten became a locus for radicals and revolutionaries as well as aspiring politicians. Across the country, different organizations were able to connect the case of the Wilmington Ten to labor unions, church groups, student organizations, and local, state, and federal elected officials who were expressing extreme skepticism of the federal government in the wake of Watergate. Combining education, agitation, and direct action, the major organizations were able to hound President Jimmy Carter and North Carolina governor Jim Hunt and force them to take corrective action.

In addition to providing a narrative and analysis of a sophisticated national strategy, chapters 4 and 5 place the campaign to free the Wilmington Ten in an international context. Building on the scholarship of Penny von Eschen, Carol Anderson, Gerald Horne, Manning Marable, and my own work, among others, these chapters demonstrate the ways in which politically conscious actors utilized the contradictions inherent in the Cold War and President Carter's human rights foreign policy to build international pressure to free the Ten.[9]

The conclusion brings the case of the Wilmington Ten from the overturning of their convictions into the twenty-first century, when they received pardons of innocence in 2012. Returning to the reality that the state of North Carolina ruined lives in order to forestall inevitable change and combat radicalism, the conclusion briefly examines what happened to the individual members of the Wilmington Ten. It also reappraises the movement to free them in light of recent scholarship on the trajectory of African American politics and black radicalism.

Since this century began, the state of North Carolina has pulsed with struggle over the types of issues that characterized the conflicts of the 1970s that are delineated in these pages. Public schools have resegregated, and state government's support for quality education for all has been hijacked by a mania for systems of charter and privatized for-profit schools. People fighting for the reform of the criminal justice system have brought to light many other cases of wrongful conviction, including people serving time on death row. Police misconduct, including excessive violence and deaths, bubble to the surface, as they have in Ferguson, Missouri; New York City; Cleveland; and elsewhere. This and more has brought forth in North Carolina collective efforts to find solutions, including the broad-based Moral Monday movement, which in the summer of 2013 led weekly protests at the state legislature that resulted in the unlawful arrests of nearly a thousand demonstrators. The point of this book is not to celebrate a heroic age of struggle or erect a totem for justice-seeking people of today to venerate. Rather, this book is a contribution to an understanding of a major episode in the Black Freedom Movement and of the circumstances surrounding it and an analysis of why and how it succeeded.

CHAPTER 1

Vigilante Injustice

The events surrounding what would become known as the Wilmington Ten began on Monday, 25 January 1971. A fight between black and white students from New Hanover High School in Wilmington, North Carolina, broke out during school hours at the Wildcat, a student hangout about a block from campus. It spilled over to the campus before being broken up by the police. Several students were injured, including Barbara Swain, an African American tenth grader who was cut with a knife by an unidentified white male student. But when Swain reported her injury to the school principal, he showed no interest in identifying the assailant, instead suspending her and four other black students. This incident capped a month of interracial conflict in Wilmington's high schools. Three days later, one hundred African American students from the city's two high schools assembled at Gregory Congregational Church to discuss their grievances. For instance, school administrators punished black students for fighting while letting whites go scot-free. The principal permitted adult-age white toughs to loiter on campus and assault black students. White male teachers harassed black students, and in one case a coach beat a black student over the head. They also demanded the establishment of a black studies curriculum and the commemoration of Martin Luther King's birthday. Connie Tindall, one of the student leaders, declared Friday, 29 January, "Liberation Day" and announced a boycott of school until the school board addressed their grievances. "We're not getting an education anyway," said another student, "so why shouldn't we stay out?"[1]

The boycott, which continued through the first week of February, was met with white Wilmington's iron fist. The school board clamped down with suspensions and expulsions. The paramilitary Rights of White People group, aided and abetted by the police and the mayor, attacked the boycotters' headquarters at Gregory Congregational Church in nighttime drive-by shootings. In response, students and community members, many of them veterans or active-duty soldiers from nearby military bases, established an armed defense of the church. Other blacks in Wilmington retaliated with arson, and property damage over the week of violence was estimated at hundreds of thousands of dollars. The violence culminated during the overnight hours of 6–7 February, when Mike's, a grocery store near Gregory Church, was burned: the police shot and killed student leader Steve Mitchell, who had gone to check on it, and church defenders shot and killed Harvey Cumber, a white man who made it through police lines, parked his truck in front of the church, and pulled out a gun. On Sunday, 7 February, the North Carolina National Guard occupied Wilmington and imposed some level of order, though racial clashes persisted in the schools and struggles for justice continued in the streets.

The case of the Wilmington Ten emerged out of the events of February 1971. In an effort to lay blame for the violence and remove the effective and popular organizer Benjamin Chavis, the Wilmington police and state prosecutor—assisted by the U.S. Bureau of Alcohol, Tobacco, and Firearms (BATF)—concocted a case against Chavis, eight other black men (five of them high school students), and one white woman. Arrested more than a year after the disturbances, they were charged with conspiracy, burning Mike's Grocery, and shooting at the firefighters and police who responded to the fire. (Ann Shepard was charged only with conspiracy.) The prosecutor, with the assent of the presiding judge, illegally excluded blacks from the jury. He solicited perjured testimony from his main witnesses to convict the Ten, who were sentenced to a total of 282 years in prison. Their convictions sparked a campaign across North Carolina, the nation, and the world to free them. This movement attracted support from religious institutions, black nationalists, leftists, and civil libertarians. It garnered the involvement of Amnesty International and successfully pressured the administration of President Jimmy Carter to take action, too. The movement forced Governor Jim Hunt to reduce their sentences in 1978, which freed most of them after five years' imprisonment. In 1980 a federal appeals court overturned their convictions, and the state did not retry them.[2]

Embedded in the story of the Wilmington Ten are imbricated themes that both define the timeline of the incident and its aftermath and were central to the transformation of black protest and insurgent action into the more recognizable black politics of the late twentieth and early twenty-first centuries. The conflict in the Port City grew from the demands of African American students for an equal and relevant education. In the early 1930s, the great attorney and legal strategist Charles Hamilton Houston identified segregated education as a concentrated expression of all the ills and indignities suffered by African Americans. Following this observation, blacks in Wilmington went to federal court several times in the second half of the 1960s to force the school system to desegregate. But for the high school students of the 1970s, occupying common space with white students was no gift. They insisted on equal access to sympathetic principals, counselors, and teachers. This core issue of educational equality touched off numerous confrontations in North Carolina and elsewhere in the 1970s and continues to do so. The outward forms of the conflicts vary—contestation over ending busing, the diversion of public monies to support vouchers and a proliferation of charter schools, continuing efforts to privatize the public schools, the criminalization of disruptive conduct of minority students while similar behavior by white students is treated as simply a school matter, to identify four that have dominated the news in the early 2000s—but the constant is the continued denial of an equal education to African Americans and other ethnic minorities.

The students who struggled for a decent education in Wilmington's high schools had to craft their own way forward. The city's traditional and established African American leaders were hat-in-hand gradualists. Their recipes for change amounted to acting with rectitude, being patient, and waiting for change to occur. Students who wanted to force change received no help from them. Sensing the shifting national spirit, the students improvised on what they had learned from the Black Panther Party and nationalist and anticolonial ideas. The students' search for protest strategies, tactics, and organization fortuitously met rapidly evolving black nationalist trends in North Carolina, which was a leader in this respect.

With these connections made, local Wilmington activists took up the concerns not just of students but of disenfranchised blacks generally and disseminated an eclectic mix of revolutionary and pragmatic black nationalism. There was a reciprocal effect as well. As the leading black nationalist and revolutionary organizations championed the cause of the struggle in the Port City, the Wilmington Ten became one of the most publicized cases of racial and political injustice. In the 1970s in North Carolina especially but also throughout the United States, women and men who wished to take part in and lead the black freedom struggle had to address this case. Because revolutionaries and black nationalists were guiding the struggle, aspiring African American politicians and race leaders were obliged to join the radicals in a united front. The Wilmington Ten became a prominent example of a new, Left-leaning black politics, one that was concerned with the substantive redistribution of power in America and not merely with a shuffling and reshuffling of names of officeholders. This energetic united front approach held sway into the 1980s, when it was overwhelmed by internal divisions, external repression, and the appearance of the "race leader" from the chrysalis of mass struggle.

African Americans who participated in the Wilmington events or observed them say that the racial trouble in the high schools began in 1968, when Williston, the high school for blacks, was closed down at the end of the school year. As elsewhere in North Carolina and the South, the New Hanover County public schools were under a federal court order to desegregate. But rather than send black and white students to all three of the district's high schools, the New Hanover County Board of Education, over the vigorous objections of the black community, shut down a critical black institution and dispersed African American students to New Hanover and John T. Hoggard High Schools, which had until that point been exclusively white. Community feelings ran high, leading to intensified distrust of the school system.[3] School board chairman Emsley Laney asserted without much explanation that

> we felt it would be very difficult to integrate Williston High School and send white students there. It was in a black neighborhood, and this was never discussed a great deal, but we felt that for the benefit of the community as a whole and the school system, the best thing to do was take the black students from Williston and split them between the two white high schools. . . . Williston was a long-time all-black school, so in the process of integration, we deemed it best to change it, and we felt the best thing to do was to send the black students to all-white senior high schools.[4]

In other words, the community good was defined by what was acceptable to whites.

The effects of such imperiousness rippled through Wilmington's black community. African American educators in the newly desegregated system were denied avenues for professional advancement and shunned by white teachers. Bertha Todd, the Williston librarian and one of the few of either race in the school system with an advanced degree, was left without employment when the school was shut down. Because of her outspokenness over the years, the school board thought to let her go rather than transfer her to an open position at Hoggard. Only the intervention of a sympathetic administrator got her, rather than a white librarian from Sampson County, that job. Still, she said, the white faculty ignored her and her black colleagues.[5] Ernest Swain, a Morehouse and University of Chicago graduate who was principal of James B. Dudley Middle School, was convinced that because of his race he was never seriously considered to be Hoggard High School's founding principal, despite a stellar administrative record. The school board, he said, hired someone whose main qualification was that he was a retired marine major and a disciplinarian. "He tried to clean it out using army tactics, or marine tactics, I guess. He kept them going and coming, suspending them[;] he did what they hired him to do, no doubt about it."[6]

For African American students, the move to the city's two previously all-white high schools was disastrous on multiple levels. Fights with racial overtones were fairly common in the years following the closing of Williston. A bump in a crowded hallway might very well be followed by racist taunts and then fisticuffs. Eight years after the fact, a black student remembered being suspended after a fight while his white opponent was not. They were called "niggers, coons, spooks," and other "racial slurs," recalled "Barnabus." "The racism was blatant, overt, it wasn't hidden, it wasn't concealed racism." "Daniel Banks," a pseudonym for another black student at the time, remembered that he and his friends formed a self-defense squad to fight whites who bothered blacks, especially black females. Timothy Tyson recalled similar episodes when he was in a Wilmington middle school in the early 1970s. In addition, fights were started by nonstudent whites who came to the high school apparently with the intention of harassing blacks.[7]

Some of the insults affected particular groups. Bertha Todd commented that Williston students who were active in student government were forcibly sidelined in their new schools. Coaches refused to play talented black athletes on an equal basis with whites. Connie Tindall, a student leader who later became one of the Wilmington Ten, was perhaps the best-known example. A star football player at Williston with the potential to be a standout in college and even in the professional ranks, Tindall was used sparingly on the Hoggard team. That there were some African American assistant coaches seemed to make no difference. They held little sway over their bosses and were regarded as lapdogs by the students, who demanded that a black coach "function as a coach and not a bell boy."[8]

Other black students were punished for speaking their minds. A student at New Hanover High School who worked part-time as a hospital janitor wrote an essay about what he termed a typical dead-end job for blacks in a typical southern town, and during class discussion he talked about racial discrimination in the labor force. The teacher accused him of being provocative, and the principal suspended him for a week. In another example, a music teacher charged Alphonso Pierce with being disruptive because he would not move to the back of the class and called her a "white bitch." In his defense, Pierce said he was moving to the back and had only mumbled "white bitch" to himself; the teacher, he said, never reacted to the white students who disrupted music. The real issue, he claimed, was that the teacher objected to the leather jackets and Black Panther emblems that he and other black students wore. Nationally, student protests against school desegregation and for civil rights often incorporated a cultural dimension related to personal appearance. Black student revolts sought not only curricular reconfiguration but also to break adult authority's control over personal expression. From students' standpoint, a large Afro hairstyle and Black Power attire were repudiations of a racial system that attempted to limit and control them. Even when articulated aesthetically and not politically, these fashion choices were understood by students and school authorities alike as overt challenges to the status quo. "Barnabus" remembered a history of abandonment of black students by white teachers: "They would take time to advise the white students, you know, go over work with the white students, classroom assignments, and the black students were neglected. . . . [I]f you were just an average student and you were black, chances are your grades were pretty bad, because the teachers didn't take the time that they took with the white students, special tutorial help, you know."[9]

Exclusion of black students from their schools' activities sparked protests. The morning of 7 May 1970 began with about 125 black students at New Hanover protesting the exclusion of black girls from the cheerleading squad and demanding the recognition of black organizations by the school principal. Representatives of the state Good Neighbor Council, which was established by Governor Terry Sanford in 1963 to manage race relations during a time of civil rights insurgency, were called in to mediate, but they could not persuade the students to stand down. Instead, the students gathered in the front of the school, where they were confronted by a group of seventy-five "out of school whites." Just after lunchtime, an adult white female drove up, got out of her car, and made "a number of distasteful comments" regarding the presence of blacks outside the school. A black female student argued with her, and when a black male student joined in, the white woman slapped him in the face. Only when he pushed her in return did the police, who had been present the entire time, intervene: they arrested the male student and struck a different black female student in her face with a billy club. Meanwhile, Hoggard High School was closed for the day following a morning full of fights, also set off by the exclusion of black females from cheerleading. Despite the presence at both schools of aggressive whites, the only arrests were of blacks, and the *Wilmington Morning Star* inflamed the situation with misleading and false reports of blacks run amok. "Tension and anger boiled over into mindless violence," was the paper's lead in reporting the incident; "throughout the troubled day, police rounded up troublemakers." As an injured student was loaded into an ambulance, the article reported, "A school bus loaded with black students rolled up alongside. 'Run over the pigs! Kill the pigs!' screamed black youngsters from the bus." By contrast, Aaron Johnson, a black Baptist minister from Fayetteville and racial conservative on the Good Neighbor Council who was present, noted that "black kids really aren't interested in violence, they just want their grievances met."[10]

Over the summer of 1970, students met under the auspices of the Good Neighbor Council to work out a basis for settling their complaints with school administrators and the board of education. They developed a fourteen-point program, which included the demands that African American students be fully represented in student government and extracurricular organizations, the schools establish a black studies curriculum, the principals administer disciplinary action fairly and become more sensitive to the needs of black students, and black guidance counselors be hired.[11]

As the new school year got underway, administrators were unable and perhaps unwilling to smooth race relations. Hoggard principal C. D. Gurganus stated over the summer that he expected disruptions, and although the schools opened on time, their steady polarization drew the attention of the Community Relations Service of the U.S. Department of Justice. Likely at the behest of the state Good Neighbor Council, two Community Relations Service workers and an attorney from the Civil Rights Division contacted Joe Wright, a protest leader at New Hanover High and later a Wilmington Ten defendant, in an effort to manage the conflict. They asked him "to use his influence as a student leader to encourage others not to resort to violence as a means of resolving their racial grievances against the school administration."[12]

African American students' concerns about safety at school underlay a major disturbance on the day before the December 1970 break. For some time, they had been complaining about the presence on campus of white nonstudents and adults whose only business seemed to be harassing blacks. This seems to have been a deliberate tactic of the ROWP, whose pattern of operation included running armed-car caravans through black neighborhoods and otherwise threatening African Americans. Prompted by the presence of "four large adult males" from Brunswick County, which was the home base of the ROWP, black students at New Hanover High

School threw stones at cars in front of the school. Nevertheless, the four white men were not arrested while seventeen students, including several leaders, were. Ten of them were convicted and given suspended sentences; eleven were expelled from school.[13]

School disturbances during this time were not limited to Wilmington. Between August 1970 and February 1971, clashes between black and white students at more than forty schools in the state—mostly high schools but some middle schools—caused them to be closed for one or more days. At North Forsyth High School in Winston-Salem, which had recently been desegregated, police could neither prevent interracial fights nor a walkout by 300 black students before Thanksgiving. When the school's principal summoned buses to take students home, about 150 black students commandeered seven buses and drove them to a mass meeting downtown. In Lenoir, about eighty miles west of Winston-Salem, 300 black students marched downtown to protest brutality by white students and police brutality and smashed windshields and storefront windows. School was closed for four days in New Bern, about eighty miles northeast of Wilmington, after fights broke out between black and white students over commemorating Martin Luther King's birthday. School officials, with the assistance of the local Good Neighbor Council, had set aside time for African American students to meet, and white students, who were not so gathered, claimed discrimination and refused to go to class. In the aftermath of the fray, the police arrested only black students.[14]

The brush fires that were combusting in individual schools and districts initially burned independent of one another. They popped up with some frequency but did not spread or directly cause another hotspot. Outside the schoolyard, however, there were local and community organizations that were prepared to support students in their struggles and inject some radical nationalist sensibility and logic into them. In eastern North Carolina, protests against racism, segregation, and discrimination in the public schools were organized by the Commission for Racial Justice of North Carolina and Virginia (CRJ), which was under the auspices of the United Church of Christ. The Reverend Leon White headed the CRJ in the state, and Ben Chavis was one of its organizers. A native of Oxford, North Carolina, Ben Chavis was in his early twenties when the 1970s debuted, but he already had substantial experience in the black freedom struggle. The son of public school teachers, he grew up on stories of his illustrious forebear John Chavis, who was born free in late colonial North Carolina and was "during his lifetime probably the most learned black man in the United States." After the American Revolution, in which he fought with the

Virginia colonists against the British, John Chavis became a Presbyterian minister and missionary, spreading the gospel in Maryland, Virginia, and North Carolina to both white and enslaved black congregations. Settling in Raleigh in the early 1800s, he opened a school for the boys of white elite Tar Heels while at night he taught black children. He prospered—until Nat Turner's rebellion in 1831. In response, the state legislature outlawed education for blacks. Chavis was soon forced to sell his property and was exiled to Oxford in Granville County.[15]

With a steady diet of heroic family lore and parents who took part in the activities of the NAACP outpost in Oxford as examples, Ben Chavis from an early age searched for opportunities to involve himself in the struggle. In 1962, at the age of fourteen, the Southern Christian Leadership Conference came to town, and he signed on as an organizer. While still a student at the segregated Mary Potter High School, he led the fight to desegregate the public library. After a year at St. Augustine's College in Raleigh, he transferred to the University of North Carolina–Charlotte in 1966, earning a degree in chemistry and a raft of experience in black radical politics on campus and in the Queen's City's black community. Upon graduation he returned to his hometown with a talent for organizing people and a radical nationalist orientation. With a bias for collective action and solidarity, by late 1970 he moved into the orbit of the CRJ, which now had the higher profile in the area.

In Vance County, Chavis led a campaign against the school board's efforts to maintain segregated schools; black protests became so fierce that Governor Bob Scott called in the National Guard "to quell what they [state leaders] considered to be an insurrection," recalled the Reverend White. The struggle led to students examining other things they wanted changed in their schools, including the observance of Martin Luther King's birthday. In neighboring Warren County, Chavis led weeks of protests against a similar situation at John Graham High School. In November, the Highway Patrol fired tear gas at demonstrators at the county school board offices; in December, several hundred students boycotted classes to demand an end to segregated schools and the hiring of more African American teachers and coaches. Soon, Vance and Warren schools were desegregated, but in many ways it was a Pyrrhic victory. African American students were not made to feel welcome in the formally desegregated curriculum, while white parents resisted the new arrangements by establishing white flight academies.[16]

Bladen County was next, in December. There, black parents fought the closing of East Arcadia High School and the consequent round-trip busing of their children sixty miles to the previously all-white Elizabeth-town High School. Students boycotted classes and with their parents pick-eted meetings of the board of education. At one point in January 1971, classes were suspended at Elizabethtown when bomb-making materials were found under a classroom trailer. School administrators expelled student leaders. The school uprising became intertwined with other issues. In April, the manager of an Elizabethtown screw factory, who was a leader of the Rights of White People organization, was the target of action and anonymous threats because he would not hire black workers. That same month, a group of whites killed a local black resident, and in retaliation, the town's largest department store was firebombed and destroyed. As it did in Wilmington, the ROWP inserted itself into the conflict by asking the governor to allow the organization to mount vigilante patrols to protect "white people in Elizabethtown." Chavis's response was unyielding: "If the white community moves on us offensively, we'll move on them offensively."[17]

The underlying cause of much of the disturbance across North Carolina was the desegregation process. Rather than integrate the schools on the basis of equality by sending black and white students in proportionate numbers to formerly segregated schools, school boards either struggled to maintain racially separate schools or closed black schools and displaced only African American students, sending them to schools where they faced hostile administrators, teachers, and white parents and students. Once there, they were placed in separate classes. "Once again white folks have made decisions that will affect black folks," said Ben Ruffin, a community organizer with the North Carolina Fund who would rise through the ranks of black politics and become chairman of the Board of Governors of the University of North Carolina system until his untimely death in 2006.[18] African American students and others in Wilmington would mount a stiff challenge to the practice of desegregated white supremacy in February 1971.

THE AFRICAN AMERICAN students at Wilmington's two high schools who embarked on a boycott arrived at their decision largely on their own. A group of leaders had emerged as students struggled with school administrators and principals. This core included Connie Tindall and Joe Wright, who were later indicted as part of the Wilmington Ten, and Roderick Kirby (who would soon take the name Kojo Nantambu), Ben Wonce, and Steve Mitchell. George Kirby graduated from high school in 1969, but he had a history of involvement in civil rights activity and lent his support.

The boycott committee addresses a press conference held at Gregory Congregational Church to announce its demands, 1 February 1971. Left to right: unidentified man with back to camera, Ben Chavis, Charles Jones, Joe Wright, Ben Wonce, Richard McKoy, Bernard Morgan, and Steve Mitchell. Photograph from the Wilmington Morning Star, *2 February 1971, courtesy of the New Hanover County Public Library.*

(George Kirby was to have been tried with the Wilmington Ten, but he jumped bail before the trial and did not return to Wilmington until the convictions were overturned.) Charles Jones, unlike the others, was a newcomer to Wilmington and did not have such deep ties to the city. But he "had the gift of gab and was knowledgeable" about protest and revolutionary movements and joined the periphery of the boycott leadership.[19]

Many of the leaders and active students were familiar with the culture and politics of Black Power. George Kirby and his friends considered themselves part of the black revolution—"but not the violent part." At the age of twelve he participated in sit-ins to desegregate downtown and was arrested. He read revolutionary theorists like Eldridge Cleaver, Mao Zedong, and Che Guevara. Wayne Moore was an active boycotter and later was indicted as one of the Ten. Like Kirby, he considered himself an adherent of nonviolence, but he also was influenced by revolutionary writers and organizations like Malcolm X and the Black Panthers. He read widely in high school—Richard Wright's *Native Son* and Chinua Achebe's classic African novel *Things Fall Apart* were two works that especially moved him. His cohort included students who believed in black pride; wore red, black, and green; and sported Afro hairstyles. It was liberating to be able to define oneself, he recalled. Charles Jones began to develop a political consciousness in the sixth or seventh grade through sports, when he read Satchel Paige's memoirs and wondered why blacks had been prevented from playing in the major leagues. Another source for his politicization was being in a military family: Fort Bragg was integrated, and he could not see the sense of segregation. A third source was the antiwar GI coffeehouse in Fayetteville, where he was introduced to the Black Panther Party and its paper.[20]

Yet for all of this interest, radical politics was more atmospheric than essential for Wilmington's African American student activists. Several participants stressed that they were focused on redress of their specific grievances. Aroused by the assault on Barbara Swain and the litany of suspensions and expulsions, they sought help not from Malcolm X, the Black Panthers, or black nationalist organizations in Greensboro but from black churches in town. However, the first three churches they asked and the Boys Club refused the students space to establish a boycott headquarters.[21] The rejection highlighted a gulf between the developing movement and Wilmington's black establishment.

Very few adults had any credibility with the student strike leaders. Connie Tindall recalled that the activists at Hoggard, of which he was the leader, had been approached by the local branch of the NAACP to be on its youth council, but they declined, citing that organization's lack of militancy. More, Tindall indicated distaste for the NAACP and the older generation because they had "rolled over" and did not fight the closing of Williston. Delores Moore, the mother of Wilmington Ten defendant Wayne Moore, had a similar observation. She was critical of Hubert Eaton, the black Wilmington physician who initiated and led the original school desegregation suit; he was a prominent middle-class advocate of civil rights, but he was "out for himself," Moore said, and was not concerned about the majority. According to a report written by a visitor to Wilmington from Duke Law School's Center on Law and Poverty, Dr. Eaton acknowledged discrimination but primarily believed that African Americans "don't want to help themselves. Several drink and are heavily absent and therefore do not make good employees." Like Eaton, the Reverend Edwin Kirton, rector of St. Mark's Episcopal Church, was satisfied by the progress of blacks in Wilmington. A member of the Good Neighbor Council and

Wilmington's Citizen of the Year for 1970, Kirton, whom Tom Jervay, the editor of the black *Wilmington Journal,* called the "fair-hair boy of the power structures," believed that racial unrest was caused by outside agitators. The report from the Center on Law and Poverty concluded that Kirton was "not impatient because he is well-off and has a fine reputation with the city." Bertha Todd, ostensibly part of the older generation of middle-class leaders, believed that her cohort suffered from an "1898 mentality," a reference to the race riot that effectively suppressed African Americans' political and economic power in the city. From that point on, she said, blacks in Wilmington, especially adults, were afraid to speak up and struggle for their rights.[22] In their cravenness, they were quick to distance themselves from the students seeking just treatment.

There were exceptions, of course. Todd, the Hoggard librarian, had the respect of students and the ear of school system administrators. From the time she started at Hoggard in 1968, she worked to ameliorate the racial tensions among students and faculty. She made herself accessible to both white and black students. One of her initiatives was a well-attended lunchtime speak-out during which students confronted each other's prejudices. She promoted African American students' participation and leadership in extracurricular and extramural activities. When the first mass meeting was called at Gregory Congregational Church in the wake of the Barbara Swain incident, Todd attended and helped the students formulate their demands. And yet she was not only in the students' corner: she also informed on them to Superintendent of Schools Heyward Bellamy.[23]

Some of the adults employed by Opportunities, Inc., a local antipoverty agency, were also helpful to the student activists. Its mission was to identify and promote grassroots community leaders and assist in their struggle to fight systemic economic inequality. In the late 1960s, Opportunities focused on correcting problems in public housing. The city's two projects for blacks were predictably dilapidated, while the one for whites was new and well maintained. The housing authority treated African American residents imperiously, often fining or evicting them for minor infractions like having guests stay overnight; housing officials also punished black residents who were active in the NAACP or complained to the black-owned *Wilmington Journal* about local government. Opportunities struggled unsuccessfully in the late 1960s to integrate the housing projects. The organization had an established after-school tutoring program and was a site where black students could ruminate about the way desegregation was proceeding. Among the adults active in Opportunities was Ann Shepard, who later became one of the Wilmington Ten.[24]

The adult Wilmingtonian who was perhaps most sympathetic to the students' situation was Eugene Templeton, the white minister of Gregory Congregational Church, which did agree to become the boycott headquarters. Templeton was born a Tar Heel and trained for the ministry at Union Theological Seminary in New York. In his desire to return to his native state, he interviewed at several churches but found the state's white UCC congregations too parochial and racially constricting. He recalled being asked at several of them which occasion he would celebrate on the second Sunday of February, Boy Scout Sunday or Race Relations Sunday. But things in Wilmington were different. It was the terminus for the Atlantic Coast Line Railroad, and black residents had ties to New York and traveled there and elsewhere outside the city. DuPont had a major factory in town, which also helped to broaden the point of view of Wilmington's citizenry. Although it was unusual for the United Church of Christ denomination to have a white minister for a black congregation, the leadership of Gregory Congregational liked Templeton, and he was hired in 1969. It was, he recollected, a solidly middle-class church, with many members drawn from the ranks of DuPont or employed as teachers.[25]

Templeton was familiar with the student activists. Gregory Congregational ran an after-school program whose tutors included some of them. Under his leadership, the church initiated black history programs that reached into the wider African American community. To connect with poorer black residents, Templeton sat on the board of Opportunities, Inc., and worked with the students, particularly on housing issues. He was impressed with their organizing abilities. They were "very good" at gathering information about discrimination and talking with people who would not talk with the authorities. So when Connie Tindall visited Eugene Templeton and his wife, Donna, in the Gregory parsonage shortly before the boycott and asked for the church's support, it was a certainty that Templeton would agree.[26]

With the permission of the church's trustees and the parents of the boycotters, Templeton organized a freedom school, drawing both on his own knowledge and on that of a group of sympathetic adults in the community, including Patricia Rhodes and Tom Houston, both of whom worked for Opportunities, and Hoggard librarian Bertha Todd. "The essential thing on the boycott as it began was that it was to be a black studies program because both of the high schools had refused to institute any kind of black studies," recalled the minister. On the first day, 29 January, between thirty and forty boycotters, including Connie Tindall and Joe Wright, attended the freedom school; by the third day, one hundred were taking part.[27]

The organizers' knowledge was uneven, but the students were highly motivated and eager to put their lessons into practice. The historical injustices of the 1898 riot in Wilmington and overthrow of the legally elected majority-black city government were known to many of the boycotters and taught to those who did not know. At the same time, while they were familiar with Dr. King, they had not heard of Frederick Douglass. Therefore, mornings were devoted to black history and culture and afternoons to strategy sessions. Observed Templeton, "They were young and they were fairly well interested in what was going on. . . . [T]hey would go through classes, lectures, talk about the strategy with the Board of Education."[28]

Templeton viewed himself not as a leader of the students but as a resource for them. After the first day of the boycott, he understood that what he had to offer the students would not be enough for them to successfully prosecute their fight. The students needed assistance to articulate demands from feelings of injustice and to figure out how to deal with the board of education and sustain a boycott. He was concerned, too, about the students' safety, as he was receiving anonymous phone calls to his home threatening to blow up the church. Though Templeton enjoyed the students' trust, he did not feel that it was his place to tell them what to do. He telephoned his old seminary friend Mac Hulslander in the United Church of Christ's offices in Raleigh to ask that African American support be sent to Wilmington, for both political and educational leadership. The Reverend Leon White, the head of the UCC's Commission for Racial Justice in Virginia and North Carolina, sent Ben Chavis, a CRJ organizer, to assist.[29]

Benjamin Chavis had just turned twenty-three when he arrived in Wilmington on 2 February. And he arrived in style. Charles Jones remembered Chavis driving into town "in a 1970, royal-blue-with-a-half-white-vinyl-top Eldorado. He was wearing a brown fur coat and a big Afro—he looked more like a pimp than a revolutionary." His youthful appearance and swagger may have caused some in authority to underestimate him. Bertha Todd believed that Chavis, as a young adult himself, could not control the student and young adult nonstudent radicals who were attracted to the boycott. Chavis was in over his head and "fell right in with them" rather than led them.[30] And yet he had considerable experience in the movement, having organized school desegregation struggles for the CRJ across eastern North Carolina in 1970, protests against the murder of his cousin in his hometown with the Southern Christian Leadership Conference, and efforts in the black community when he was a student at UNC–Charlotte. He had also attempted to organize a Charlotte chapter of the Black Panther Party and apparently maintained friendly ties to the party after the national headquarters decided not to let his organization affiliate.[31]

Chavis's impact was immediate. He and Jim Grant, a seasoned participant in the civil rights and anti–Vietnam War movements of the 1960s who was now a reporter-organizer for the Southern Conference Education Fund's *Southern Patriot* and other publications, helped to focus the students' demands, publicize the struggle, build community support, and defend the boycotters and Gregory Congregational Church from the attacks by the ROWP.

On 29 January, four days before Chavis arrived, Benjamin Wonce, who led the six-person boycott steering committee, and others met with a board of education advisory committee to present their demands. Their leaflet, "What We Want: What We Believe," was a rough and not always coherent announcement of their grievances that focused primarily on the unfair behavior of the principal of New Hanover High School. How they would elicit fairness from him was not clear, though they vowed to continue "after action has been taken on these matters or as we recognize them (our EIGHT POINTS)."[32] But with Chavis's guidance the boycotters sharpened their demands and course of action. Significantly, Chavis had identified those activists who for a variety of reasons "had a broader view of problems concerning Wilmington." In a leaflet appealing for parental support, the students placed their grievances clearly within a larger context of "white oppression and racism." They claimed that the school board's denial of their demands for a black studies curriculum and relevant black speakers amounted to mental enslavement. They asked their parents to support their efforts to "be respected, not as colored nor Negro but as Black Students," and to join them when they "walk out the slave masters['] classrooms" and rally at the board of education. If there was any doubt about the new mood, it was dispelled with the closing statement on the leaflet: "POWER PEACE and LIBERATION TO ALL BLACK PEOPLE."[33]

At a press conference on 2 February, Chavis insisted that the students' demands were just and that their struggle was not an isolated one. Across eastern North Carolina, black students were paying the price for desegregated schools and were protesting the multiple ways they were shunned in them. Wilmington was simply the latest instance, and he hoped that with the help of the UCC and the CRJ, the local struggles would combine and pursue their grievances on a statewide level. African Americans in Wilmington and across New Hanover County had to come to the aid of the boycott, because "this is not only a student struggle, this is a struggle to the black community and the white power structure." It would be wrong to allow the students to be isolated and have to carry on the struggle by themselves. He specifically appealed for the support of the churches and their ministers, "because the church is the only institution that black folks control." As the boycott's new spokesperson, Chavis set a deadline of noon the next day, 3 February, for the school board to respond to the students' demands.[34]

Chavis was experienced enough to know that the conflict might spread beyond the schoolyard. He disputed the canard that outside agitators had stirred up otherwise peaceful blacks in Wilmington. Asked by a reporter whether his tactics were designed to provoke a confrontation with the police, Highway Patrol, and National Guard, Chavis said unequivocally that was not the case. The students' complaints were with the school board, not law enforcement. However, he said, "the system" had a history of bringing in outside police to keep the movement down, and "if the National Guard and the Highway Patrol come in and try to run interference for the school board, now that [is] another question. . . . [T]he black community will defend itself now if the Highway Patrol or National Guard inflicts offensive maneuvers against the black community." And if the government chose to bring in these outsiders—or vigilantes—to stop the boycott, he could also "bring in outside support to make our movement more strong. You know, we are not playing, this is very serious. This is about the liberation of the black community in Wilmington, and this is what . . . this struggle will amount to—the total liberation of black folks in this county."[35]

Superintendent Heyward Bellamy rejected the students' demands. At a community meeting at Gregory Congregational Church on the evening of 2 February, Bellamy told the assembled students, their parents, and others that they needed to respect the established chain of authority and bring their grievances to the school principals—the very persons in authority who had been showing African American students such little regard. He dodged the issue of a black studies curriculum by saying that the schools would try "to include the contributions of all ethnic groups in all appropriate areas of the curriculum." But the students' and parents' experience completely contradicted Bellamy's assertion, as neither Hoggard nor New Hanover, unlike the old Williston High, devoted any class time to African American subjects. In addition, Bellamy contemplated no changes in the coaching ranks to include blacks, and he asserted that the police would continue to be a presence on campus, as he was committed to a partnership with Police Chief H. E. Williamson, despite the department's racist reputation in the black community. Furthermore, Bellamy said he would no longer discuss the students' grievances unless they called off the boycott. Students who returned to school with a note from their parents would be offered amnesty but would still have to make up late assignments. Those who continued the boycott would be suspended. The county commissioners lauded Bellamy's "forthright actions" and supported in advance "any measures" he and the school board thought were necessary to squelch a protest. The *Wilmington Morning Star* similarly supported the school administration against the students.[36]

The noon deadline for a favorable response from the school superintendent passed as students met at Gregory Congregational. In response they voted to expand the boycott to include all grades, not just high school, and then 250 students—mostly black, but including a "smattering of whites"—marched to the school board. About half of the system's high school students stayed out of classes; by the following day, nearly 80 percent of the black students from the two high schools were absent. Bellamy again declared that nothing the protesters could do would close the schools.[37]

School and city officials were intransigent. Not only would they not negotiate with the boycotting students, they also rebuffed mediation by racial moderates in state government. Mayor Luther Cromartie and Chief Williamson invited the state Good Neighbor Council to send a representative to Wilmington to help sort things out, but when the representative turned out to be the Reverend Aaron Johnson, a black man, they wanted nothing to do with him. Johnson said that white city leaders then wanted to deal only with the governor. The Good Neighbor Council concluded that city and school officials were "derelict" in responding to the complaints of black students. Referencing the knife attack on Barbara Swain in January, the council stated that if a white student had been assaulted, administrators would have written up a report, and Chief Williamson would have had the culprit in custody that evening. In response, Williamson blamed "out-of-town persons involved in the boycott and racial strife in the city," and the *Morning Star* opined that the council's criticism was "far-fetched . . . a dispiriting example of the bad habit too many of us fall into in striking out injudiciously with our blame."[38]

Although the situation remained relatively quiet at Gregory Congregational during the evenings of 1 and 2 February, with students staying overnight, friction was building in the surrounding area. A fight between black and white student spectators erupted during a basketball game at New Hanover High School; police reports indicate that only African Americans were arrested. Rocks and bottles were thrown at police and at

On 3 February, Schwartz's Furniture, a white-owned store in a black neighborhood, was burned, and Lum's Restaurant on Oleander Drive, in a white neighborhood, was firebombed in the overnight hours of 4–5 February. Both fires were blamed on black protesters. Law enforcement authorities, however, determined that Lum's was burned by its owner to collect insurance, and many blacks believed the same was true for Schwartz's, which is pictured here. Photograph from the Wilmington Morning Star, 5 *February 1971, courtesy of the New Hanover County Public Library.*

cars on Dawson Street. Violence escalated the evening of Wednesday, 3 February, and white opinion further hardened. That night Schwartz's Furniture, a white-owned store in the black community, was burned, the first of several arsons over the next week. In the overnight hours of 4–5 February, another firebomb destroyed Lum's Restaurant on Oleander Drive, in the middle of a white neighborhood. The Wilmington paper linked both arsons to the African American protest and even quoted an unidentified bystander as saying that he saw a black man running from the store shouting, "L. Schwartz is gone now!" Yet no one was arrested for the crime, and separate observations by several people across decades cast doubt on the claim. Delores Moore, mother of Wilmington Ten defendant Wayne Moore, and Eugene Templeton noted that although Schwartz's building and inventory were destroyed, the account books were not, and customers continued to be billed without delay. Moore, Templeton, George Kirby, and even the moderate-to-conservative Aaron Johnson believed that at least some of the arsons were committed by the storeowners for the insurance. Their suspicions are confirmed by a newly declassified report from the FBI that concluded that Lum's was burned down by its owner, who hoped to use the racial unrest to collect the insurance on his business. This, of course, was never reported at the time.[39]

The press's inaccurate and provocative reporting captured the attention of the ROWP, which responded by inserting itself into the conflict and dramatically escalating the violence. On Thursday, 4 February, Reverend Templeton called for the city to impose a curfew to prevent bloodshed. The police chief and mayor refused, just as they refused earlier requests to provide protection when anonymous callers menaced Templeton and his wife. Instead, Chief Williamson suggested that the troubles would end if Gregory Congregational was closed. That night armed whites organized a drive-by shooting at the church, in which two African Americans, including Wilmington Ten defendant Marvin Patrick, were wounded. Police limited themselves to watching the church and spying on boycotters and did nothing to stop the assailants. A few blocks from the church, whites shot at black individuals or couples. "There were a lot of isolated incidents," remembered Kojo Nantambu.[40]

The escalation of violence, the police's apparent collusion in it, and the vilification of the school boycott in the press changed the contours of the struggle. On 5 February, a crowd estimated by the *Wilmington Morning Star* of between three hundred and four hundred students— but estimated by the black weekly *Carolina Times* at more than two thousand—marched to city hall to demand protection from both the vigilantes and the police. African American residents near Gregory Congregational expressed support for the students and criticism of the school board and were understanding of the continuing incidents of arson aimed at white businesses in their neighborhood. At the church, students armed themselves after expressing to Templeton a desire to defend the church. They gathered mostly small arms in poor repair, according to Nantambu: "We had a lot of old guns that the brothers had stole from their fathers out of the garage or something that was all taped up. Now a few brothers had two or three .22s up there which were in better shape than the shotguns we had up there." However, that students armed themselves did not mean that they knew how to shoot. Charles Jones commented that he did not know how to use a gun, and he suspected that most of the other students did not know how, either, so it is reasonable to conclude that talk of armed struggle by protesters was largely rhetorical.[41]

The escalating violence brought help from two groups of black Wilmingtonians who did know something about guns: so-called brothers

On 5 February, students demonstrated in front of city hall to demand protection from the Rights of White People vigilantes and the police. Photograph from the Wilmington Morning Star, [6] February 1971, courtesy of the New Hanover County Public Library.

of the street and servicemen from nearby Camp Lejeune in Jacksonville and Fort Bragg in Fayetteville. While they were not inclined to become involved in high school students' grievances, once the church was attacked they felt an obligation to defend it—and to take revenge against aggressive whites. Wilmington native Larry Reni Thomas, who has been prominent in efforts to memorialize the 1898 race riot and who interviewed many participants in the February 1971 events, described the "street brother" typology in his *Rabbit! Rabbit! Rabbit! A Fictional Account of the Wilmington Ten Incident of 1971*: "Most of them were either high school dropouts, ex-convicts, winos, heroin addicts or former students who had been expelled from school for discipline reasons. Most of them were not afraid to say that they hated white people and that they loved the idea of 'blasting some Cracker Klansmen in they white asses!'" Unemployed or sporadically employed, they existed on the margins of the economy and society. Despite their addictions, they were radicalized—some in prison, where they encountered Malcolm X, and others after Dr. King's assassination. Many of the servicemen were older brothers of students involved in the struggle. C-Man, a street brother, remembered that after the first drive-by shooting, "brothers came up from Jacksonville dressed all in black and carrying .45s." Ben Chavis, who coordinated the defense of the perimeter of Gregory Church, paid tribute to the soldiers from Fort Bragg for standing guard and preventing the outmatched students from being overrun by armed white supremacists.[42]

For these radicalized nonstudents, the issue was clear and was ably summarized by C-Man: "The way I saw things, and maybe the way a lot of dudes saw things[,] is that the crackers were trying to take the church. . . . [I]t was more or less a thing whereas we gonna make a stand, we gonna dig in and whatever it takes to keep the crackers from coming in, we gonna keep them out." The convergence on the neighborhood near Gregory Congregational was not orchestrated by outsiders, as was alleged by the chief of police. (The issue of outsiders was a red herring, brought up by authorities so as to deflect attention from substantial issues.) "No one said, 'let's do a military-style plan' or anything of that nature. Folks just came prepared to defend the church," remembered Jim Grant. "People just showed up and organized themselves."[43]

With the arrival of reinforcements, there were now two distinct groups of persons engaged in what Robert F. Williams called armed self-reliance. One group consisted of students and their allies who had been involved in the boycott from its inception. They remained in the close vicinity of Gregory Congregational Church and concentrated on fending off attacks on the church. Erecting barricades outside the house of worship and posting armed lookouts up to two blocks away, for three nights they exchanged gunfire with vigilantes who menaced the church and its surrounding neighborhood. On the evening of Saturday, 6 February, around eight o'clock, some of this group were outside Gregory Congregational engaged in a discussion with the Reverend David Vaughn of Central Baptist Church, who was pleading with the students to lay down their guns and work for a peaceful solution. A caravan of armed whites drove through the barricades and fired at the people standing outside the church and sprayed the Reverend Vaughn with buckshot. Kojo Nantambu, who was supervising the guard, and another student, William Boykin, returned fire. When the skirmish was over, Nantambu sent Boykin and his brother to muster more defenders and weapons, but they were arrested for "going about armed to terrorize the populace."[44]

A second group—the reinforcements from the military and Wilmington's streets—was more amorphous than the first, and less is known about it. While the boycotting students and their leaders were relieved when the soldiers and brothers off the block appeared, they operated independently from the boycott and not under its direction or discipline. While members of this group likely participated in the direct defense of the church and its occupants—at different times Chavis saluted them for their assistance—it was most probably they who extended the violence beyond the church perimeter and attacked white targets. As no one has taken credit for the actions of this group and as its members were able to act without being detected or infiltrated by the authorities, their reasoning cannot be fully known but may be inferred.

It is this confederation that was probably responsible for the rash of firebombs that were set from Thursday, 4 February, to Saturday, 6 February. Many of the burned buildings, like Mary's Grocery, Carney's Supermarket, Johnson Grocery, and Smitty's Shoe Shop, were white-owned mom-and-pop stores. Businesses like these are often targets during racial violence as manifestations of blacks' resentment of higher prices, inferior goods, and often hostile or indifferent service. Other buildings that were damaged had more tangible connections to the students' struggle: the New Hanover High School field house and some offices of the Wilmington Housing Authority symbolized institutions that oppressed them.[45]

One building in particular commanded the attention of some participants in the struggle: Mike's Grocery at the intersection of Sixth and Ann Streets, a block from Gregory Congregational Church. Once during the overnight of 4–5 February and again in the early evening of Friday, 5 February, some persons, presumably from the group of nonstudent participants, tried unsuccessfully to burn Mike's down. Firefighters put out the blazes but in the process were shot at by unknown persons. On Saturday, 6 February, the arsonists were successful. Mike's was destroyed.[46]

Given that the arson of Mike's became the centerpiece of the prosecution of the Wilmington Ten, it is appropriate to understand why the store was such a focus of attention during the days of violence. When the Ten were put on trial, the prosecution argued that they burned Mike's because the owner disrespected a black girl and had to pay the price. Among the student boycotters, Mike's indeed had a bad reputation, but according to Kojo Nantambu the students talked only of "taking the cracker's food and that would hurt him that way." While one might conclude that one attempt to burn Mike's was the result of black resentment, the complaint against Mike for mistreating a single customer does not seem to merit trying to destroy the store three times. A more likely explanation for the determination to burn Mike's came from student leader Ben Wonce, who said at the time that many of the white vigilantes' attacks came from near the store.[47]

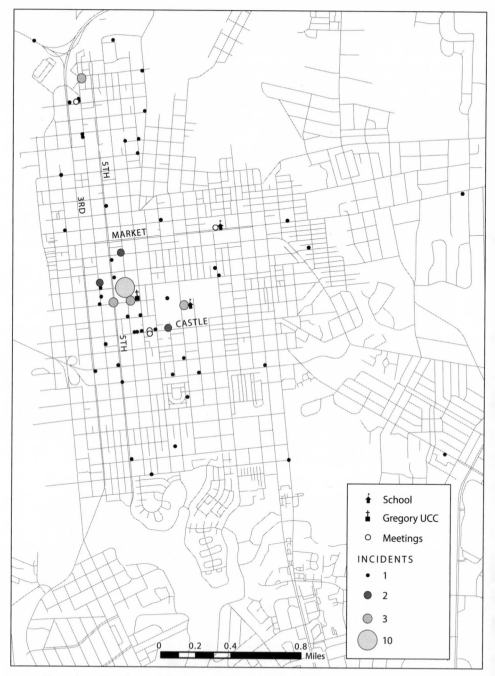

Clustering of incidents of shootings and firebombings related to the Wilmington school boycott during the period 2–11 February. Based on a map by Elizabeth Hines.

Location of shootings and firebombings related to the Wilmington school boycott during the period 2–11 February. Based on a map by Elizabeth Hines.

On 4 and 5 February 1971, there were two unsuccessful attempts to burn Mike's Grocery, which was located one block north of Gregory Congregational Church. Over those days, violence escalated, as the members of the Rights of White People group drove by the church and shot at the building and its occupants. On 6 February, around 10 P.M., there was a third, successful attempt to burn Mike's. Photograph from the Wilmington Morning Star, 7 February 1971, courtesy of the New Hanover County Public Library.

The attacks intensified and reached a climax on Saturday, 6 February, and early Sunday, 7 February. Around 7 P.M., Wilmington police knew of several meetings of whites on Castle Hayne Road north of Gregory Congregational Church who were organizing armed raids on the church. "It's getting so the white people in this town don't have a chance the way the school board and chief Williamson are giving in to these blacks," said one of the participants. Said another, "What we need in this town are some dead agitators. They should be shot and left out in the street as a reminder for three days and then bury them. I've got my gun. If two or three more of these men will go with me, I'm ready to go get some things straightened out." The police made three arrests but did not break up the meetings. One officer expressed his solidarity with the vigilantes: "It's a sad situation when people can go around sniping and killing and there's nothing you can do about it without the Supreme Court blowing your head off. . . . I really think we should go down there and clean it out now." These were the meetings that resulted in the shooting of the Reverend Vaughn.[48]

Around 10 P.M. there was the third, successful attempt to burn down Mike's Grocery. When Mike's and two adjacent buildings caught on fire, Steve Mitchell, age nineteen, was on guard duty outside the church. The police claim that Mitchell pointed a shotgun at Patrolman Jackie Shaw, but when he pulled the trigger, it misfired; Shaw then used his weapon and killed Mitchell with a single shotgun blast to the throat. The police chief immediately claimed the killing justified, and Mayor Cromartie said, "I see the shooting tonight as a deterrent."[49] Those on the other side tell a different story. They said that when Mike's caught on fire, Mitchell handed his weapon to his partner and made his way down the street to pull the alarm, as the burning store endangered nearby homes. That is when Officer Shaw shot Mitchell. But according to neighbors who watched out their windows, Mitchell was not dead, and he was moving while police officers roughed him up. They put him in a patrol car and drove him to New Hanover General Hospital; in the ninety minutes it took the police to travel the two miles to the emergency room, Mitchell died. To observers, it was a clear case of a police murder.[50]

Gunfire continued in the overnight hours as police continued to allow out-of-town and out-of-state whites—whom the *Morning Star* identified as "sightseers"—to cruise by the church; Reverend Templeton claimed that the parsonage was riddled with fifty bullet holes that evening. Then around 8 A.M. Sunday morning, 7 February, Harvey Cumber, a white supremacist, was killed in front of the church. Police told the newspaper that Cumber, who lived four blocks away in the 200 block of Nun Street, was shot while walking home after purchasing a carton of soft drinks. In fact, the department's own log (and later news reports) stated that Cumber drove through police lines, parked his pickup truck near the church, got out, and brandished his gun. He was shot and killed by unknown guards, both in defense of the church and in retribution for the killing of Steve Mitchell. That same day, three out-of-town whites, who were likely recruited for the mob, were injured by gunshot after crossing police lines.[51]

For days, even as the ROWP assaulted the church, the mayor, police chief, and city manager had refused to impose a curfew, because they felt they had the situation well under control. But with the death of a white man, the situation was now officially out of control. The mayor imposed a curfew beginning at 7:30 P.M., and the governor sent the State Highway Patrol, which had already been patrolling the city's perimeter, and the National Guard into Wilmington. On Monday morning, the Guard stormed Gregory Congregational. The building was empty, save for the church caretaker and one other person. Police and Guard spokespeople claimed to have found shotgun shells, .22 caliber casings, ammunition cartons, and emergency medical supplies. The next day, Chief Williamson claimed that his officers found dynamite that had been overlooked in the first search. The curfew remained in effect for three days and the six hundred National Guard troops patrolled the city for a week, but the violence was slow to wind down.[52]

The combined force of the paramilitary ROWP and law enforcement put an end to the boycott, but whites continued to suppress student dissent. Most of the expulsions and suspensions were upheld. Scrums between black and white students continued in the school hallways. White high schoolers demanded that the school board exclude African Americans from New Hanover and Hoggard. Singing "Dixie" as they marched to the board of education building in mid-March, one hundred of them, with a smattering of their parents, proclaimed that "the time has come for the white students to gain back their lost rights." Principals had to stop listening to black students, and those "causing the trouble [must] be removed from school immediately and permanently." They demanded that the school board refuse black students permission to hold a Martin Luther King memorial service, and they threatened their own school boycott should they not be heeded. New rounds of disciplinary action against black students followed for the remainder of the school term. In March, police arrested nearly three dozen students, most of them African American, at the two high schools and Williston Middle School. Black students testified before a meeting of the North Carolina advisory committee to the U.S. Civil Rights Commission that they were "egged into arguments by racist white teachers, brutalized by local police and judged unfairly by local judges." The advisory committee found these charges credible as well as one by Ben Ruffin that black students were being used as "pieces of equipment" by school authorities, who tolerated their presence only to receive federal funds.[53]

As if to prove this point, *Morning Star* newspaper editorials labeled black students who continued to protest their conditions in school "hoodlums," decried their "arrogant defiance of this community's order," and, supporting the Nixon-era refrain for law and order, demanded the

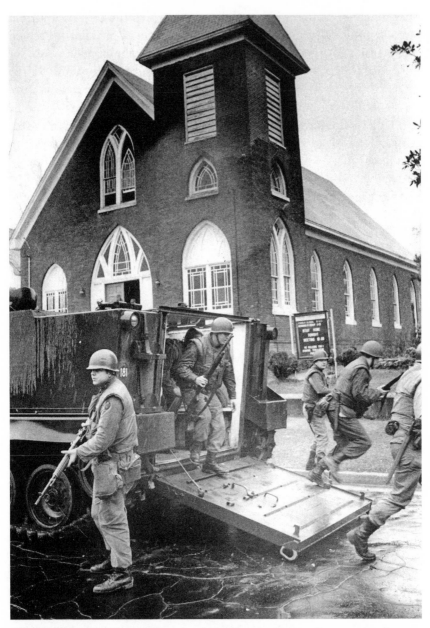

Members of the North Carolina National Guard storm Gregory Congregational Church in response to the killing of Harvey Cumber, a local white supremacist who had menaced the boycotters in front of the building. Photograph from the Wilmington Morning Star, *[14 February 1971], courtesy of the New Hanover County Public Library.*

punishment of "both the kids and the adults" who ostensibly manipulated them. A group calling itself the Concerned Citizens Association presented the city council a petition with five thousand signatures calling both for the police chief's removal because he was soft on the boycott and for the establishment of an auxiliary police force. When the county commissioners responded by approving the hiring of a dozen sheriff's deputies to be placed permanently in the schools, the New Hanover County Taxpayers Association instead suggested that retired military personnel be deployed to enforce order on campus; the police, said a spokesperson, mollycoddled criminals.[54]

The most brazen expression of whites' determination came from district court judge John M. Walker, who presided over the early March trial of William Boykin and Gary Robinson for going about dangerously armed, one of the first trials related to the February uprising. This trial occurred at the same time as the war crimes court martial of Lieutenant William Calley for the mass murder of Vietnamese civilians at My Lai. In an unusual hour-long questioning of police chief Williamson, whom he thought not aggressive enough, Judge Walker demanded to know why he had not ordered a raid on Gregory Congregational Church earlier. More blacks should have been arrested, the judge said, including the church trustees. "Maybe we should have brought in Lt. Calley to go in and clean the place up," Walker stated. If he had been chief of police, lectured the judge, "I'd have led my men over there and I'd have cleaned that church out."[55]

Withal, this unremitting tocsin drowned out the occasional letter to the editor, such as one from a "white, Protestant, and Anglo-Saxon" woman that criticized "the arrogant aristocracy or the low income whites or the ignorant but well-heeled middle class" who refused to constructively engage black Wilmingtonians in a search for racial peace. And it all but overwhelmed a new biracial Hoggard student club whose members pledged to "make a special effort to respect each other" and achieve interracial understanding.[56] The boycott and uprising had been violently suppressed, and the students returned to school with their demands largely unrealized. More, the state and federal governments were set on extinguishing whatever embers managed to continue glowing after the uprising. Through means both legal and illegal, overt and covert, they meant to hammer Ben Chavis and cripple a developing insurgent radical movement, no matter the cost in damaged lives and tattered civil liberties.

On the other hand, the armed defense of the church, the killing of Harvey Cumber, and the widespread damage to local businesses altered the balance of power, which in the years to come would help this new movement withstand assaults. As Bertha Todd and others had commented, black oppression in Wilmington was predicated in part on the "1898 mentality"—a paralyzing fear. White vigilantes and the police had previously figured that they could act with impunity. But during the first week of February 1971, student boycotters, street brothers, servicemen, and their supporters taught Wilmington's whites that the cost henceforth would be dear, future armed assaults would be imprudent, and that paramilitary groups like the ROWP and the Ku Klux Klan would eventually have to be restrained.

But self-defense, while important in the Wilmington struggle, was never a sufficient basis on which to build a movement, a fact that was clear to all activists. In the aftermath of the uprising, Black Power politics embarked in new directions.

CHAPTER 2

The Making of a Movement

Across eastern North Carolina in the late 1960s and 1970s, racial conflict was most often ignited by struggles about education. In Wilmington, Pitt County, New Bern, Clinton, and elsewhere, court-ordered desegregation was met with stiff opposition from whites who wished to maintain segregated schools and from blacks who objected to their exclusion from the decision-making process as dual school systems were dismantled. The open conflicts that developed were frequently short lived, and a common characteristic of these local flare-ups was the youths' rejection of their elders' gradualism and the donning of at least the accoutrements of Black Power, including firebrand oratory and Black Panther attire. Yet if they gravitated to a common rhetoric to express their grievances, most of the struggles remained local and for the most part isolated from each other, with little attempt on the part of local activists to join forces.[1]

Wilmington was the most notable exception to the localized rule. Certainly the genesis of the boycott was local grievances acted upon by high school students who simply desired their resolution; while some boycotting students expressed an incipient political consciousness, many others did not, and none of them had connections or communications with political movements beyond the city. But between the Wilmington uprising of February 1971 and the arrest of the Wilmington Ten defendants the following year, Black Power and black nationalist activists developed in the city and kept a high political profile. They interacted with like-minded organizers in other parts of the state and developed theoretical frameworks that guided their practical activity.

The student boycott and subsequent rebellion were crushed, but visible struggle continued in Wilmington, as this chapter makes evident. Also apparent in the months after the uprising was the authorities' commitment to hobble Ben Chavis. He was the object of police surveillance, petty harassment, court injunctions, and arrests on serious federal and state charges. Local, state, and federal authorities tried to put Chavis hors de combat, and Chavis in return likely viewed the attacks on him as serious but hardly unexpected.

There is a difference not simply of degree but of kind between the serial instances of low-grade warfare and the extensive roundup of suspects in March 1972 that led to the Wilmington Ten trials. Chavis and other movement figures and organizations had experience with the former and could more easily adjust to them. The dragnet, though, coming as it did a year after the events, was potentially catastrophic and seemed to catch many by surprise. This chapter is concerned with the year-long period before the Wilmington Ten frame-up became public, when Black Power organizations embedded themselves in the daily lives of African Americans and became hegemonic in the freedom struggle in Wilmington and North Carolina.

In Wilmington and eastern North Carolina, three main Black Power trends both cooperated and competed to amplify the power of the students' protest. Together and separately they strove to interpret the chronic conflict in the schools for the students and adults in the communities. They explained how localized battles over education were both linked together and symptomatic of larger structural inequalities. In sum, they worked to politicize students' grievances and bring African American students and adults into a discussion and practice of strategies for race liberation. The shifting practical struggles and discussions of strategy in the period before the trials of the Wilmington Ten were significant on at least two counts. Engaging communities in the state on a full range of issues was important for mobilizing African Americans in large numbers, and the process of mass consciousness-raising helped to create an educated citizenry that could advance sophisticated political demands. Because of this two-pronged approach, African Americans would be able to use the case of the Wilmington Ten to make progress on other issues that might have looked unrelated but were in fact intimately connected to the celebrated case of political repression.

Foremost was the United Church of Christ's Commission for Racial Justice of North Carolina and Virginia, whose main organizer, Ben Chavis, had been invited to Wilmington by Eugene Templeton, the Gregory Congregational Church minister. Begun in 1963 as an ad hoc formation within the UCC, it became a formally recognized body of the denomination in 1969, with Albert Cleage, a prominent black Christian nationalist from Detroit, as its first chairman. In North Carolina and Virginia, which made up the Southern Conference of the UCC, the CRJ enjoyed at best tepid support from the predominantly white church hierarchy and a significant number of white congregations. This complicated the work of the CRJ, whose fieldwork enjoyed broad support among both black UCC congregations and black communities in general.[2]

Second, the Southern Christian Leadership Conference (SCLC), led in eastern North Carolina by Golden Frinks, arrived in Wilmington after the uprising but was nevertheless able to attract some of the student protest leaders. The SCLC's start-up was the Wilmington Movement, which projected a broad program, including black community control over a reestablished black high school, proportional representation in elected offices, improved city services in black neighborhoods, jobs in local government, and a boycott of local retail businesses that did not hire black workers.[3]

Third, news of the struggle in Wilmington was also broadcast and influenced by the Youth Organization for Black Unity (YOBU) and its newspaper, the *African World*, whose correspondent, Jim Grant, traveled around North Carolina as "a community organizer and a reporter." (His work also appeared in the *Southern Patriot*, the publication of the Southern Conference Education Fund.) Grant was a black nationalist, a believer in Malcolm X. But practically speaking, he thought that blacks would have to form interracial alliances because, even in North Carolina, they constituted less than one-third of the population. YOBU did not have a sustained presence in Wilmington, but its reporting and commentary on the situation there and in public schools across the state did reach the Port City and significantly influenced the thinking of black nationalist activists and the direction of Black Power in the state.[4]

IN THE IMMEDIATE aftermath of the uprising, two organizations supported by the CRJ became active to further the students' momentum. The Black Youth Builders of the Black Community (BYBBC) was started by eighteen-year-old Roderick Kirby (Kojo Nantambu) and united between fifty and one hundred youth to lead the "people in our struggle for liberation in totality." Occupying the same building as the BYBBC on Castle Street was the First African Congregation of the Black Messiah, whose pastor and assistant pastor were Ben Chavis and Nantambu, respectively. Because of the organizations' overlapping membership and leadership, it makes sense to explore them together.

Writing at the time of their founding, Chavis offered the view that "Black Liberation Struggles . . . will always be revolutionary and holy." In a number of ways the BYBBC modeled itself on the Black Panther Party's example by combining serve-the-people programs with political education. And like the Panthers, the organization labored in an atmosphere of aggression by white vigilantes. Using CB radios and police scanners,

Rights of White People members gathered quickly and rode armed into the city's African American neighborhoods. In the months following the February uprising, more than forty African Americans, most of them between the ages of sixteen and twenty, were shot and wounded. These assaults went unsolved. Ben Chavis reported to police that while he was standing in front of the Black Messiah church, a pickup truck drove by and a white passenger pointed a pistol out the window and said, "This is for you." Other whites drove by and took pictures of the building; the Wilmington police confirmed that the whites riding through the neighborhood were in cars registered to members of the ROWP. On the first anniversary of Steve Mitchell's killing, the ROWP opened a headquarters on Castle Street, one block from the BYBBC building. Black Wilmingtonians responded to these provocations, to be sure, by sniping at whites driving through their neighborhoods or attacking white-owned businesses. Nantambu took cheer in the community's response to the white invasion: "In my mind it was a victory," he told the *SOBU Newsletter*.[5]

It was under these conditions that the BYBBC and the Black Messiah church conducted their work. Armed self-defense figured in the mix, but more for projecting esprit de corps than as the central strategic component. Among the first things the organizations did was form a drill team similar to that of the Panthers. On a few occasions, FBI informers reported that members of both groups had a session of weapons training, including one lesson devoted to gun safety using a .22 caliber rifle and a 12-gauge shotgun. Likewise, there were occasional reports of old rifles on the premises. But the FBI was unable to find any evidence of serious armed training, and rumors of stolen military rifles being shipped to the groups' headquarters proved to be just that. Ideologically, the groups were eclectic. They promoted the rebirth of a "total 'Black Nation'" as seen, for instance in the launch of a food and clothing drive with a goal of meeting the needs of five families per week, dubbed Operation SOUL (Save Our Underprivileged Liberals). The BYBBC was determined to "go back to our natural culture" and "resolve [the race problem] not through integration but rather through setting up their own institutions in the Black community." At the same time, the BYBBC proclaimed adherence to "socialistic/democratic principles" and Leninist rules of democratic centralism. The group substantially incorporated Chairman Mao's "Three Main Rules of Discipline and Eight Points for Attention." Whether the BYBBC absorbed these ideas from reading the Black Panther newspaper or *Quotations from Chairman Mao Tse-tung*, the organization's outlook was much like nationalist formations across the country in the early 1970s.[6]

The Congregation of the Black Messiah was a youth-oriented United Church of Christ congregation inspired by the Reverend Albert Cleage's Black Christian Nationalist Shrine of the Black Madonna in Detroit. Since the mid-1950s, Cleage had been increasingly frustrated with the integrationist bent of both the black clergy in his native Detroit and his own UCC denomination. The Shrine of the Black Madonna, which he opened in 1967, attracted young activists who likewise were dissatisfied with the direction of black churches. Cleage's new congregation was fluid, drawing members who had been regular attendees of the Socialist Workers Party's Militant Labor Forum as well as people who had worked in the South with the Student Nonviolent Coordinating Committee and the Congress of Racial Equality. The ideological plasticity was contained by the overriding belief that the concern of the new congregation, like the original Disciples of Christ, was not the bodily resurrection of Jesus but "the resurrection of a 'Black Nation.'"[7]

The same could be said for the Wilmington Congregation of the Black Messiah. It was formed to attract blacks under thirty because, as Kojo Nantambu explained, most local churches were not available to black youth when they needed them. Wayne Moore remembered that the church required members to read a book a week concerning some aspect of black history or culture. The church's prayer service included a "Pledge to the Black Flag," the "Black Christian Pan-Africanist Creed," the "Black National Anthem," an antiphonal "Nation Building" prayer, and various Civil Rights Movement–era freedom songs, some of which were revised to include Black Power lyrics.[8]

Three events typify the BYBBC's political profile in Wilmington. First, in June 1971, shortly after its founding, it brought Howard Fuller of the Malcolm X Liberation University and an important black nationalist and pan-Africanist figure to speak in Wilmington. Second, in August 1971, the BYBBC protested the murder of George Jackson in Soledad Prison in California; marching through several black neighborhoods, fifty protesters rallied at the county courthouse and heard Nantambu speak against busing and the presence of police in black communities. And third, on the anniversary of the Wilmington uprising, the BYBBC sponsored Steve Mitchell Week, "in commemoration of the FIRST BROTHER to give his life for us in our very indigenous struggle here in 'JR. BABYLON.'"[9]

Kojo Nantambu's staunch position earned him close scrutiny by law enforcement and the ROWP. The ROWP itself patrolled and policed black neighborhoods in Wilmington, meting out punishment and inviting retaliation. A profile of ROWP leader Leroy Gibson in the *Greensboro*

Daily News explained the organization's logic: "The way Gibson sees it, Wilmington's troubles result from 'all of them blacks wanting to come in and demand everything and expecting white people to give it to them. Well, they've finally hit an organization that's going to stop that.'" And yet despite the police department's alleged irritation at the ROWP's usurpation of authority, city officials blamed the continuing violence on Nantambu. Though he had no evidence of his involvement, the Wilmington city manager said that "everyone assumes he is" responsible for the violence.[10]

Attempts to suppress Kojo Nantambu and to intimidate blacks in Wilmington reached a peak in the fall of 1971. Clashes between the ROWP and African Americans had become a regular occurrence when, on the evening of Friday, 1 October, the Hoggard High School football team played New Hanover High at Legion Stadium. Toward the end of the game, Nantambu, who was in attendance with other members of the BYBBC, heard that about two hundred whites were menacing black spectators outside the stadium on Carolina Beach Road. He sought out the Wilmington police officers on duty to control the threatening whites. The police refused, turning attention instead on a group of African American teens who were preparing to use belts to defend themselves from the white crowd. Angry words between a police officer and Nantambu escalated into pushes and shoves and culminated in more than a dozen officers descending on and beating Nantambu. He was arrested on misdemeanor charges of assaulting an officer and hindering an officer in the line of duty; the following month he was convicted on the assault charges and sentenced to a year in jail despite evidence that the injured officer may have been hit by his colleagues' own billy clubs.[11]

This altercation sparked a week of street fighting. But this was not the BYBBC's only method of struggle, and soon afterward Kojo Nantambu joined the city's Good Neighbor Council, which was refashioned as the Human Relations Commission. Largely the creation of Aaron Johnson, who served on the State Human Relations Commission and was the governor's representative in Wilmington, the local group aimed to encompass all points of view in the community. From Johnson's perspective, the ROWP and the black activist organizations had the same concern—integration—and he wanted to open a dialogue between them. The New Hanover Human Relations Commission officially debuted in December 1971, with thirty-seven members—twenty-two whites and fifteen blacks—including representatives from the ROWP, the First African Congregation of the Black Messiah, and the A. Philip Randolph Institute. Bertha Todd, the Hoggard librarian who played an important role in supporting the student boycotters, also was a member.[12]

Kojo Nantambu, the Black Messiah church's representative on the commission, struck a positive and principled note. He attributed the racial polarization in Wilmington to the powerlessness of African Americans and their exclusion from public life by whites. The situation was intolerable, and its continuation would lead to a "race war." And yet, violence was counterproductive: "The only thing we can gain by violence is the incarceration of brothers and sisters, and injured people lying in the hospital." A nonviolent and peaceful solution had to be found. Nantambu thus proposed a series of meetings to "discuss and agree upon an equitable and just distribution of power within the City of Wilmington."[13] The response of most of the rest of the commission was not encouraging. Bill Cullom, a DuPont executive and the chair of the Human Relations Commission, set the tone. He formally welcomed Nantambu into the dialogue but focused his attention on dismantling the BYBBC's defense of the community from ROWP drive-by shootings. Despite good reasons to the contrary, he tried to persuade black residents to trust the police to protect them. He was joined by black members of the racial-moderate axis of the commission. Rutherford Leonard, the local president of the International Longshoremen's Association, the principal organization of black labor in Wilmington, articulated what Cullom only dared imply: the unrest in Wilmington was caused by black "groups looking for a disturbance." Leonard, who had been accused of being distant from black Wilmington's struggles, admitted he did not know what black Americans were disturbed about, because "I'm not out there with those people." The Reverend Edwin Kirton, rector of St. Mark's Episcopal Church, "found no evidence of discrimination" in Wilmington's high schools. The Reverend W. J. Baskerville of the Chestnut United Presbyterian Church opined, "If I read the paper right [Ben Chavis and Leon White] seem to express the idea that discrimination here is unbearable. I do not feel it is to that extent." After four months of useless palaver, Nantambu resigned from the commission in April 1972.[14]

Chavis and Nantambu continued the work of establishing relations with other nationalist organizations in North Carolina, especially in the eastern part of the state. Their network was enlarged to include organizers in Granville, Bladen, Vance, Warren, Cleveland, and Wake Counties, and they merged under the banner of the African Peoples United Front. They developed ties with the Winston-Salem chapter of the Black Panther Party, which appeared interested in extending its presence in the state eastward, and sought to coordinate their activity with the Malcolm X

Liberation University in Durham. The two leaders also allied themselves with the Greensboro-based Student Organization for Black Unity (which, by 1972 had changed its name to Youth Organization for Black Unity) as a way to tap into networks of African American college students, and they pledged to work with those involved in both grassroots and electoral politics who were interested in founding an independent black party. Further, Chavis and Nantambu participated in the summer and fall 1971 protests in Greenville, Pitt County, against the murder of a black day laborer by a state highway patrolman and offered their perspective on the way forward in that struggle, which was led by Golden Frinks. Thus, the leadership of Chavis and Nantambu, who enjoyed the patronage of the CRJ, was instrumental to the beginnings of a radical- and nationalist-led movement that had geographic reach, bridged different organizations, and utilized varied forms of political activity, including self-defense, "insider" activity on the Good Neighbor Council, electoral politics, and direct protest.[15]

GOLDEN FRINKS AND the SCLC appeared in Wilmington in March 1971 as renewed physical confrontations rocked the city's schools and some neighborhoods. On the thirteenth of that month, seventeen-year-old Clifton Eugene Wright was shot to death in the home of Mollie Hicks, who was not home at the time. (Hicks was one of the comparatively few black adults who supported the students' boycott, and her daughter Leatrice was active in it, too.) Wright and two friends were gambling; whether there was an argument or simply some roughhousing, one of them shot and killed Wright. They immediately called Kojo Nantambu for help. Nantambu then called Chavis and James Ferguson, the Charlotte attorney who was handling much of the legal representation of those who had been arrested during the protests. Fearful of what would happen to them, the friends concocted a story that a white man had approached Hicks's apartment in the Taylor Homes public housing project and fired a shotgun at Wright when he answered the door. Chavis and the SCLC, not knowing the true circumstances of the killing, claimed the violence was racially motivated and demanded that the authorities act to solve the crime. Such calls were echoed by the U.S. Civil Rights Commission. For more than a week, Wilmington's schools were turned upside down with protest and interracial clashes. Telephoned bomb threats forced the evacuation of the schools, and after one such call, students at Williston Junior High engaged in a rock-throwing fight that shattered more than two hundred windows. More than a dozen students at one high school were suspended for demanding the principal lower the flag to half-staff in honor of Wright.

Governor Robert Scott sent fifty state troopers to Wilmington, and agents of the State Bureau of Investigation and the Bureau of Alcohol, Tobacco, and Firearms stood ready to act.[16]

Frinks announced his presence in the city and the formation of the Wilmington Movement at a press conference. One of the state's best-known black activists, Frinks had been involved in civil rights protests since the 1950s, first in a local branch of the NAACP and from 1963 as the SCLC's field organizer. In the 1968–69 school year, Frinks had led a successful boycott of the Hyde County schools over the same issues that smoldered in Wilmington and across eastern North Carolina: the closing of historically black schools, dispersal of African American students to previously all-white schools, and exclusion of blacks from the decision-making process. Setting up headquarters in the International Longshoremen's Association union hall, Frinks outlined an ambitious agenda, much of which transferred strategy and tactics that worked in Hyde County to Wilmington. Whereas the earlier boycott in Wilmington had aimed to include African American students in the schools on the basis of full equality, Frinks questioned the value of desegregation as it had been practiced in eastern North Carolina. The educational system was "repressive to blacks," he said, and the closing of Williston two years earlier was "an act of destruction against the black community." He rejected as "poppycock" and "hanky panky" the idea that black students should bear the brunt of desegregating the schools and society and called for another boycott of indeterminate length to pressure the school board to reestablish Williston as a predominantly, but not exclusively, black high school. Frinks's reasoning was reminiscent of that found in W. E. B. Du Bois's essay "Does the Negro Need Separate Schools?" For Frinks, as for Du Bois, the salient issue was not segregated or integrated schools but whether African American children would receive a good education and be taught by teachers who respected and empathized with them. Reclaiming the Williston traditions would allow for "a crash program of education among our people so that we will be educationally qualified to move ahead on equal terms with anybody in anybody's school anywhere." Somewhat later he promised to picket and disrupt local businesses until they hired black Wilmingtonians.[17]

The political establishment wished he had not shown up to forecast nothing but doom. The black and white moderates of the Good Neighbor Council, too, were disturbed by his presence; they called him polarizing, to which he retorted that the real problem was that the council was ineffectual, uninformed, and elitist. The Good Neighbor Council, said Frinks, could not know what was in the interests of the black community because none of its members were ghetto residents. The exchange of volleys continued, with some white moderates meddling to try to isolate Frinks. Through intermediaries, the associate schools superintendent persuaded Dr. Hubert Eaton, a pillar of the city's black middle class, publicly to state that African Americans in Wilmington would "settle matters ourselves without any outside interference." But resorting to the trope of "outside agitators" reveals the compromised position of the moderates of the Good Neighbor Council. Appointed by city leaders—the same people who tried to suppress student protest—the council incorporated the same bias against "outsiders." In the council's view, Frinks—and Chavis, too, for that matter—disrupted the paternalistic relationships between local whites and blacks that defined the boundaries and pace of change in Wilmington's race relations. Eaton recognized the Good Neighbor Council's conundrum, even as he opposed Frinks: the blacks to whom whites turned were not the same ones blacks followed. And in particular, the black students simply did not recognize the established black leadership.[18]

The young people's initial reactions to Golden Frinks were generally positive. Rallies at the International Longshoremen's Association hall regularly drew five hundred persons or more, a number of whom responded to his call for a renewed school boycott. Attendance at school was down significantly on Monday, 22 March, and two hundred African American students instead attended lectures and film sessions at the longshoremen's union hall. The school board responded by going to federal district court and getting a temporary injunction against Frinks, Chavis, Eugene Templeton, the CRJ, the SCLC, eighteen other named individuals, "and other persons and organizations 'known and unknown.'" The court found that the boycotts, protests, picketing, and demands for an all-black high school interfered with its desegregation orders. The following month, Judge Algernon Butler made the injunction permanent, which effectively ended organized protest in the schools.[19]

But unlike the CRJ's approach to organizing, Frinks's politics depended on practically continuous and flamboyant public actions. (Decades later, Wilmington activists laughingly and dismissively recalled his threats to disrupt the 1971 Azalea Festival by releasing chickens along the parade route. "They can't arrest the chickens, all they can do is eat them," Frinks said.) So when protest in the schools was made untenable because of the court injunction, Frinks and the SCLC dropped the quotidian work of organizing students and parents as advocated by the BYBBC in favor of another high-publicity project, a march from Wilmington to Raleigh. Hastily conceived as one of the local actions in the SCLC's nationwide "War against Repression" campaign, the Wilmington Movement subsumed the boycott's principal demands under calls for an end to the Vietnam War, a guaranteed annual income, and welfare rights.[20]

A caravan of 500 people, including Ben Chavis and Jim Grant, sixteen cars, and a U-Haul truck crossed the New Hanover Memorial Bridge out of Wilmington on the morning of 30 March. As planned, most of those soon turned back to town, but 150 people continued on to East Arcadia, where they were joined by another 60 protesters en route to the first night's stop in Elizabethtown. Both of these towns had seen recent intense protests over school desegregation and white supremacist organizations like the KKK and the ROWP. The march encountered its first serious trouble in Smithfield, a Johnston County white supremacist stronghold, on 1 April. Dominating the landscape on the main highway at the city limit was a billboard that stated, "Welcome to Smithfield. This is Klan Country. Join and Support the United Klans of America, Inc. Help Fight Communism and Integration!" Local authorities threatened to arrest any marchers if they entered town. The police chief said they lacked a parade permit, and for good measure he added that he would refuse any organizers' request for one. The Klan threatened to confront physically any challenge to white supremacy, and the mayor declared an overnight curfew. Before repairing for the evening to a church outside the town limits, the march's leaders again proclaimed their growing list of demands, now including the abolition of capital punishment and the repeal of right-to-work laws and the statute that prohibited the state and local governments from negotiating contracts with labor unions. Smithfield's bluster about blocking the march turned out to be for the cameras, as the next day the town issued a permit and 130 people marched through the city. Perhaps wishing to avoid other such confrontations, at Smithfield's western limit, the group boarded buses to take them the remaining thirty miles to Raleigh, where SCLC director Milton Fitch presented the Wilmington Movement's program to state legislators.[21]

Despite misgivings that, from an organizing perspective, the SCLC represented flash over substance, at least three leaders of the February boycott endorsed the march. Ben Chavis recognized the Wilmington Movement at one of its first rallies and pledged his support to the SCLC and its program. Ben Wonce, perhaps surprised by both the intensity of the violence and the lack of adult support the previous February, joined the Wilmington Movement. "If non-violence will get me my freedom, then I will be nonviolent," he declared. Recognizing the belated interest of black adults, Wonce said that he was glad that they were now supporting the struggle. He was, he said, "willing to forget what they had not done in the past because they were here now." At another rally preceding the march, he put "the power structure" on notice: "The structure cannot ride a man's back who stands erect, it is only those who are bent over who are ridden. Therefore, I say to all black people, let's stand up for freedom." Joe Wright called for unity among all those in eastern North Carolina who were fighting against the unjust way school desegregation was being implemented.[22]

Though they could identify injustices and initiate actions, it did not appear as if Golden Frinks and the SCLC could focus on sustaining a *movement*. Coincidental with the march to Raleigh, the Wilmington Movement initiated a boycott of retail businesses that did not hire African Americans in other than the lowest positions and did not make financial contributions to the "poor people's co-op," another of Frinks's initiatives. George Kirby, a local organizer, emerged as a central figure in these campaigns. He was listed as one of the incorporators of the "Poor People's Consumers Corporation" and took the lead in the actions to force the A&P grocery chain and other businesses to hire black managers and cashiers in local stores and invest a percentage of their local profits in the cooperative. Rallies at the longshoremen's headquarters and marches to city hall in May culminated in store protests in June. Kirby organized fifty teenagers to enter A&P stores in Wilmington and fill shopping carts with merchandise: fresh meats on the bottom, ice cream and frozen foods next, and canned goods on the top. They proceeded to the checkout line, but when they asked if there were black cashiers, managers, or assistant managers and were told there were not, they said they did not want the food and walked out. Kirby and the teens were nonviolently disruptive, and after a week and a half of action, A&P agreed to change its hiring practices. The Wilmington Movement followed that victory by challenging employment discrimination at Piggly Wiggly grocery stores, J. M. Fields, the Piece Goods Store, and Simons Store. Kirby and teen activists entered the shops, made a commotion, disorganized some merchandise, and scared shoppers into not making purchases. Kirby was arrested, charged with inciting a riot and engaging in a riot; he was convicted and sentenced to four years in prison. The co-op, however, was short lived and came under suspicion by other activists for shady bookkeeping.[23]

But in late August 1971 the peripatetic Frinks abandoned the struggle in Wilmington and took his followers into neighboring Pitt County, where earlier that month State Trooper Billy Day murdered a black day laborer named William Murphy on a rural road near Ayden. Being in the news was a priority for Frinks. He assembled an impressive coalition to fight for justice for Murphy and march under the twin banners of "Black Power" and "Soul Power," including the Black Panther Party, the CRJ, the Pitt County NAACP, and an organization of Pitt County black ministers. The *African World* wrote extensively about the murder and subsequent protests. In September, coincident to the SCLC's work in Pitt County, students at Ayden-Grifton High School launched their own struggle that combined outrage at Murphy's murder with objections to teacher indifference and hostility, a "Racist, Fascist, Pig" administration, and a mind-numbing curriculum. Frinks's theatrics helped to make him among the most effective mobilizers in eastern North Carolina, and he was able to recruit some of the ablest Wilmington organizers to the SCLC. At the same time, as his various simultaneous enterprises suggest, Frinks had an attention deficit. His furious pace of activity tended to crowd out more sustained work by the CRJ and the BYBBC, and when he and the SCLC left town, they left nothing behind.[24]

Chickens on the loose, hundred-mile marches to Raleigh, shopping pranks in downtown businesses—these grabbed publicity, but many of Wilmington's activists came to see them as distractions. Chavis, who was seeking ways to raise the national profile of the students' struggle and establish permanent organizations to deal with the issues they raised, was astonished that the SCLC was flitting from one issue to another. "The original movement evolved around the school crisis and soon became a survival crisis for the entire black community of Wilmington," Chavis wrote in an open letter to the black community. But with the arrival of Frinks, "the movement mysteriously shifted to evolve around economic development, abolishment of capital punishment, and the resegregation of an all black high school. . . . Brothers and Sisters what has happened to our original demands? Check it out!" To black nationalists like Kojo Nantambu, Frinks's emphasis on jobs and economic boycotts diverted from the principal task of building a nationalist consciousness and obtaining better education. Frinks's Azalea Festival antics were clownish. The march to Raleigh, coming so soon after the February uprising, was a safety valve. SCLC members were "moderate civil rights organizers" who were trying to hijack a militant mass struggle.[25]

Militant activists had long complained that the SCLC took action that blurred confrontation rather than accentuated it. In January 1965, the Student Nonviolent Coordinating Committee (SNCC) opened a campaign for voting rights in Selma, Alabama, which the SCLC belatedly joined. Meetings, rallies, and marches to the courthouse to register blacks to vote were punctuated by police and vigilante violence, including the murder of Jimmy Lee Jackson by Alabama state troopers. SNCC wanted to continue to intensify the local movement, create havoc, and compel President Lyndon B. Johnson to force Governor George Wallace to put an end to violence and the state's obstruction of African Americans' citizenship rights. SNCC's commitment to heightening the contradictions to the point of resolution was captured in a speech by the organization's chairman, James Forman: "It's not just the sheriff of this county or the mayor or the police commissioner or George Wallace. This problem goes to the very bottom of the United States. And you know, I said it to them and I will say it again. If we can't sit at the table, let's knock the fucking legs off, excuse me." By contrast, the SCLC expressly tried to step back from the confrontation and calm people down by organizing a march from Selma to Montgomery, the state capital. SNCC believed this to be an unwise and perhaps dangerous detour for the movement and did not support it; in fact the march was notable for the rout at the Edmund Pettus Bridge. Kojo Nantambu responded to a similar mode of operation when he opposed Frinks and charged that he offered "a soft line solution to Wilmington's problems."[26]

Nor did Frinks help his case by acting like the new sheriff in town and putting the activists around the CRJ on notice. Among his first utterances upon arriving in Wilmington was a dismissal of the student activists: "All their action is spontaneous. They read something, maybe about Fidel Castro or Che Gueverra [*sic*] or Adolph Hitler[,] and they say this is the way to get things done. That's why they followed Ben (Chavis). When he came along, he was their great fuehrer." He accused the CRJ of "causing polarization in the community" and the Congregation of the Black Messiah of wanting "'self defense to black determination,' guns and bullets and a new church that will send all black people to a segregated Heaven." And he clearly stated that he was the only one able to resolve black Wilmington's problems.[27]

Faced with this rhetoric, Ben Chavis branded Frinks and the SCLC as "professional 'confusers.'" Nantambu complained about the rumors Frinks spread about the BYBBC and others being sources of violence in Wilmington. Nantambu believed that Frinks's talk of the BYBBC as "gun-toting militants" split the movement and ultimately had the effect of driving adult support away from the nationalist project. As the Reverend Leon White reflected, the SCLC, with its emphasis on theatrics and addiction to publicity, "overwhelmed" the more militant work of the CRJ.[28]

ALTHOUGH IT DID not have an organizing presence in Wilmington, the Student (later Youth) Organization for Black Unity was important to the development of the Wilmington struggle in a couple of respects. First, the organization's biweekly newspaper, the *African World*, originally called the *SOBU Newsletter*, aspired to report on the struggles of black college and high school students, especially in North Carolina, and to link these domestic events with struggles in Africa against colonialism and neocolonialism. Milton Coleman, who retired in 2009 as deputy managing editor of the *Washington Post*, was the *African World's* editor. With a combined in- and out-of-state circulation of around ten thousand, Coleman said, the paper and the organization were "respected." The *African World*, reflecting YOBU's desire to spotlight issues in which it wanted to become involved, was a clearinghouse for information about students' struggles; it also contained extensive, detailed, and informative articles on Africa. The reporting on the Wilmington uprising and the 1972 arrests and trial of the Wilmington Ten was particularly textured, helping black nationalists across the state to be aware of the struggle and to take up its cause. No figures are available for the number of copies sold in Wilmington, but members of the Congregation of the Black Messiah and the BYBBC distributed the paper.[29]

The paper situated the Wilmington events in a broader context of struggle and complemented the efforts of Chavis, Nantambu, and the CRJ. While Chavis and Nantambu reached out to students at the University of North Carolina–Charlotte (Chavis's alma mater), attended regional black nationalist conferences, and assisted the United Black Students Association's fight in the Portsmouth, Virginia, schools, YOBU's newspaper highlighted student discontent and organizing across the state. From the reporters/organizers that YOBU sent into the field, readers learned of the similar conditions animating vigorous protest. The situation in Kings Mountain, near Charlotte, was typical. There, college students helped to form the Black Awareness Organization over the 1971 summer vacation. This group attempted to address a number of issues in this small Cleveland County mill town, including dilapidated housing and a lack of public services in the black community. At summer's end, the college students left, and leadership passed to high school students who focused attention on issues in the recently desegregated school system. Among these were instances of the high school principal calling African Americans "Black monkeys," the expulsion of black pupils, an inadequate black studies curriculum, and the refusal of the schools to meet the extracurricular needs of African American students. What made this new iteration of the Black Awareness Organization notable was its determination to concentrate on quotidian work rather than on "flag waving, press conferences, and not-to-be-met proclamations."[30] This was the same approach advocated by Chavis and Nantambu in Wilmington.

Struggles for black studies and larger numbers of black faculty and administrators filled the *African World*'s pages. In Trenton, North Carolina, the full complement of black students, with the support of the community's adults, struck the Jones County schools and shut them down for more than two days to stop the firing of an African American teacher. In the southeastern South Carolina town of Cross, the Black United Students Association rejected concessions by the Berkeley County board of education to set up a special, seniors-only black history class that would be taught by white U.S. history teachers. Students objected on two grounds: that the teachers were not qualified, or else they would have brought the history to light before, and the proposed curriculum ignored Africa. Student organizers were prepared to launch an independent, community-based African American history program. "Black Studies would tell us the truth about white folks. And why should [the superintendent] give us something that we're going to use against him?" quipped one female activist. Summing up the changes percolating within the younger generation, the *African World* observed, "It was a deep revelation for a girl whose parents still say 'yessir' to every white man they see."[31]

As this comment illustrates, the *African World* sought not only to catalog instances of resistance but also to chronicle and promote the change in black consciousness. A significant manifestation of this new consciousness was the Day of Solidarity to Save Black Schools on 25 October 1971. Organized by SOBU, this rally of five thousand at the state capitol in Raleigh brought together black student governments, student unions, and high school groups to protest proposals that would have hurt the public black colleges and universities in the state. This coalition had also lent support to high school struggles in the state such as at Ayden-Grifton High School in Pitt County and in Wilmington. Ben Chavis was a featured speaker at this demonstration. "Even though we're in an armed struggle in Wilmington, we have a consciousness about the problems you brothers and sisters are engaged in today. And we are supporting you wholeheartedly," he said.[32]

SOBU's revolutionary nationalism provided ideological consistency to Black Power in the state. The organization was founded in May 1969 on the campus of North Carolina A&T State University in Greensboro, nearly coincident with the beginning of a student uprising at that city's historically black Dudley High School that would quickly consume both it and the A&T campus. Similar to events in Wilmington two years hence,

SOBU actively cultivated relationships with college and high school students and community residents fighting discrimination on a number of fronts.[33] Envisioning itself as a successor to SNCC, which had dissolved partly due to ideological conflict, SOBU rejected nonviolence while simultaneously searching for other principles on which to base a united student movement.[34] It aimed to rectify the shortcomings of earlier advocates of Black Power, and by its second national meeting in April 1971, SOBU emphasized pan-Africanism as its guiding ideology.

The rejection of integrationism and the adoption of a pan-African ideology raised a series of questions: What was the essence of pan-Africanism? How should SOBU activists link their theory to the practical struggles they engaged? SOBU rejected a cultural-nationalist interpretation of pan-Africanism, which emphasized a depoliticized bond between African Americans and Africa. John Mendez, a SOBU adherent who in 1971 helped Ben Chavis start the Congregation of the Black Messiah in Wilmington, explained what he found lacking in the cultural-nationalist approach: They "would give you a good rap, run the line down . . . but they never really did anything, as far as getting involved in movements and struggles." Ed Whitfield, one of the founders of SOBU, whose black nationalist credentials extended back to the armed student takeover of Willard Straight Hall at Cornell University to demand the establishment of Afro-American studies on campus, believed that cultural nationalism expressed an "unhealthy" identity with Africa: "There was a fatalism around what was here, that you could hardly do anything about what was here. We Africans, what we need to do is to try to figure out how to integrate and relate to the African continent, which does not get you a lot of respect in a lot of neighborhoods. It's like [laughter] the African stuff and cultural heritage stuff, all that's nice, but what about right here?" According to Whitfield, SOBU's pan-Africanism had a political thrust: "So much of what we did in the beginning years was to look at ourselves as an African people intimately connected with the continent of Africa. . . . We're here and involved in a whole lot of kinds of things, and the vast majority ain't going nowhere and need to figure out how to make this work or how this struggle in it is tied to the struggle around the world."[35]

Surveying the black student movement since the ascendance of Black Power, SOBU coordinator for student programs Mark Smith stated that the lack of a guiding ideology had caused the movement to drift. Activists and organizations were hostage to the spontaneous eruption of movements against instances of injustice, which meant that they were reacting to events rather than initiating and sustaining struggles. Black students often were successful in achieving their demands because their passion caught administrators off guard; but once their initial fear wore off, Smith said, officials worked to co-opt the very concessions that they made. This state of affairs meant that relying on mass spontaneous outbursts was a bankrupt strategy and was likely to lead to deleterious results. (Readers in Wilmington would have understood this also as a criticism of Golden Frinks and the SCLC.) SOBU argued that reliance on popular outrage rather than taking part in the ordinary tasks of organizing resistance frequently degenerated into stereotyped rhetoric and "blacker-than-thou" posturing. Nelson Johnson, SOBU national chairman, criticized faux-militancy in his regular column in the *SOBU Newsletter*, titled "The Struggle in Perspective." Without a deep and intimate connection to popular struggles, wearing the activists' uniform of overalls or camouflage fatigues amounted to little more than posing. "Wearing military garb does not make you revolutionary," he wrote; neither did an ability to quote Malcolm X and Stokely Carmichael. Johnson went further. He found that students who spoke most often about "unity . . . struggle, sacrifice, seriousness, apathy, etc." engaged in empty rhetoric while promoting trivial issues like university funding for a "stereo-equipped Black house." He challenged blacks who wanted to be part of the struggle to pay attention to the "variation in interest of those to whom unity is proposed" and promote a program "around the proper principles for the purpose of creating a social order based on cooperative work and a joint and equitable distribution of goods and services." In another article, he wrote, "What we are pleading for here is a move towards seriousness and commitment in order to get away from the romantic and false notions that have so perverted our struggle."[36]

Ben Chavis was aware of and participated in the activities of SOBU. He was devoted to the black church and to the CRJ, but as he put it, "I had also an identity. I kept my nationalist credentials." As it worked to promote a political pan-Africanism, YOBU and Chavis joined forces with each other and a variety of black political tendencies to publicize the struggle in Wilmington and advance a practical agenda of Black Power.[37]

In the months between the Wilmington uprising and the September 1972 trial of the Wilmington Ten, Ben Chavis, the CRJ, and local leaders like Kojo Nantambu worked with others in North Carolina to build a Black Power movement that cut across class lines and political affiliations. The result was a vital coalition led by radicals and revolutionary nationalists that intervened in issues related to political repression, African American education, the criminal justice system, and the formation of an independent black political movement.

An early participant in this coalition was the Winston-Salem chapter of the Black Panther Party. It originally formed as a chapter of the National Committee to Combat Fascism, which was a kind of probationary stage for groups around the country that wanted to affiliate with the Panthers. Like other party chapters that had free breakfast and other serve-the-people programs, the Winston-Salem Panthers had developed an ambulance service for African Americans who were denied transportation to the hospital. The chapter also experienced significant harassment by the police and the FBI, which resulted in arrests and disruption of its activities. On 7 March 1971, the chapter organized a Revolutionary Intercommunal Day of Solidarity, which rallied support for imprisoned activists like Angela Davis and Black Panther Party cofounder Bobby Seale and for the recent struggles in eastern North Carolina. Held outdoors in cold weather—city officials refused to permit the use of a high school gymnasium—the event brought to town the principals from the Wilmington struggle. Milton Fitch and Golden Frinks of the SCLC spoke. Fitch set aside differences between the SCLC and the Panthers over nonviolence; he addressed the audience, he said, "for one special reason. You see, I'm black and you're black. You're oppressed and I'm oppressed. And I'll be damn[ed], we got to stick together until we get this thing off our backs." Frinks's remarks connected the need to free all political prisoners, the destruction of black education, and the fight against the Vietnam War. Chavis reviewed the struggles against racism in the public schools in the state and then issued a strong endorsement of the Panthers. "As a result of this," he said, "the man has become very repressive, not only to our brothers and sisters struggling in the educational system, but oppressing for any movements to our liberation. . . . We have to stand behind the Black Panther Party all the way because they're the vanguard party and they have proven to be a party for the people, and the people has [*sic*] to stand behind that party."[38] Chavis, the CRJ, and the Black Panthers crossed paths periodically afterward, particularly during the protests in Pitt County over the murder of William Murphy by State Trooper Billy Day, as the Panthers tried to extend their influence to other parts of the state. But despite his strong early endorsement of the party, Chavis and the Panthers appear to have established only episodic relations. A plausible explanation is the admonition by the Reverend Leon White, Chavis's superior in the CRJ, not to have truck with secular radicals. Chavis was a controversial figure within the United Church of Christ's southern white congregations, but White pledged his support if he kept his distance from the Panthers.[39]

The nationalists represented by Chavis, the CRJ, and SOBU were involved in work to reform the criminal justice system and to build an independent black political movement. Racism in the criminal justice system had long been a concern of the CRJ. Its formation was spurred, in fact, by the case of Marie Hill, a seventeen-year-old black girl from Rocky Mount, North Carolina, who was convicted of murder and given the death penalty in 1968. Upon her arrest, Hill had been denied legal representation and forced to write a confession. She later pleaded not guilty, but at trial her race, class, and sex counted heavily against her, while the murdered man's reputation as the operator of an illegal gambling establishment and a child molester figured not at all in the jury's and the judge's mind. The CRJ defended Hill on appeal (employing the Ferguson Chambers law firm that represented the Wilmington Ten) and in 1971 successfully argued before the U.S. Supreme Court to have her sentence overturned.[40]

The commutation of Marie Hill's death sentence provided impetus for more work in this area. In May 1972 the CRJ, SOBU, and the SCLC held a statewide meeting on criminal justice issues at Raleigh's historically black Shaw University. According to Leon White, the gathering would "develop plans to aid political prisoners and to finalize plans to organize black communities to guarantee equal justice for Blacks in state and federal courts." This was to be no legalistic session; rather, participants would strategize about a campaign to reform the system through mass protest, legal defense, and legislative pressure. Participants were drawn from the ranks of movement attorneys like James Ferguson and Irv Joyner, grassroots organizers like Owusu Sadauki of the Malcolm X Liberation University and Nelson Johnson of SOBU, black elected officials like Chapel Hill mayor Howard Lee (the first southern black mayor of a predominantly white town) and state representative Joy Johnson (the second black member of the General Assembly elected in the twentieth century), and aspiring politicians like Dr. Reginald Hawkins (the Charlotte civil rights activist who made a respectable showing in his two campaigns for the Democratic Party gubernatorial nomination in 1968 and 1972 and who helped clear a path for succeeding waves of black elected officials). Among the specific results of the conference was the formation of the North Carolina Criminal Justice Task Force. This group brought together black legislators, lawyers, and civil rights and Black Power activists and held a series of ten hearings across the state. The one in Wilmington was held in August at the Congregation of the Black Messiah; Leon White, Ben Chavis, Irv Joyner, and Joy Johnson presided. Witnesses testified about previously undocumented instances of police misconduct, the glaring absence of African

Americans from law enforcement, the exclusion of blacks from juries, and other facets of racial discrimination. The hearing panel directly linked this abuse to the illegal seizure of power by whites in the 1898 race riot and concluded that a major reason for the racial revolts in Wilmington was the "inability of the Black community to gain relief from police brutalities through the legal channels." The panel issued fourteen recommendations for rectifying the situation that members said depended on the extensive political mobilization of black people.[41]

Criminal justice reform was important to SOBU, too. In a perceptive opinion article in the *African World*, Nelson Johnson reviewed the history of black people's ensnarement in the criminal justice system. In a "profit oriented society," the majority of crimes "are the result of exploitative relationships between people." The society's laws favor the few who control the wealth at the expense of the majority, whose labor augments the minority's wealth and power. American society followed the Golden Rule—the one who has the gold makes the rules: "Thus the materially hungry must steal to survive, and the psychologically hungry must commit anti-social acts because their human needs cannot be met in a property oriented state." But while most persons considered criminals were themselves victims of exploitative socioeconomic relations and racism, and while some of them became politically conscious while they were incarcerated, it was important not to romanticize them and elevate them to the status of "political prisoners." Johnson argued that there was misguided activity that focused on so-called political prisoners and perhaps even claimed that incarcerated people would lead the revolution. Some advocates of this view, Johnson believed, were involved in questionable fund-raising and "monetary rip-offs." Idealizing prisoners was counterproductive; becoming involved in prisoner education programs and infusing the curriculum with pan-Africanism, however, would have salubrious results.[42]

The movement had to be selective in who it labeled a political prisoner and worked to free. Campaigns to free political prisoners like Angela Davis, Huey Newton, and later the Wilmington Ten were valuable in awakening African Americans. But a mode of operation that focused on campaigns to free all manner of incarcerated persons was not sustainable, and it distracted from the task of building a comprehensive movement to tackle the ills facing black people. "The only solution to solving the problem of political prisoners, dope-addiction, hunger, fratricide, etc. is by a fundamental transformation of our society . . . in the form of a mass based political party of politically conscious individuals, that are totally committed to the struggle, and not just enthusiastic and emotionally aroused," Johnson argued.[43]

Ben Chavis, Owusu Sadauki, Nelson Johnson, their respective organizations, and other black nationalists worked to harness the political energy generated by African Americans into a left-wing political movement that united both grassroots activists and aspiring politicians. In the estimation of Johnson and others, the spontaneous protests characteristic of the early Black Power era of the late 1960s had exhausted themselves, and rather than agitating, trying to manufacture outrage, and stimulating street demonstrations, activists needed to lower their profile and get on with the business of political education. "We are not at this time in this country, in a revolutionary situation," Johnson observed. Among the earliest attempts to direct and coordinate political activity, developed at a conference at the UCC-owned Franklinton Center in Bricks, North Carolina, was the idea of establishing an information clearinghouse. Chavis was tapped to head the organization with the endorsement of movement attorneys; the CRJ; the Malcolm X Liberation University; future members of the U.S. House of Representatives Frank Ballance, Eva Clayton, and G. K. Butterfield; radical students; and others.[44]

This particular venture seemed not to materialize, but there were soon meetings around the state whose initial purpose was determining an appropriate course of action for African Americans in the 1972 election cycle. As discussion occurred about the necessity of defeating incumbent Richard Nixon and identifying an acceptable Democratic candidate, the radical nationalists enlarged the parameters of the conversation. While some of the most influential African American politicians, like U.S. Representatives Louis Stokes and John Conyers, advocated for separate black caucuses while committing to work within the two-party system, black nationalists in North Carolina seemed to gain traction for their argument that this approach would lead African Americans into a cul-de-sac. A focus on "the promise that a Black man will one day sit in the whitehouse [sic]" was no substitute for building black political power. They argued for political independence and for developing an agenda that would address the needs of the majority of African Americans and would remove "ourselves from spheres of influence of white control such as the Democrat and Republican factions of the white party." In April 1971 they began to lay the foundation for an independent black political party, which debuted at the end of the year. While it planned to field candidates for the 1972 elections, according to future Wilmington Ten attorney and influential African American politician Frank Ballance, the Black People's Union Party would begin with small-scale initiatives such as survival programs followed by agitation for jobs and educational reform. It planned to build a presence in more than twenty locations across North Carolina, including Raleigh, Wilmington, and Rocky Mount, and would be organized around issues rather than around the projection of a personality.[45]

The political momentum continued into 1972, sometimes changing names but converging with the nationwide drive toward a black political assembly. Founded in March 1972 in Gary, Indiana, whose black mayor, Richard Hatcher, hosted the affair, the National Black Political Assembly was an experiment: Could the nascent class of black elected officials who were emerging in post-segregation America and the local and national networks of revolutionary nationalists effect a working alliance to advance the demands of black people? Would African Americans' demands concerning police brutality, political repression, jobs, education, and the like advance along independent lines, or would they be subsumed in the two-party system despite being gilded with a patina of radical rhetoric? Four thousand African Americans from forty states, the District of Columbia, and all walks of life gathered in Gary under the slogan "Unity without Uniformity" to find the answer.[46]

In North Carolina the initial results looked promising. As part of the run-up to the Gary convention, the Black People's Union Party organized a statewide meeting at Raleigh's Shaw University that drew five hundred participants and led to the formation of an even broader organization named the North Carolina Black Caucus. The meeting adopted a resolution on Wilmington that linked causes of the February 1971 uprising to the illegal overthrow of the city's integrated Fusionist government by white supremacists in 1898. The resolution called for an investigation of the criminal justice system and for the Congressional Black Caucus to investigate the historical and contemporary situation in Wilmington. The meeting at Shaw, which brought together Democrats, Republicans, and blacks not affiliated with either party, passed resolutions on important economic issues, too, such as favoring the establishment of a guaranteed annual income and free day care and health care.[47] The momentum continued with the annual meeting in April 1972 of YOBU at North Carolina Central University in Durham. About 1,500 students from both historically black and predominantly white colleges across the state convened and pledged themselves to continue the political organizing begun at Gary and in particular to campaign for freedom for the recently arrested Ben Chavis and the Wilmington Ten.[48]

Nationally, the tensions between black activists who aspired to electoral politics and those who sought change through revolutionary mass organizing were palpable soon after the Gary convention. Most black elected officials opposed political independence; they wanted to use the convention's agenda to rate candidates and secure votes for Democrats. The revolutionaries and nationalists were highly distrustful of such vote bartering and skeptical that any major party candidate, from presidential hopeful down to dog catcher, would keep any promise to black people. "Obviously the Convention's slogan of 'unity without uniformity,'" opined the *African World*, "was replaced by 'opportunism without accountability' as soon as people left Gary." The point was not to debate whether Democrats or Republicans could better represent the interests of black people. Rather, "surviving the illusion of a populist McGovern thrust and the ridiculous Blacks for Nixon wave, the remaining alternative was to consolidate the power of Black people and aim at the fundamentals instead of engaging in silly 'McGovern or Nixon will save us.'"[49]

This tension, however, was not so acute in North Carolina, as the revolutionary nationalists were able to develop a program of action that won the approval of those who sought change through electoral means. An April 1972 meeting of the Black People's Union Party selected Ben Chavis and Owusu Sadauki as its leading members. The next month a meeting of the North Carolina Black Caucus debated whether to throw its support behind any of the major Democratic candidates in the 1972 gubernatorial election; but while there was some sentiment for this approach, probably among elected officials like Chapel Hill mayor Howard Lee and Raleigh city councilmember (and influential funeral home operator) Clarence Lightner, radicals like Owusu Sadauki, Nelson Johnson, and Leon White were able to prevail and prevent an endorsement.[50]

The debate was a healthy one and did not lead to schisms. In July, 350 people attended a meeting at Shaw University of the North Carolina Black Convention, which was the first statewide meeting of the group since the Gary convention. Preceding the gathering, about 75 participants, including representatives from the Black Panther Party, the CRJ, the SCLC, and the Republic of New Afrika rallied at the steps of the state capitol to protest the incarceration of African Americans and to call for the reform of the prison and criminal justice systems. The *African World* observed that the all-day meeting was notable for the absence of the political opportunism that marred the convention movement on the national level. The meeting's cochairs were Owusu Sadauki of the Malcolm X Liberation University and YOBU and Representative Joy Johnson. Clarence Lightner and Nelson Johnson "assumed leadership roles in the broadly based gathering." In addition to deciding how to relate to the national convention movement, the meeting devised a statewide agenda for work in social welfare, education, criminal justice reform, and voter registration as "suitable projects everyone could work on." The spirit of the meeting was best captured by the speech given by Representative Johnson. For this pioneer elected official, the important thing was not ensuring dominance for his agenda or political persuasion; rather, the important thing was ensuring a strong united front and allowing the views of all trends—reformist and revolutionary nationalist alike—to be heard: "To those blacks who wish to work inside the system—right on. To those who wish to work outside the system—right on. To those who favor violence—right on. To those who favor non-violence—right on. To the integrationists—right on. To the non-integrationists—right on. To the young—right on. To the old—right on. To all of you this convention says right on if it means we work together in a spirit of unity."[51]

This catholicity of spirit continued long after the closing gavel of the convention. And when the Wilmington Ten were put on trial and convicted, there already existed a broad-based foundation for a movement that not only could fight to free them but also could raise a host of questions related to racism, political repression, and the necessity for a new African American political activism to address these issues in a militant and productive way.[52]

CHAPTER 3

They're Taking Our Boys Away to Prison

I t took more than a year before state and local authorities felt ready, in March 1972, to make the mass arrests that they hoped would sideline for a long time Ben Chavis and other Wilmington black liberation fighters. During these months, Chavis, Kojo Nantambu, and other Black Power advocates continued to organize in Wilmington and eastern North Carolina, but they did so in conditions that were hostile and disruptive. The comprehensive pressure on the movement in Wilmington culminated in the arrests and trial of the Wilmington Ten.

One significant point of pressure was continued white vigilante activity. The Rights of White People organization was given wide berth to operate in Wilmington and New Hanover County. The group was out in force when the new school year opened in September, protesting the board of education's busing program for integration, and 150 members picketed Superintendent Heyward Bellamy's home that month. ROWP leader Leroy Gibson threatened "extreme measures" if busing was not stopped, and rallies of upward of 500 people featuring Gibson's incendiary rhetoric against integration and employment of African Americans in downtown businesses became a regular part of the political landscape that fall. Gibson publicly offered to train members and supporters in the production of Molotov cocktails; he instructed whoever would listen in committing sabotage. ROWP armed rallies in Hugh McRea Park and armed patrols through black neighborhoods resulted in skirmishes in October. On the fourth of that month, William McGhee, a black longshoreman, was threatened at gunpoint by David Joyce, a Klansman at whose Castle Street store McGhee was shopping. McGhee then shot Joyce in self-defense and turned himself in to the police. The United Klans of America called for their members to descend on Wilmington the next evening. In response the city declared a state of emergency, and while police chief H. E. Williamson called out the ROWP for "inflaming the situation," the state of emergency was enforced almost exclusively in black neighborhoods. The Good Neighbor Council took no measures against the ROWP but rather worked to disarm the black communities by persuading black residents to aid police in identifying "snipers and troublemakers." The city manager predictably blamed African Americans for the violence. At the same time, the police and sheriff's deputies were in contact with the different Klan factions and the ROWP, offering them advance notice of the impending state of emergency. The *Baltimore Afro-American* reported that "very few days go by without shots being fired into the black community by passing white motorists."[1]

A second point of pressure was the police campaign of harassment of Ben Chavis. One day he was arrested on the pretext that his car's turn indicator was not working. On the evening of 6 October, as he returned to Wilmington from his Oxford home, police stopped his car "to see if he had any type of arms, but he didn't," according to a report filed by Fred Cooper of the state Good Neighbor Council. His vehicle registration, however, was in his briefcase, which was in the trunk of the car, not the glove compartment. But rather than let him produce the registration, the police arrested him. Perhaps recognizing their recklessness, the police tried to release Chavis on a promise to appear for a trial or hearing. "Chavis, however, preferred to remain in jail and he said that he would stay . . . until the Messiah came," wrote Cooper.[2]

The Wilmington authorities' harassment of Chavis was situated within a growing federal plan devised and implemented by the Federal Bureau of Investigation with the knowledge and approval of the Johnson and Nixon administrations to suppress black nationalism and criminalize radical political dissent. The FBI's BLACKPRO was begun in 1968 and went beyond the traditional attempts to pin the civil rights movement to the Communist Party. BLACKPRO paid particular attention to black nationalist groups, including not just the Student Nonviolent Coordinating Committee but "new groups" that might emerge. FBI agents were directed to work their informants to keep tabs on "obscure community activists" who might become agitators. In 1968 the FBI developed an Agitator Index of individuals the agency believed exhibited potential for disruptive activity. The bureau tracked members of the Congress of Racial Equality, SNCC, the Southern Christian Leadership Conference, the Revolutionary Action Movement, the Nation of Islam, the Black Panther Party, and others. With the blessing of Lyndon Johnson's and Richard Nixon's attorneys general, bureau agents worked with the Department of Justice's Community Relations Service, the Bureau of Alcohol, Tobacco, and Firearms, and various military intelligence services to spy on black communities and individuals across the United States. The special agent in charge in the FBI's Charlotte field office enthusiastically embraced the espionage program, which was named COINTEL. Ben Chavis was added to the Agitator Index in 1969, and in Wilmington, FBI agents and local authorities began to develop informants who reported on the activities of the city's black nationalists. When the Agitator Index was merged into a larger spy list called the Administrative Index in 1971, Chavis was identified as a Key Extremist who was armed and dangerous.[3]

Arresting and trying Chavis on spurious but serious charges in quick succession was a third point of pressure. On 10 December 1971, Chavis and Jim Grant were arrested on federal charges of helping two fugitives, Theodore Hood and David Washington, escape. As described by historian Timothy Tyson, in 1970 Hood and Washington had been participants in the protests in Oxford, North Carolina, related to the murder of Ben Chavis's cousin Henry "Dickie" Marrow by a local white supremacist and his son. The police and justice system were unable and unwilling to punish the murderer, and the Good Neighbor Council was ineffective in containing African Americans' anger. Blacks exacted retribution for Marrow's murder (and other grievances) by setting fire to the town's tobacco warehouses. It was during that time that Hood and Washington drove their Buick into a police roadblock, where authorities discovered high-powered rifles and explosives in the trunk and arrested them. Out on bond, they hightailed it to Canada. Upon their return, they named Chavis and Grant as facilitators of their escape. In April 1972, Grant and Chavis were tried in federal court in Raleigh; Grant was convicted, but Chavis was acquitted. While it was known at the time that Hood and Washington received immunity for their testimony, it was not known until later that they were FBI informants and had exchanged their false testimony for immunity from prosecution and a variety of material inducements.[4]

A week after his and Grant's arrests, Chavis was charged with accessory to murder after the fact in the March 1971 shooting death of Clifton Eugene Wright. Wright and two other teenage boys had been visiting the home of Mollie Hicks, whose daughter Leatrice was involved in the Wilmington school protests. The boys had said that a white man came to the apartment door and shot Wright when he answered. In a panic, they had called Kojo Nantambu, one of the Wilmington student leaders and assistant pastor at the First African Congregation of the Black Messiah, for help. Wright's death jolted Wilmington's black community. City authorities asked for and received state law enforcement assistance. The SCLC called on Governor Robert Scott to "intervene in the tense and explosive situation in Wilmington." Chavis, who had been traveling across North Carolina organizing for the Commission for Racial Justice, stated from Raleigh that Wright's death was a racist murder. According to the State Highway Patrol, Chavis told the *News and Observer* of Raleigh that Wright was "assassinated" because he knew Mollie Hicks, who was one of the few adult supporters of the school boycott and who Chavis said received "numerous" death threats. The U.S. Civil Rights Commission called on the Justice Department to investigate, arguing that the police department's continued intimidation of Mollie Hicks was a clear violation of the law. Police chief Williamson angrily denied the charges, criticized Chavis for his "irresponsible" statements, and castigated the Civil Rights Commission for its inflammatory language. There was no evidence, Williamson insisted, that the killing was racially motivated or that there was even a white man involved. He believed that the two teenagers knew what had happened in Hicks's apartment but were not telling the police. Likewise, Mayor Luther Cromartie blamed "uninformed publicity-seeking individuals" for "a major percentage of the misunderstanding and ill feeling between the races."[5]

Pressing into service the tired trope about outsiders stirring up trouble, the police chief and mayor were patently wrong to evade responsibility for the dreadful state of Wilmington's race relations. Significantly, however, they were right about the death of Clifton Eugene Wright being neither an assassination nor a racially motivated murder. While the details are not entirely clear, Wright and his friends—Donald Reddick (aka Don Nixon) and Jerome McClain—were playing cards in the Hicks apartment. Gambling devolved into roughhousing, and a shotgun in the apartment was brought into the mix with tragic results: Nixon shot Wright. To cover up their crime, they claimed that the assailant was a white man. The police were unable to make headway solving the crime until later that year when they arrested Nixon for misdemeanor larceny and receiving stolen property. According to Kojo Nantambu, Nixon was then charged with killing Wright and told that if he implicated Chavis he would receive some consideration. (The chronology contained in Nixon's North Carolina Department of Public Safety offender record offers corroboration for Nantambu's assertion, as does the court record for Nixon in which the murder charge was dropped to involuntary manslaughter and sentencing was postponed until he testified against Chavis.) Nixon then told police that when he told Chavis what really happened, Chavis told him to continue to say that a white man committed the shooting. With Nixon providing all the evidence, Chavis and Mollie Hicks were arrested on 27 December as accessories after the fact to murder.[6]

Nixon's story lacks veracity. Why would he call Nantambu and tell him one account of the shooting and then immediately tell Chavis another? The authorities' pattern of using informants and false statements to ensnare Chavis also casts doubt on Nixon. And as Kojo Nantambu recollected, he and other activists were wary of Nixon from the beginning, harbored doubts about his story of Wright's death, and wanted to steer clear of him, all of which made any arrangement with Chavis improbable.[7]

Yet Chavis agitated the issue of Wright's death. His statement that Wright was assassinated roiled blacks in Wilmington and contributed to the authorities' decision to call in state troopers, who mostly patrolled black neighborhoods. Chavis was also the likely source for the Black Panther Party's report that Wright was killed by the Ku Klux Klan during a meeting of progressive African Americans in Hicks's apartment. In death, Wright was martyred, with the Panther newspaper reporting that others attending the so-called meeting, upon hearing the shotgun blast, ran to the door, only to discover "the body of a potential revolutionary." Chavis's statement that the police were aware of death threats against Hicks and had her under twenty-four-hour surveillance unmistakably implicated the police in the shooting.[8]

Given Nantambu's skepticism of Nixon, it is likely that Chavis, too, had doubts. His unwillingness to probe them points to a tactical shortcoming in the radical organizing tradition and had serious consequences for the movement in the Port City. One of the ways radical movements historically have presented their cases to the public is through the emotional appeal of the innocent victim. The Haymarket martyrs, Julius and Ethel Rosenberg, and the Communist Workers Party Five who were murdered in 1979 by an alliance of Klansmen and American Nazis with the assistance of the Greensboro police department and an informant for the federal BATF were all unfairly condemned by a repressive state apparatus. At the same time, they were serious activists involved in the business of making a revolution. Portraying them as more or less innocent reformers both does a disservice to what they stood for and creates suspicion and disillusion among potential allies when evidence appears that they partook in activity that contradicted the pure status their supporters projected. In the case of Clifton Wright's death, fixing blame on the wrong party dented the movement's credibility.

Chavis posted bail in the amount of $10,000 soon after his arrest and continued to organize. But the charge hung over him. In February 1972 during a speech at Queen's College in Charlotte, Chavis mentioned that he would one day like to visit Africa. District Court judge Gilbert Burnett heard of Chavis's remarks, rearrested him, and raised his bail tenfold, labeling him a flight risk. Chavis denounced this move, linking it directly with the authorities' attempts to control African Americans ever since the 1898 Wilmington Race Riot. Unable to make the higher bail, Chavis remained in jail for a week until attorney Frank Ballance successfully argued for a lower amount before another judge. Not until June 1973 did the case come to trial, and Chavis was acquitted of the reduced charge of accessory after the fact to involuntary manslaughter. In a well-publicized campaign that included mass protests, coalitions of local and national organizations, and an appearance in the courtroom by Angela Davis, the legal defense succeeded in conveying the tattered nature of the state's case. North Carolina's authorities suffered a significant defeat, but they nevertheless succeeded in monopolizing the time, energy, and resources of Chavis and many Wilmington activists that otherwise would have been directed against school segregation and other forms of inequality in the Port City and eastern North Carolina.[9] Charges of abetting a fugitive and being an accessory to murder, while serious and distracting, were a sideshow compared to federal and state authorities' attempts to punish Chavis directly and explicitly for the uprising of February 1971.

FROM THE POINT of view of the Wilmington police, mayor, and the district attorney, Chavis and his outsider associates had riled up the normally pacified African American community. The unrest had been put down only with great difficulty. The state was compelled to make an example of someone, and Chavis was the obvious choice. At the federal level, there was great interest in removing Chavis as part of COINTELPRO. The state solicitor (what North Carolina district attorneys were called until 1975) and the Wilmington police department worked closely with the FBI and the BATF to arrest and incarcerate Chavis. They were presented with such an opportunity in May 1971 when Allen Hall, a teenager with a peripheral connection to the school boycott, was arrested on unrelated charges.

In 1971, Allen Ray Hall was eighteen years old. His family life had been unstable, and he had had to fend for himself. His mother was not married and still in school when she gave birth to him, and he went to live with Allen Hall, who was his guardian and gave him his name. When the elder Hall died, he lived alternately with a foster family and his mother, who in the meantime had married a longshoreman. In the seventh grade Hall began to have difficulty in school, owing to a teacher who had a tense relationship with his mother and stepfather, criticized him in front of his classmates, and called attention to his out-of-wedlock birth. He dropped out of school in the ninth grade. He entered a life of marginal employment, sometimes working in a nursing home or odd jobs. Like other "brothers of the street," Hall was attracted to the February events. Though he was not, contrary to his insistence, intimately involved in the events at Gregory Congregational Church or a confidant of Ben Chavis, he was active enough in the boycott and protests near the high schools to be named in the federal court injunction that the school board successfully sought. After the uprising he came to the attention of SCLC organizer Golden Frinks, who employed him to help at meetings and set up and break down equipment.[10]

Hall also had a problem controlling his temper. On 8 or 9 March—arrest warrants contain both dates—he went to New Hanover High School and got into a fight with two white school employees, smashing each with a glass bottle. Within a couple of days the police issued warrants for Hall's arrest on charges of assault and assault with a deadly weapon. Hall fled first to New York and then to Washington, D.C. For a short time he worked in a Coca Cola bottling plant but became homesick and returned to Wilmington in May. On the fourteenth he was arrested and remained in jail because he could not make bail. His requests for assistance from Chavis and the Black Youth Builders of the Black Community went unfulfilled. As Kojo Nantambu remembered telling Hall's mother, the BYBBC was feeling the sting of the police and city officials and was not able to help Hall, especially since he was not an active member of the organization. Nantambu speculated that Golden Frinks then interjected himself and cultivated the idea in Hall's mind that he was stewing in jail while Chavis was free because Chavis and the BYBBC refused to help him. This version of events is plausible, given the sometimes-toxic competition between the CRJ and the SCLC in Wilmington and the hyperventilated rhetoric that these groups exchanged in the months following the uprising. Confined to his jail cell, Hall began to turn against Chavis and the movement.[11]

If Hall thought he was being ignored by Chavis and wanted to exact a measure of revenge, he received further encouragement from the district attorney. Two weeks after his arrest, Hall was charged with shooting at police and wounding Wilmington police sergeant H. F. Genes a few blocks from Gregory Congregational Church on the evening of 5 February and burning Mike's Grocery the following night. From the time he was charged until Chavis and the Wilmington Ten were arrested in March 1972, Hall received multiple visits from police detectives W. C. Brown and D. L. Monroe and the assistant district attorney Jay Stroud. They cajoled and pressured Hall into incriminating Chavis and Marvin Patrick and concocting statements that provided the basis of Hall's testimony against

Allen Hall in an undated photograph. Photograph from the Raleigh News and Observer, *8 March 1977, courtesy of the State Archives of North Carolina, Raleigh.*

the Ten. Hall met them alone without his court-appointed attorney, Frank Cherry, who questioned his mental competence. After more than three months in custody but before Hall entered a guilty plea in the burning of Mike's and shooting at emergency personnel, Cherry secured a court order committing him to Cherry Hospital, the formerly segregated state mental institution in Goldsboro, for a psychiatric evaluation; he was discharged after sixty days with a diagnosis that he was competent to stand trial but was returned to the facility in February 1972. Two notable occurrences happened during Hall's time in the mental hospital: he continued to receive visits from Stroud and the two detectives, and he came into contact with Jerome Mitchell, a youthful offender from Wilmington who was charged with murder and robbery but who claimed tangential connection to the events of February 1971. Hall and Mitchell, facilitated by Jay Stroud, the Wilmington Police Department, the FBI, and the BATF, fabricated a tale in which Chavis commanded his minions to commit arson and attempt murder. They finalized their version of events in February 1972 during joint interviews.[12]

Right after Hall and Mitchell made their joint statement to investigators, Stroud acted to present them as witnesses before a grand jury. Shortly after, District Attorney Stroud and the federal authorities believed that Allen Hall and Jerome Mitchell were solid enough as witnesses and their stories sufficiently synchronized to begin the process of taking Ben Chavis and other Wilmington activists into custody. Except for Chavis, who exactly would be caught up in the dragnet seemed to be arbitrary. Ann Shepard, a white VISTA volunteer and mother of young children in her thirties who had taken up the boycott cause, was on the list from the beginning. Stroud considered charging the Reverend Eugene Templeton of Gregory Congregational Church and his wife, Donna, for their hosting the student protest in February 1971 but decided not to; likewise, student leader Benjamin Wonce was considered and then discarded. Joe Wright and George Kirby, who would later be added to the Ten, were also considered but not picked up. When the arrest warrants were executed beginning 16 March, seven of the twelve persons taken into custody were eventually tried as part of the Wilmington Ten: Chavis, Ann Shepard, Connie Tindall, Jerry Jacobs, James McKoy, Willie Earl Vereen, and Marvin Patrick. They were held on bonds of between $10,000 and $75,000. Five others—Jerry Leon Jacobs, James Bunting, Cornell Flowers, Tommy Atwood, and Mike Peterson—were also arrested. But the lineup of suspects kept shifting. When the probable cause hearing was held two weeks later, Jerry Leon Jacobs had been dropped. George Kirby was arrested in late April and

Joe Wright two days later. By the first week in May, Wayne Moore and Reginald Epps had also been indicted by a grand jury. All who would go on trial as the Wilmington Ten were now in custody, but neither the police nor prosecutors could say what linked them together.[13]

The Wilmington daily newspaper reported that the warrants, which were kept secret until Ben Chavis could be located, were executed beginning at 2 A.M.; the operation, which was conducted by police officers volunteering their time, was mostly finished by 4 A.M., with one final arrest coming shortly after seven in the morning. While the paper stated that eager police took the suspects by "complete surprise," those arrested were not unprepared. Almost immediately the CRJ articulated a strategy. The day after he was arrested, Ben Chavis was visited by a girlfriend, Alfreda Jordan, who tried to leave with a letter he had written to the Reverend Leon White with thoughts on mobilizing public opinion:

> Rev. White somehow we have go[t] to move quickly to bring mass political pressure on this system down here. My bond is too high to consider wasting that much money. However if you could get with [Roderick] Kirby, and Irv [Joyner] if possible and plan an immediate strategy on how to start local, state and national demonstrations protesting our illegal captivity this would help. The Chief of Police is lying, they have no positive evidence—just hearsay (I should know the Chief has also stated that he knows there will be no reaction from black people as a result of our arrest. We cannot let his statements prove to be true.)
>
> Contact John Mendez[;] some kind of protest could be held in Raleigh.

Within two days the CRJ and Wilmington local activists had begun to raise their voice in protest. They mounted a daily picket line with signs demanding freedom for "political prisoners" in front of the New Hanover County jail. Led by Irv Joyner, an attorney with the CRJ, twenty students at historically black St. Augustine's College in Raleigh marched through a surprise snowstorm from their downtown campus to the state capitol. (Students from nearby Shaw University, also historically black, found themselves snowed in and unable to participate.) They held press conferences, too, during which they articulated radical critiques of the political and criminal justice systems. They also paid attention to developing a front that united African Americans of different political orientations, for appearing with the CRJ's Irv Joyner were the revolutionary nationalist Kojo Nantambu, the nonviolent and slightly erratic Golden Frinks of the SCLC, and the aspiring electoral politician Reginald Hawkins, a Charlotte dentist and candidate for the 1972 Democratic gubernatorial nomination.[14]

Two strands of thought informed the political offensive after the arrests. First, the CRJ situated the arrests in the history of Wilmington since the 1898 riot. The Wilmington government was "illegal," constituted as it was in the aftermath of the coup d'état, and thus the arrests were illegitimate. The arrest of Chavis and others was not simply an unfortunate or singular miscarriage of justice. Rather, it was embedded in a history of vigilante justice and organs of authority doing the bidding of the extreme elements of white supremacy. In 1898 white Democratic Party leaders and their newspapers called for the overthrow of the city's biracial Fusion government and the summary killing of African Americans who tried to exercise their right to vote, and in 1971 it was the mayor and police chief who ensnared Chavis and more than a dozen others in response to ultimatums from the ROWP. Making this connection was of vital importance to the consciousness-raising that underpinned the campaign to free the Wilmington Ten from the beginning. This historical lesson, communicated in press conferences, street demonstrations, and articles in the *African World*, was useful for reaching a variety of audiences, including the white congregations (South and North) that coexisted with the southern black ones in the United Church of Christ; labor advocates and organized labor who saw parallels with repression against the working class and the low rates of unionization in North Carolina; and African Americans in Wilmington, the state, and the nation.[15]

Another skein of thought continued the language and analysis of black nationalism and pan-Africanism. Written and verbal speech was peppered with references to Africa and African liberation. From the New Hanover County jail, Chavis wrote open letters to "Dear African People," described his longing for the "motherland" and the necessity of "African-Americans relating back to Africa," and invoked terminology from Maulana Karenga's cultural-nationalist Kawaida philosophy. Analytically, Chavis linked the oppression of black Wilmingtonians with the oppression of Africans. DuPont, General Electric, and Gulf Oil—all with a significant presence in the Port City—"are exploiting and oppressing our brothers and sisters in Angola and all of southern Africa. These are the same corporations that are stealing the riches of our Motherland." Nationalists formed an African Peoples United Front in Wilmington to demonstrate and agitate against the exploitation of African Americans and Africans alike and to organize self-defense against the ROWP and its backers in local, state, and federal law enforcement.[16]

The arrests compelled Wilmington radicals to rethink their strategy. Kojo Nantambu announced his withdrawal from the New Hanover County Human Relations Council (formerly the Good Neighbor Council). For those in the BYBBC orbit, his presence on the council was an experiment: Could something positive and substantial be accomplished by joining with black and white moderates? The answer was no. He apologized for not recognizing this sooner and called for a renewed mass protest. Other North Carolina black nationalists had been moving in that direction for a while. The North Carolina Black Caucus, meeting at Shaw University on 26 February, adopted a "Resolution on Wilmington," which was subsequently presented to and approved by the Gary convention of theNational Black Political Assembly. Outlining the history of struggle in the Port City, it called for Wilmington to be a point of attention for African American activists and elected officials. The caucus attracted black Democrats and Republicans as well as unaffiliated African Americans and those advocating a separate black party, but it was the radicals' agenda that steered the meeting. The meeting adopted resolutions in favor of a guaranteed annual income, free day care, and free health care. In the weeks following the Gary convention, these same radicals were able to check efforts to hijack independent black politics into the Democratic Party. They gained important leadership positions in the caucus and fended off discussion of which white candidate to support in the Democratic gubernatorial primary. Because they were effective organizers and had a knack for finding common ground with black North Carolinians who aspired to office or inclusion in the two-party system, they were able to keep the moderates in the caucus despite the radical agenda. At the same time, the Left had the ability to organize separately from moderates and centrists, as seen by a meeting of the Youth Organization for Black Unity in April 1972 at North Carolina Central University in Durham, which drew 1,500 participants from across North Carolina.[17]

That the arrests came at a time not only of increasing struggle but also of heightened black unity was not lost on Irv Joyner, Kojo Nantambu, or the Hoggard High School student and member of the African Peoples United Front called "Mighty X," who appeared at a press conference after the roundup. "It was no accident that Reverend Chavis and the Wilmington 9 were arrested at the conclusion of the first national Black political convention," Joyner said at the conference:

The convention voted at that meeting to demand the dismantling of the present illegal Government of Wilmington and that [local] and state elections be held to guarantee that all of the citizens of Wilmington have a voice in the selection of a new city Government. The convention also voted to begin a national campaign to inform black people across the country about the [repression] of black people in Wilmington and to provide technical aid and assistance to aid in the struggle here. . . . Wilmington is a symbol of all that is wrong and ugly in America. . . . White people have gone mad in the city. We are planning a long-range campaign to free Rev. Chavis and the Wilmington 9, to bring justice to the black community, to empower black people to have control over the operations of the Government of this city, and to bring the spirit of the Lord to civilize a mad, hungry, and greedy people.[18]

In fairly short order, then, the CRJ was ready to fight the arrests and indictments. By the time of the probable cause hearing, which took place two weeks following the arrests, mass protest was a visible part of the strategy. When the hearing opened just before 11 A.M., a group of between seventy-five and one hundred people maintained a vigil outside the New Hanover County courthouse with signs reading "We Shall Avenge 1898," "African Power," and "Judge Burnett Would Hang His Own Mother." Periodically they broke out in civil rights songs and chanted loud enough to disrupt the court proceedings. A reporter for the *Wilmington Morning Star* described the scene: "Large throngs of youthful blacks congregated in the vicinity of the Court House and crowded into the second floor District Court room. At one point over 225 people sat in the crowded court room or stood along the walls. A majority of the spectators were black and many were dressed in the blue denim garb characteristic of activists or wore green, black and red Black Power buttons."[19]

They had their work cut out for them. The judge, Gilbert Burnett, was not an obvious racist in the manner of his fellow jurist John Walker, whose comments about clearing out Gregory Congregational Church like Lieutenant William Calley at My Lai alarmed Wilmingtonians of goodwill a year earlier. Still, Judge Burnett had his prejudices, both racial and generational. The presence of more than two hundred young African Americans in his courtroom had an effect on him; he could feel the black community's interest in the case and seemed to be bothered by it. Reflecting on the hearing from a distance of three decades, Burnett made this comment apropos nothing: "Now keep in mind, the place is packed—90% of 'em black people—I mean, you know, in the courtroom. It was a good sized court room." He was dismissive of Chavis, "who came

in with his bible and his reversed collar—you know, he says he's a minister, maybe he is, I don't know. But uh . . . later he headed up the NAACP.
And I told my wife, I said, 'He will ruin 'em—you watch.'" Burnett was
determined to keep the press from investigating too independently the
charges against the defendants. For the two days that the hearing lasted,
he invited journalists into his chambers and schmoozed with them. "We
had coffee, we chatted, shook hands—you know, all that stuff, went back
in [to court]. . . . I wasn't betrayed by one, not one."[20] For a hot beverage
and face time with the judge, the press accepted largely without question
the veracity of the charges against the Wilmington defendants.

Burnett had been on the bench for a decade and had some sympathy
for blacks who protested their exclusion from public accommodations. In
some way he identified with them and speculated that he might have done
the same things they were doing were he in their subordinate position.
But as a well-situated white North Carolinian, he just could not conceive
that black Wilmingtonians could disrupt Jim Crow on their own; as he
described it, the first sit-in cases he heard as an assistant judge around
1962 were instigated by northern whites "to stir up the kids and to try to
make the courts look like fools." Burnett's staple tactic was to diffuse the
confrontation—rather than jail demonstrators, he would fine them, and if
they could not afford the fine, he would waive it. His goal was to take "the
wind outta their sails" and show the outsiders the way out of town.[21] But
if this approach worked to Burnett's satisfaction in the early 1960s, it was
ineffective in 1972, as activists increasingly rejected civil disobedience and
the perceived respect for authority that went with it. Not only was their
rhetoric more provocative and incendiary, but also they did not exhibit a
shred of faith in the judiciary or in the concept of rule of law as guardians of
their rights. Rather, they saw the courts as another instrument of coercion.

Burnett had no patience for a movement that did not exhibit deference
to his court or to the established order. When the probable cause hearing
opened, he took the spectators to task for including in their midst youth
under the age of sixteen; he threatened the organizer of the crowd—"some
adult Black male," he said—with arrest for contributing to the delinquency
of minors and the youths with a visit from a truant officer. After this tongue
lashing, he changed to a paternalistic tone. "We love our children here
in this county, black or white," he said, and for good measure he passed
along what he said was ten-year-old advice from Tom Jervay, the older
and moderate owner of Wilmington's black weekly paper, to the effect
that black students should not skip school to protest for civil rights. "This
was good advice then and it still holds true," he wagged. The continued

protest exasperated him; as he responded to one of his critics soon after the hearings, Wilmington was a delightful place to live and "98 percent of the citizens, black and white, would like to forget the race issue and work together for the good of the community." And he justified his harsh pretrial rulings, especially in matters of bail, by making unfavorable—and ahistorical and disingenuous—comparisons between nonviolent demonstrators like "the James Merediths and the Doctor Kings" and the defendants now before him. Before a meeting of the racially moderate Human Relations Commission, Burnett declared, "I think it is time all of us—black and white—recognize that the criminal element has infiltrated the civil rights movement. . . . You have this criminal element which has entered the picture as it often does for a given cause."[22]

Judge Burnett's insistence on what historian William Chafe termed "civilities" and his evident animosity toward the defendants and the direction of the movement in the city and state guaranteed an unfavorable outcome for the Wilmington activists. Even so, the state's case was surprisingly leaky, which was apparent even to journalists whom the judge claimed to tame. The two-day hearing was a dress rehearsal—minus a stacked jury—of the trial that would take place in September and October. Reported the *Wilmington Morning Star* about the state's main witness, "Serious contradictions and confusion was apparent in portions of the witness testimony. . . . In addition, he showed confusion . . . and had difficulty relating" the events of February 1971.[23]

Answering Stroud's often leading questions, Allen Hall narrated a story about the night of 6 February 1971, during which Mike's was burned and police and firefighters were allegedly assaulted. Around 9:30 that evening, Hall claimed, he left the boycott headquarters at Gregory Congregational Church in the company of Ben Chavis and Marvin Patrick; he and Chavis had pistols, Patrick a shotgun. They walked one block west to Nun Street and Sixth Street. They remained near that intersection for around fifteen minutes, discharging their weapons in the direction of police cars a block away at Nun and Fifth, and then returned to Gregory. Hall's recollections were specific and his descriptions exact.[24] But he unraveled under cross-examination by James Ferguson and his cocounsels John Harmon, Matt Hunoval, and Frank Ballance.

There were factual inconsistencies, as when Hall said he had a .38 caliber pistol and then said it was a .25. He stumbled over his recounting of where he, Chavis, and Patrick went in the neighborhood and could not correctly identify street names or where they went, confusing, for example, the order and direction of numbered streets; it was as if he was visiting the environs of Gregory Church for the first time. Inexplicably, he could not identify the color of an undercover police car even though it was directly under a streetlight but could easily identify Marvin Patrick, who was down the street enveloped in shadows.[25] Hall's testimony on cross-examination was riddled with such errors.

Equally revealing were statements elicited by the defense attorneys of possible motives for Hall's testimony. Ferguson got it into the record that Hall had been arrested in May 1971 and convicted in January 1972 on the very charges that were currently being brought against the defendants. He tried to find out whether District Attorney Jay Stroud offered Hall leniency in return for his testimony; Hall admitted that he talked to police and implicated Chavis and others because he thought they would go easier on him. But when Stroud objected to this line of questions, the judge stopped it. The judge could not, however, stop Hall from announcing another motive for his testimony. Under redirect examination, he pointed a finger at Chavis and told Jay Stroud that he had agreed to testify because he was angry at Chavis for not helping him. In his re-cross-examination, Ferguson probed Hall's admission, suggesting that the police and Golden Frinks of the SCLC separately exploited his grudge in order to get Hall to implicate Chavis. And Ann Shepard's attorney Matt Hunoval, in his cross-examination, brought to light a February 1972 letter Hall wrote to her from jail that threatened her life if she did not corroborate his story.[26]

In a bizarre twist that should have caused Judge Burnett to question the core of the state's case, Allen Hall at the conclusion of his testimony leaped from the witness stand and tried to attack Ben Chavis:

MR. FERGUSON: You want Chavis bad, don't you?
HALL: No, sir.
MR. STROUD: OBJECTION
HALL: No, sir, BECAUSE TO ME HE IS NOTHING . . .
MR. BALLANCE: Can we have the reporter indicate with exclamation points he answered with hostility? . . .
([As attorneys discussed with the judge whether to end for the day] Mr. Hall left the witness stand and there was commotion in the courtroom.)
THE COURT: Sit down! I don't want any demonstrations.
MR. FERGUSON: I would like the record to show the witness came down from the witness stand and came straight for Mr. Chavis and had to be restrained by law enforcement officers.[27]

The most startling evidence to emerge from the probable cause hearing was not any of Hall's fabrications of fact but the active role of the district attorney and the police in constructing Allen Hall's testimony. From the first hint that Hall met with police detectives after he was jailed in May 1971 because he thought he would receive some consideration, Ferguson probed his relationship with the authorities. Hall acknowledged that when he was arrested for burning Mike's and assaulting emergency personnel, he did not implicate Chavis or the others. But after three days in jail, Hall said, he then gave a full accounting of the crimes of Ben Chavis and the other defendants to Wilmington police detectives Brown and Monroe and signed that statement. He then said that he met the detectives not just once but "several" times between his arrest in May 1971 and a week before the probable cause hearing in March 1972 and that his statement about Chavis's crimes evolved over those interviews. "I told them a section of it at a time," he said, which contradicted his earlier testimony about making a full statement.[28]

The importance of this discovery was immediately apparent both to the defendants and to the district attorney. Did Hall's story change over time? Did the district attorney and the police tell Hall what to say? Each time Hall met with authorities, did he sign a statement? James Ferguson tried to force the district attorney to turn over the records of Hall's interviews and his written and signed statements. "We made a request as early as we could because we made it as soon as we found out that there were such statements in existence. Prior to today, we did not know about them," he told the judge. Jay Stroud resisted turning over the records. More, he tried to prevent the defense from questioning Hall about his interaction with the authorities. Stroud stated that he would stipulate that he and the police detectives met with Hall several times. But as Ferguson pointed out, that stipulation raised the question of the substance of those meetings, and what Stroud wanted was to be able to have Hall testify but not be cross-examined. Judge Burnett sided with the prosecution, which allowed Stroud to hide evidence that Hall was not being truthful and to conceal the state's role in suborning his testimony. The withholding of this evidence handicapped the defense's efforts to challenge the credibility of the state's main witness.[29]

At the conclusion of the hearing's second day, Judge Burnett ruled that there was probable cause and bound the defendants over for trial. The stated had secured a victory after months of manipulating Allen Hall, stopping Chavis in the street, looking the other way at ROWP aggressions, and charging Chavis with other serious crimes; the police and prosecutors finally ensnared Chavis and the movement in Wilmington. But prosecutors were like the proverbial dog that chased a car and caught it: What would it do next? The district attorney had a big sloppy case that rested on the testimony of two young men—Allen Hall and Jerome Mitchell—who had been marginally involved with the protests, had been incarcerated for other unrelated crimes, and had incentive to lie for the state. With the shifting cast of characters and key witnesses' shaky accounts, the state's attorney found the cases becoming unmanageable. State Solicitor Allen Cobb concluded that "there is no way in the world we can try all the cases at once." The indictment of Chavis and Marvin Patrick for the murder of Harvey Cumber was put on hold, and four of the remaining defendants (Atwood, Bunting, Flowers, and Peterson) had their trials postponed—permanently, it turned out—as the state prepared to try eleven for burning Mike's Grocery, conspiracy to burn Mike's, and conspiracy to assault emergency personnel.[30]

Because they were unable to post bonds of between $7,500 and $50,000, Chavis, Jacobs, McKoy, Patrick, Tindall, and Vereen remained in jail. When Wright, Epps, Moore, and George Kirby were arrested, their bail was set at between $10,000 and $15,000, which was subsequently reduced to $5,000. But their families were unable to raise that amount, and they, too, were locked up pending trial. Only Ann Shepard, who like Kirby was charged only with conspiracy, made her $4,000 bond. The state made it difficult for them to prepare their defense. First, they were scattered across at least four prisons in eastern and central North Carolina, which was a strain on their lawyers. Many times the attorneys needed to see them together or have them meet with potential witnesses. The inconvenience did not end when they were housed in the New Hanover County jail at the start of the trial. In an instance that James Ferguson strongly implied was typical, his meeting with his clients was delayed by four hours, and even then the only place available for the meeting was a large cell, with him on the outside conferring with them through prison bars. Despite the evident hardship—and despite the facts that Chavis never failed to appear in court and that his codefendants had deep ties to their communities, had jobs that they could return to, or had parents who swore to guarantee their children showed up for trial—the court refused to lower their bail or release them on their own recognizance.[31]

In the months between the probable cause hearing and the June trial date, defense attorneys attempted two measures to ensure justice for their clients. At the beginning of May, James Ferguson, Frank Ballance, and John Harmon petitioned the U.S. District Court to remove the trial from state court to the federal court. They complained of roadblocks put up by the prosecution and state judiciary: they were not given adequate time to prepare their case, they had not received the written transcript of the probable cause hearing, and the district attorney was determined to bring a series of charges in separate trials against the defendants, which would keep them wrapped up in court for the foreseeable future. At its core, they argued, the state's case criminalized political activity, and their clients were "being persecuted because of their alleged involvement in protesting racial discrimination against black citizens." While they waited for a ruling from U.S. District Court judge Franklin Dupree, the state could not move forward with its case, but at month's end Dupree denied the petition and returned the case to superior court. Upon this setback Ferguson and his colleagues sought and obtained a change of venue, and the trial was moved to Burgaw, the seat of neighboring Pender County. On 5 June 1972, with Judge Joshua James presiding, the curtain rose on another act of political theater masquerading as a criminal trial.[32]

JUDGE JAMES WAS sixty-five years old when the eleven defendants appeared in his courtroom. He was not a career jurist, having been appointed to the bench only two years previously to complete the unexpired term of Rudolph Mintz, who had died in office. His sensibilities were shaped both by his prosperous family's roots in North Carolina, which stretched back to before the American Revolution, and by his and his family's political connections. His father was a state legislator, and a brother was a state supreme court justice. When James was two years out of law school in 1949 (he matriculated late, after operating the family farm and enlisting in the Army Air Force during World War II), Governor Kerr Scott appointed him to the Public Utilities Commission; two decades later another governor appointed him chair of the North Carolina Industrial Commission, which administered the workman's compensation laws. As an attorney in private practice and in his government posts, Judge James was used to protecting the established order. Like other white racial moderates of his day, he desired a smooth management of the transition from segregation to a new racial order, any deviation from which he viewed as extremism. Black radicalism especially was anathema to him.[33]

And yet his did not appear to be a malignant "law and order" courtroom in the fashion of a legal lynching courtroom like the Scottsboro defendants faced in the 1930s or that Richard Nixon was trying to recreate in the 1970s with his "tough on crime" rhetoric. He seemed particularly sensitive to actions that could stir racial resentment. When attorney Ferguson told the judge that transporting the defendants to the front of the courthouse and taking them off the bus and handcuffing them together was both humiliating and possibly prejudicial should potential jurors see them, Judge James stopped the practice. The judge, too, removed the large number of armed deputies flanking the bench when Ferguson argued that their presence implied his clients were dangerous and could adversely affect the jury. Judge James denied defense motions to sequester potential jurors during voir dire so as to minimize the influence of racially charged statements during jury selection, but on balance the legal team believed that the judge protected the defendants' rights to a fair trial.[34]

Observers got further hints of the quality of fairness that would be available to the defendants during jury selection. The rules governing the selection of the jury were this: All who were called to jury duty were sworn in, and twelve potential jurors from the venire were called to the jury box. They were questioned both as a group and individually, first by the state prosecutor Jay Stroud. The prosecutor, who had available to him four preemptory challenges per defendant, for a total of forty-four, could also ask the judge to excuse a juror "for cause," meaning something about the juror—a connection with potential witnesses or preconceived opinions about the case—prevented her or him from reaching a fair verdict. A dismissed potential juror was replaced in the box by another person called from the venire. Once Stroud had assembled a jury with which he was satisfied, it was passed to Matt Hunoval, who represented Ann Shepard, who repeated the process followed by Stroud. When he was satisfied with the jury, it was James Ferguson's turn. At the end of the first round, any juror approved by the prosecutor and both defense attorneys was seated as a juror; the remainder of the jurors was passed back to Stroud, and the process was repeated until a jury of twelve was selected.

On the first day of jury selection, the initial composition in the box was eight whites and four African Americans. Stroud's questioning was generally unremarkable, as he tried to fashion a jury that would be sympathetic to the state. A couple of whites were excused for cause, including one whose racial animus was too evident even for Stroud, but he also excused jurors for what appeared to be the simple reason that they were black. When he passed the jury to Ann Shepard's attorney, the jury was ten whites and two blacks. Hunoval's questioning seemed to be directed at getting potential jurors to understand that his client was not on trial for arson, only conspiracy. When he was satisfied and passed the jury to Ferguson, its composition was nine whites and three blacks.

James Ferguson, the lead attorney for ten of the eleven Wilmington defendants, had a substantial investment in this case on several levels. He grew up in segregated Asheville, North Carolina, in the 1950s, and much like other African American teens of his generation, he chafed at the restrictions. In 1959, as president of his high school's student government, he organized protests against the construction of a substandard addition to the school. He and his classmates felt that the school should be equal to the white high school, "which looked basically like a college campus," and that blacks should be able to attend the white high school if they chose to do so. Their protest rallies and meetings with the school super-intendent halted the expansion and put into motion the construction of a new and improved black high school and eventually the desegregation of the system's secondary schools. The following year, in the wake of the Greensboro sit-ins, Ferguson helped to found and was the first president of the Asheville Student Committee on Racial Equality, which tackled the desegregation of public facilities in town. With training in nonvio-lent direct action by representatives of the American Friends Service Committee, the Asheville Student Committee on Racial Equality learned strategy and tactics for sit-ins and negotiating skills that led to victory. Before the protests began, Ferguson approached the only two black attor-neys in Asheville about the legal implications for what his group was about to do. Instead of the lecture he expected, they offered their sup-port and encouragement and promised their legal assistance if they were arrested or otherwise needed it. The lawyers' answer both surprised and inspired Ferguson; probably without knowing fully what it entailed, he determined that he would become a movement lawyer. After graduating from high school and then North Carolina Central University, he attended law school at Columbia University; instead of interning during summers in law firms—on Wall Street or otherwise—he deliberately sought jobs that put him in contact with the poor folks he was determined to serve.[35]

Ferguson earned his juris doctorate in 1967 and moved to Charlotte to join a law partnership with Julius Chambers and Adam Stein, forming the first integrated law firm in North Carolina. Within a few years the firm had a strong general practice to pay the rent and a robust devotion to civil rights law. He met Ben Chavis, who was then a student at UNC–Charlotte and attracting attention from the police and FBI. Ferguson made the same commitment to Chavis he had received a few years earlier from the two black attorneys in Asheville. He traveled to Wilmington to work on the federal suit Julius Chambers filed to desegregate New Hanover County schools and met student activists there like Joe Wright; when racial friction developed between black and white students and blacks were arrested on criminal charges, Ferguson was on hand to defend them. Perhaps those cases were a dry run for him, as he came to realize that the practice of civil rights law and criminal law were imbricated in a criminal justice system that has historically been used to silence society's critics.[36]

For two and a half days Ferguson probed potential jurors, seeking to uncover submerged biases against his clients in particular and popular struggles for racial equality in general. His questioning hinted at a strategy that both asserted his clients' innocence and aimed to educate jurors and the larger public about the racial and political contexts in which the trial was taking place. Prospective jurors, black and white alike, were reminded that the alleged crimes for which Chavis and the others were on trial took place during a time of racial and radical protest; jurors were asked if they recognized a right to protest oppressive conditions. They were told that several of the accused were members of the First African Congregation of the Black Messiah and asked if they were bothered by the concept of a black messiah. Because one of the charges involved guns, they were asked if they recognized the right of protesters to armed self-defense. Did jurors believe, he further asked, that because there were a large number of defendants on trial that some must be guilty of some charges? What was notable about the process was the number of jurors Ferguson successfully challenged for cause. It was not a difficult call for the judge to dismiss Mr. Edens, who had recently belonged to the Ku Klux Klan and subscribed to white supremacy. But a Mr. Thompson, a white juror, while professing remarkable open-mindedness about religion and integration, did not believe in a right to self-defense; and a Mrs. Alford, another white, said she would want to hear testimony from the defendants in order to clear away whatever doubt she may develop. In both of these and other instances, Judge James excused them for cause upon Ferguson's request. And while such jurisprudence may seem commonsensical, it was far different from the contentiousness that saturated the second trial of the Wilmington Ten. In any event, at the end of the day on Thursday, 8 June, James Ferguson pronounced the defense satisfied with the jury. There were nine blacks and three whites, including two blacks and one white agreed upon by all sides. The overwhelming majority of the remaining members of the jury pool were African American, virtually assuring a majority-black jury even if Stroud exercised all his remaining peremptory challenges.[37]

On Friday morning, Assistant District Attorney Stroud took control of the jury. From the transcript, it appears as if he was acting erratically. His questions were often abrupt, and he called jurors by wrong names.

Sometimes he did not make it clear whom he was addressing, prompting jurors to ask him if he was addressing them. He tried to question the three jurors who had already been seated, prompting Ferguson to object, which the judge sustained; Stroud, though, did it once more and once again was corrected by Judge James. He engaged in a particularly contentious exchange with one potential juror, a middle-aged black man, as he tried to shake the man's position that he would be influenced by nothing save the evidence. But when it came time for the afternoon break, he had neither removed nor challenged for cause any of the jurors. Then something bizarre unfolded, with significantly adverse consequences for the course of the Wilmington defendants' legal fortunes.[38]

When court reconvened after lunch, Solicitor Stroud was not in the courtroom. State Solicitor Allen Cobb, who was Stroud's boss and co-counsel, explained to the judge that Stroud had taken ill and was running a fever. With the consent of the defendants the judge adjourned the proceedings for the weekend. On Monday morning, 12 June, Solicitor Cobb in open court told Judge James that Stroud remained sick with some type of gastrointestinal virus or infection—he did not know the specifics—and was unable to be present, and it was not clear to him when he would be healthy enough to return to the job. He claimed that Stroud was the only attorney of the four in his office who was familiar with the case—the state's attorney's office, with all of the resources at hand, apparently had a strict division of labor to avoid overburdening each lawyer. Given the uncertainty of Stroud's condition, Cobb moved for a mistrial. Matt Hunoval and James Ferguson objected to a mistrial. The defense had gone to considerable effort to mount its case, especially so since the accused could not make bail and had been incarcerated in jails and prisons widely scattered across the state; a repeat of this process would create a significant hardship on and expense for the attorneys, as well, who were compelled to devote their attention practically exclusively to the case and forgo cases that supported them. As Ferguson argued subsequently, why should the accused have to pay for deficiencies in the organization of the prosecutor's office? As Cobb stated to the court, Stroud knew he was becoming ill as early as Wednesday—why did the state make no provisions for preparing another prosecutor to step in?[39]

Judge James reluctantly granted the mistrial. He was mindful of the time, expense, and hardship to the defense. He granted, too, that the trial was proceeding in an orderly and fair fashion and that none of the security precautions he had put in place—he had authorized a large show of armed force in the aftermath of the courtroom shootings in the Jonathan

Jackson trial in California, for which Angela Davis had been tried and recently acquitted—proved necessary. He also expressed satisfaction in the fact that the white citizens of Pender County had remained calm. But he did not question the state's explanation of how it deployed its staff and felt that he had no choice but to end the trial.[40]

The circumstances surrounding the mistrial were until recently not definitively known. Stroud's odd behavior offered his defenders and those who are still convinced of the Wilmington Ten's guilt proof that he was in fact ill, even if the malady was not physical, but mental—Stroud's son subsequently claimed that his father had suffered from bipolar disorder since he had been a law student in the 1960s.[41] But at the time and for the past forty years, the defendants and their supporters scoffed at Stroud's claim of stomach distress. In September 2012 the *Wilmington Journal* published newly discovered documents that definitively show that State Solicitor Stroud feigned illness in order to get a mistrial and a second chance at a favorable jury. On the back of a legal pad, Stroud weighed the disadvantages and benefits of a mistrial. The chief drawbacks, Stroud reckoned, were wasted time and "inconvenience to all concerned." But the advantages were clear—and evidently persuasive. A mistrial would bring a different judge; allow him better to prepare for jury selection; give him the chance to argue for a jury venire from Jones County, which he figured would be less sympathetic to the defense; and enlist the assistance of a special prosecutor.[42]

The evidence strongly suggests that the mistrial was not unanticipated but premeditated, at least by Stroud. Ben Chavis believed that the driving force was the overambitious assistant district attorney and that District Attorney Allen Cobb did not want to prosecute the case in the first place. What can be stated with certainty is that the state got a mulligan. Based on how the jury selection went over the first week, it is reasonable to assume that the jury's composition would have been fair to the defense. Despite Judge James's refusal to lower bail, he was vigilant in protecting the rights of the accused. And, too, although the defense argued from the beginning that Pender County's method of constituting a jury pool discriminated against African Americans and young people, it appeared that the citizens who were summoned to jury duty were indeed fair-minded and honest. Evidence for this observation comes from the state's effort to impanel a jury from a different county.[43] Such attempt was unsuccessful, but with a new jury venire, a new judge, and reinforcements from the state attorney general's office, Stroud thanked his stars and prepared anew to frame the Wilmington Ten.

Disadvantages of Mistrial	Advantages of Mistrial
1) waste of a week	✓1) different judge
2) could affect Hall's attitude & other witnesses.	✓2) better prepared to select jury & to handle motions / more organized
3) possibly waste of 2 weeks unless Allen can set up quick docket	✓3) avoid longer jury selection & hang jury in Pender because of their concern about retaliation.
4) inconvenience to all concerned	✓4) fresh start w/ new jury from another county.
5) possibly get Judges Chess, Godwin or Copeland on new trial	✓5) avoid reversible error & new trial on back of Def - witness interviews
6) delaying getting cases over with	✓6) can enlist Dail Johnson's help
would be true even if Pender if got a Special Venire from Jones.	✓7) opportunity to separate Shephard from others to keep out Hall's letter.
	✓8) time to have case well prepared & organized.

As he was allegedly battling an illness that landed him in the hospital, prosecutor Jay Stroud found time to write a list that detailed the reasons to ask for a mistrial in the first (June 1972) trial of the Wilmington Ten. That trial, which was in the jury selection phase, would almost certainly have resulted in the impaneling of a majority-black jury. Among Stroud's reasons to push for a mistrial was the strong possibility of getting a new judge to take the place of Joshua James, who treated the defense fairly; the likelihood of a more favorable jury, which to Stroud meant fewer blacks and more possible KKK members; and a chance to be better prepared and organized. Courtesy Timothy B. Tyson Papers, Southern Historical Collection, Wilson Library, University of North Carolina at Chapel Hill.

WITH A NEW trial on the calendar for September in the Pender County seat of Burgaw, the state of North Carolina began afresh its preparations to send the Wilmington Ten to prison. (Between the two trials, George Kirby jumped bail and was not put on trial with the others, thus reducing the number of defendants to ten.) Perhaps concluding that the trajectory of the aborted June trial was preventable, state attorney general Robert Morgan assigned Dale Johnson, who was the first statewide special prosecutor, to the case; the position of special prosecutor was created to assist local prosecutors in complicated cases, Johnson remembered, and his assignment came after a request by Wilmington district attorney Allen Cobb. While this probably did not surprise revolutionary Black Power organizations in the state like YOBU, it irritated allies like Dr. Joy Johnson, who accepted the legitimacy of the political system. And even the racial moderates who otherwise opposed the Black Power activities represented in Wilmington by the First African Congregation of the Black Messiah and the BYBBC were rankled. Said New Hanover Human Relations Commission vice chairman James Chambers, "I do think they (authorities) are overreacting. . . . They are just making people think they're out to get Ben Chavis."[44]

The selection of Robert Martin to preside over the trial reinforced this belief. Born in 1912 and raised in Northampton County near the Virginia border on land granted to the family by the colony's lord proprietor, Martin was an enterprising farmer and businessman before studying the law first in a night school in Rocky Mount and then at Wake Forest Law School in Winston-Salem. As a young attorney in High Point he developed political connections and found mentors and friends among the state's railroads and industrial commissioners. He counted as a patron a former law professor, I. Beverly Lake, who in 1960 and 1964 mounted unsuccessful campaigns for governor on a hard segregationist platform. Martin's perspective was that Lake's race-baiting was merely a blemish; African Americans' sit-ins and challenges to North Carolina's obstructionism to school desegregation that rocked the state were of little consequence to Martin. "He was an all-out segregationist; there's no question about that," Martin remarked. "But that didn't affect me at all, personally." His loyalty paid dividends in 1965 when on Lake's recommendation newly elected Governor Dan K. Moore appointed Martin a special superior court judge. Unlike their elected counterparts, special judges are traditionally patronage appointees, are more insulated from political crosscurrents, and are better positioned to preside over controversial cases. With blithe disregard for the struggles for racial justice that bloomed all around him, Martin was on the bench for the trial of Robert and Larry Teel, two white men accused of murdering Henry "Dickie" Marrow, Ben Chavis's cousin, in Oxford in 1970. The two were acquitted in a trial replete with irregularities, which the *News and Observer*, a paper not known for its friendly voice to African Americans, pronounced a "sham and mockery."[45]

Procedurally, the chief justice of the state supreme court decides when and which special judge will be assigned to a particular case. The Wilmington Ten defendants believed that Attorney General Robert Morgan had a hand in persuading the chief justice to appoint Martin, though there is no paper trail to support such a belief. But Morgan and Martin were friends, enough so that the two took the ethically questionable step of taking lunch together during the trial. The Wilmington Ten lost their chance of a fair trial the moment Robert Martin was named the trial judge. Not only did he and the prosecution enjoy a cozy relationship implied by sharing a meal, but in at least three critical phases of the trial Martin's rulings placed the defendants at a clear disadvantage and made it practically impossible for Ferguson and his colleagues to mount a case.

Selecting a jury is fundamental to the course of a trial. That this process in the first trial was about to yield a majority-black jury that pledged to keep an open mind about both the prosecution and defense was enough for Stroud to ask for a mistrial. In the second trial, which was called to order on 11 September, the prosecution had two advantages it lacked in the first. The list of potential jurors from Pender County was disproportionately white, which in North Carolina's polarized social climate made it difficult for the defense to find a fair jury. And the judge routinely denied defense motions to excuse for cause jurors who plainly stated that they had preconceived ideas that the defendants were guilty. From the beginning, James Ferguson probed the jury pool to uncover potential biases or other impediments to a fair trial. For example, on the second day of jury selection, after both sides had agreed on only one juror, Ferguson asked one of the remaining eleven persons in the box if he knew anything about the case and where he might have gathered that information. The juror, who was a postmaster, answered that he read the *Morning Star* and the right-wing *Hanover Sun*. He further said that he had discussed the cases a fair amount in the course of his daily routine, had formed opinions about the defendants, and would need to have evidence of their innocence to change his opinion. Another juror stated that the defendants would need to prove that they were not guilty, because he already was of the opinion that they were. But Judge Martin denied Ferguson's motion to have them removed for cause. In another instance, a white juror stated that he was retired from the Wilmington Fire Department and considered one of his duties as a juror to "uphold the Police and Fire Department of Wilmington." The judge refused to excuse the juror for cause, and Ferguson continued to question him. When this juror revealed that his son was in the National Guard and was on duty in Wilmington during the February 1971 events, Ferguson renewed his motion and was again denied. But perhaps recognizing that he was acting obviously unfairly, Judge Martin excused this juror on his own discretion.

A white female juror stated strongly and in many ways that she would believe a police officer's testimony over any other person's testimony. Even the judge asked her questions, to which she gave the same answers, yet Martin refused to excuse her for cause. Right after, Ferguson solicited the view from all but one juror that they believed that an indictment was evidence of guilt; said one juror, "I don't think our officer just drove up on the corner and says, 'Here, you guys, go with me.' I think there is something to it." Ferguson again moved to exclude these jurors, and when the judge denied the motion, Ferguson used his preemptory challenges to excuse nine jurors who had not been seated. This pattern repeated itself over the course of the ten days of jury selection until the defense used up all of its discretionary challenges.[46]

Judge Martin not only disabled the defendants with his prejudicial rulings during jury voir dire but also allowed Jay Stroud and Dale Johnson a free hand to shape the jury to the state's liking. And according to Stroud's handwritten notes, he was pleased with prospective jurors who were white and racist: "Bryant (KKK) good"; "possibly KKK good"; "Pridgen (KKK?) good"; and "does not have record KKK!!" are four typical comments scrawled on the legal pad. Stroud made a note to himself to "stay away from black men," though he was favorably disposed to one African American man, whom he described as "sensible, Uncle Tom type."[47] Early in the selection process Stroud was able to disqualify a black woman when she admitted that she had some sympathy for the defendants, though she said she would listen to the state's case with an open mind and would follow the law and the judge's instructions. The judge's allowing of the juror's dismissal for cause was in stark contrast to his insistence that jurors who expressed bias against the defendants be kept on the jury. Most times, however, Stroud did not have to challenge jurors for cause—he simply used his preemptory challenges to remove black jurors. On the second day of selection, for example, with ten jurors still to be chosen, there were eight whites and two African Americans in the box; Stroud and Johnson excused the two blacks, who were replaced by whites. When the jury was passed back to the defense, three jurors had been chosen—including a black woman. At the conclusion of the second day, Ferguson and his colleagues passed the jury back to the state, with African Americans accounting for four of the nine outstanding jurors; at the beginning of the third day, Stroud dismissed the four blacks and none of the whites. Among those called to the box was another African American, whom Stroud promptly dismissed.[48] By the time the jury of ten whites and two blacks was impaneled, the state had taken advantage of a racially skewed jury pool—in a county whose population was 43 percent z cousin

- stay away from black ~~women~~ men   Leave off Rocky Pt., Maple Hill

                                          Put on Burgaw, Long Creek, Atkinson
                                                          Blacks

1) Prevdgen (KKK?) (good)

2) Justice (O.K.) (on basis name)

3) Suggs

✓ 4) Thompson

5) Rooks (hosp.)

6) Heath (O.K.) (KKK?)

✓ B 7) McIntyre (leery)

✓ 8) Rivenbark (O.K. on basis name)

B 9) Murphy (worth chance because from Atkinson)

✓ 10) Edens (good)

✓ B 11) Graham (knows; sensible; Uncle Tom type)

✓ 12) Wells (good on basis name; good)

13) ~~Speaks~~ Spayd (good on basis name) (Blueberry)

14) Wallace (Gene Wallace husband; fish camp) (not to be intimidated)

15) Baucom (outstanding)

✓ B 16) Sidbury (leave off)

✓ B 17) Wooten (leave off)

✓ 18) Alford (C. represented; good)

✓ B 19) James (stay away from)

20) Derby

✓ 21) Shingleton (C knows; good)

✓ 22) Jones (?) (O.K.) (part of rough family)

23) Flynn (good; fine)

✓ B 24) Moore (no)

25) Smith

26) Turner (little white woman, fine)

B 27) Stringfield (no named black on jury)

28) Aikens (probably o.k.) if white

B 29) Randolph (no) on basis Maple Hill

B 30) Aikens (as good as any; with no)

31) Murray (good!!)

32) Barge (good!!!)

Prosecutor Jay Stroud's jury selection notes from the second Wilmington Ten trial, September 1972. Stroud illegally worked to exclude African Americans from the jury and to include KKK members and sympathizers. Courtesy Timothy B. Tyson Papers, Southern Historical Collection, Wilson Library, University of North Carolina at Chapel Hill.

African American, only 35 percent of the prospective jurors were—and had used all but one of its preemptory challenges to excuse blacks. Presented with a renewed argument about the flawed selection process and biased jury composition, Judge Martin remained unmoved.[49] The next phase of the miscarriage of justice was about to begin.

The prosecution's case wobbled on two withered legs and was propped up by Judge Martin's rulings. First, Stroud blew a lot of chaff in the jurors' faces to convince them by the sheer volume of exhibits and testimony that the Ten must be guilty. A parade of prosecution witnesses swore that something occurred in February 1971: rock throwing, gunfire, damage to a police car, a fire, and so on. Stroud submitted into evidence piles of pictures of Gregory Congregational Church and environs *taken months after the events* and taken during the day, while the events at the heart of the trial occurred at night. The desired effect of this photographic welter was to bolster the credibility of witnesses who gave their version of what happened around Gregory Congregational, even though the photographs did not accurately represent what occurred in February 1971 or in any way implicated the defendants in the crimes of which they were accused. In one instance, Stroud used a shot of Gregory Congregational to have a witness point out where authorities found explosives after the National Guard raid, yet none of the charges against the Ten concerned explosives; in another instance he introduced a police photograph of Chavis, a Black Panther, and others at the funeral for Steve Mitchell. Defense counsel objected to all of these, but Judge Martin allowed them. In most instances, the state's witnesses could not tie any of the Wilmington Ten to the crimes of which they were accused. But by larding on visual exhibits and witnesses who testified that there was violence in the neighborhood in February 1971, Jay Stroud took advantage of the widespread belief among jurors prior to the trial that some crime was committed and that at least some of the defendants must be guilty as charged.[50]

The main witness who provided eyewitness testimony that the Wilmington Ten defendants committed the crimes of burning down Mike's Grocery, shooting at emergency personnel, and conspiracy was Allen Hall, the second wasted leg of the state's case. For the most part, Hall, who took the stand for five days beginning 26 September, repeated his performance at the probable cause hearing in March, combining vivid recollections of the defendants' criminal actions with vague and contradictory statements about those same events under questioning from the defense.

Hall's behavior was hostile and bizarre regardless of who was questioning him. At one point during his direct testimony, the jury was sent out of the courtroom while attorneys for both sides argued a point of law. Hall remained on the stand and taunted the defendants:

> MR. FERGUSON: . . . Your Honor, Allen Hall is on the stand is making "son of a bitch, mother fucking"—
> (Solicitor Stroud stepped in front of Allen Hall.)
> MR. HUNOVAL: My client said she observed him.
> COURT: The Court did not observe this. We'll take about a 10 minute break.
> MR. FERGUSON: I'd like to call attention that he did the same thing as he went out of the courtroom.
> MR. HUNOVAL: My client said the same thing . . .
> MR. FERGUSON: We would observe to the Court that at the preliminary hearing this witness came off the stand and approached the counsel table in a menacing manner.[51]

Ferguson's reminder to the court was prescient. On his fifth and last day as a witness and unable to provide any satisfactory answers to Ferguson's questions, a visibly agitated Allen Hall, who stood over six feet tall and weighed more than two hundred pounds, tried to attack the defendants and their attorneys. The trial record recorded the pandemonium:

> Q: You don't have any idea what time it was whenever you did any of these things?
> SOLICITOR STROUD: OBJECT
> A: I don't know what time it was. I have told you and told you.
> Q: I want you to tell me what time it was—
> (The witness came off the witness stand and attempted to reach the defense table. Chairs and tables were pushed around and upset. The witness was subdued. All the jurors had left the courtroom with the exception of juror 8. The jurors returned to the jury box and were asked to retire to the jury room by the court.) . . .
> [After a short recess court reconvened.] (Defendant Shepard started breathing heavy and moved to the opposite end of the defense table from the witness stand.)[52]

Guided by Jay Stroud, Allen Hall had presented what he said was firsthand knowledge of the crimes of the defendants. Hall testified that on Friday, 5 February 1971, the day before Mike's Grocery was burned down, he was among the "approximately 95 or over a hundred" persons at Gregory Congregational Church who heard Ben Chavis expound on his "Chicago strategy"—setting fire to a business and then laying an ambush of the police and firefighters who responded. Chavis, said Hall, stated that the Chicago strategy would be used on Mike's because the owner was a white man making money in a black neighborhood and had "cussed out this colored girl." Further, according to Hall, Chavis said that Mike should have been making donations to the boycott but did not and so would have to suffer the consequences of being burned down. Hall had exactingly specific recollections about conversations at Gregory Church concerning shooting at whites. He described in detail driving with Chavis, Marvin Patrick, Jim Grant, and two others to an Oleander Drive pawnshop to purchase guns, bullets, and gunpowder and then to a service station to buy gasoline. He stated with certainty that Chavis ordered him to make gasoline bombs, using for wicks cloth that Hall said he saw Chavis remove from a "set of luggage" that was under his bed in the Reverend Eugene Templeton's home, where he was staying. Also in that luggage, Hall said, was a plastic bag of dynamite, which Chavis supposedly said was for blowing up police stations and white businesses. Along with all of the defendants and some unnamed children, Hall said, he assembled the Molotov cocktails; when they were done, Hall and most of the defendants left the church to shoot at cars on Nun Street between Sixth and Seventh. On Saturday, 6 February, Hall testified, Chavis said that Eugene and Donna Templeton were scared and that if they tried to call the police or sheriffs "concerning what was happening at the church for us to kill them." He had a vivid and unambiguous recollection of how Mike's was burned that night and which defendants threw Molotov cocktails through which windows.[53]

But under cross-examination, his unreliability as a witness became evident. He could not correctly recall the geography around Gregory Church that he described so clearly to the prosecutor. His vivid memory of the purchase of gasoline, guns, and ammunition that he conveyed in both his direct testimony and his February 1972 signed statement to authorities now grew fuzzy and contradictory. "I haven't the least idea because I don't know," echoed through his answers to Ferguson. His precise description of the burning of Mike's was now heavily qualified by "I don't know." In his direct testimony he spoke definitively about planning the attack on Mike's on Friday, 5 February, but in his signed statement to the Wilmington police, Jay Stroud, and BATF agent Bill Walden, he said he was drinking that day and was not at Gregory. Though he clearly identified under oath the Ten as having committed the crimes of which they were accused, his February 1972 statement to authorities contains no mention of Wayne Moore and Joe Wright and says nothing about Reginald Epps and James McKoy throwing firebombs.[54]

When pressed to explain the discrepancies both internal to his testimony and between his testimony and his signed statement, Hall's default response was that over the course of "several" subsequent meetings he verbally made revisions and corrections to his statement to Stroud, but that Stroud had neither typed up a new statement nor asked him to sign the old one with the corrections. To explore the veracity of Hall's claims, the defense tried to obtain copies of what became known as the "amended statement." Once it became known that Hall had met many times with Stroud and law enforcement and that Hall's story had evolved in response to questions posed to him, the state solicitor had no choice but to acknowledge it. But he succeeded —with the judge's help—in keeping it from the defense. The additions and amendments were purely for his benefit, Stroud argued, and so should be considered work product and thus not subject to inspection by defense attorneys. This jesuitical exegesis allowed Hall and Stroud to explain away the untrustworthy testimony as little more than clerical errors. The judge upheld the convenient fiction that the defense had access to everything it had a right to see.[55]

James Ferguson suspected that the "several" additional meetings Hall had with prosecutors and police were for the purpose of coaching the witness and aligning his story with Stroud's version of events. Notes in Stroud's own handwriting on various trial-related documents are persuasive evidence that Stroud did just that—and from almost the instant that Hall was arrested. Hall's first extensive contact with police concerning the events of February 1971 concerned the shooting of Harvey Cumber, which he said he witnessed. Hall fingered Chavis for the shooting and also said Marvin Patrick and Jim Grant were armed and present on the scene. Hall had said nothing in his statement dated 7 June 1971 about the burning of Mike's or other crimes for which the Wilmington Ten were tried. Yet scrawled across the fronts and backs of the three-page statement were Stroud's detailed notes about Mike's and the shooting at police and firefighters. Stroud claimed that he made those notes during a subsequent interview of Hall but did not write them up and have Hall sign it. Interestingly, between the time Hall gave the statement on 7 June and when he gave his statement in February 1972, the narrative of the burning of Mike's was embellished, including references to the so-called Chicago strategy, while the shooting of Cumber disappeared altogether; in fact, the latter statement by Hall specifically states that he was not at Gregory Congregational Church in the morning when Cumber was shot. Then there is the matter of Stroud's actions during James Ferguson's and Matt Hunoval's cross-examination of Hall. Stroud's notes of the questioning include what appear to be instructions to Hall about how to answer. "Say, I don't recall"; "say didn't mention in written statement—did in discussion!"; "how many times talked with police before your trial"—these and similar remarks implicate Stroud in Hall's web of lies.[56]

The "amended statement" and evidence of Stroud's solicitation of Hall's perjured testimony was not all that was kept from the jury. So, too, were many instances of the apparent inducements with which Stroud purchased it. Hall was serving a twelve-year sentence, but when he was being prepared to take the witness stand, he was treated in a most unusual fashion. The jury did not hear that Hall had been transferred from a correctional facility in Lumberton, about ninety minutes from Wilmington, to the Onslow County Jail, half as far from his home. His meetings with Stroud and Wilmington police officers often took place at his mother's home, where he could also visit with her. He was allowed several private visits with his girlfriend, Sandra Mitchell, including as recently as the opening of the trial. Rather than returning to prison or jail, Hall was housed at the Holiday Inn on Wrightsville Beach for periods of time before and during the trial. He was sometimes joined there by Eric Junious, a thirteen-year-old who had until recently been in reform school for committing robbery and who claimed to have witnessed the Wilmington Ten commit their crimes. Hall and Junious were not confined to their room but had access to the beach and alcohol. On this critical point of preferential treatment, Judge Martin refused to let the jury hear Hall say that he was not being kept in a prison or jail but was being "kept with deputies and policemens [sic]" largely to keep defense attorney Ferguson from interviewing him.[57]

Judge Martin's wrongheaded rulings—during jury selection, allowing prosecutors to present evidence that was irrelevant to the charges but nevertheless prejudicial to the defendants, hiding Allen Hall's multiple statements from the defense, preventing the jury from hearing about Jay Stroud's favorable treatment of Hall—effectively turned His Honor into an adjunct of the prosecution and a collaborator with the state of North Carolina, which was trying to incarcerate the Wilmington Ten. With him on the bench, judicial temperance vanished and along with it a chance for a fair trial.

Given his reputation as a judge with political connections and ambitions and given James Ferguson's prior encounters with him during the electric Teel trial in Oxford, the defense could not have been surprised by Martin's deportment, behavior, and rulings. From the outset the legal defense had to decide how to try the case under adverse circumstances. Ferguson and his colleagues understood the political dimensions of the trial, and they saw that Stroud presented his case as one of "legitimate government . . . being undermined by the powers or ideas represented by the defense."[58] During the different phases of the trial they objected consistently to the prosecutor's criminalizing of their clients' political activity. Ferguson made his living as an attorney and devoted considerable time and energy to lawyering for the cause of racial liberation. But he knew that in the emancipatory process, the practice of law was of secondary importance and was subservient to building a mass movement. Overemphasizing or restricting the struggle to the courtroom could in fact kill a movement because trials are by their nature slow, reactive, and confined by rules.[59] This restrictiveness, which is present in all trials with political implications, was amplified by Judge Martin's collusion with the prosecution.

On 17 October, at 5:20 in the evening, after weeks of jury selection and witness testimony, days of closing arguments, and a full day of listening to Judge Martin's instructions, the jury of ten whites and two African Americans retired to deliberate the fates of Ben Chavis, Ann Shepard, Connie Tindall, Marvin Patrick, Joe Wright, Willie Earl Vereen, Jerry Jacobs, James McKoy, Reginald Epps, and Wayne Moore. Barely three hours later, the jurors returned a verdict: all defendants guilty on all charges. The speed with which the jury reached the decision was astonishing and redolent of the haste with which the Mississippi jury freed the killers of Emmett Till. The verdict itself could not have been a surprise to the defendants or the spectators in the crowded courtroom, though the repetition of the word "Guilty" surely was wrenching. As the verdicts were read, some in the crowd, many of them wearing "Free Rev. Chavis" buttons, gasped audibly; at least one person burst into tears. Given the late hour, Judge Martin delayed sentencing until 9:30 the next morning. The defendants received a total of 282 years in prison, with Chavis receiving the largest sentence of twenty-nine to thirty-four years behind bars. Outside the courthouse, a knot of demonstrators organized by the CRJ with the assistance of Golden Frinks and including friends, family, and supporters waited for hours while the defendants, now convicted, were processed and led in shackles to the prison bus to take them to Raleigh, their first stop in the prison system. Ben Chavis's mother, Elizabeth, swooned, and supported by two daughters burst out, "Isn't this beautiful! They're taking our boys away to prison." On the bus, stunned but not defeated, the Wilmington Ten began to sing.[60]

The defense team made decisions that affected the trial, its outcome, and the ability to continue the fight in the streets afterward. The defense attorneys rejected a strategy of "introduc[ing] ideological matters in order to win jury sympathy and to turn the case into a forum on the major issues of the day."[61] Such an approach had been used to some effect in earlier political trials, such as Angela Davis's in 1971, in which she was acquitted. Likewise, the defense dismissed a strategy of turning the trial into political theater and an indictment of the judicial, social, and economic system, as was the case with the Chicago Seven conspiracy trial of 1969. Ferguson had two qualms about a strategy of confrontational theatrics. Whereas in other trials defendants believed they had a chance to win the jury's sympathy, that was not a likely outcome in the Wilmington Ten trial. Perhaps a strategy of disruption and defendant outbursts, as happened in Chicago, was based on the premise that the law and the courts were illegitimate. As became manifest in the Chicago trial, the well-known attorney William Kunstler had little but contempt for Judge Julius Hoffman and the legal system. Ferguson saw matters differently: the legal system in place in North Carolina and the South was unjust, but he did not view the system as illegitimate.[62] A significant reason he was a respected and effective litigator was because his adversaries saw that his concerns were with rights and principles of the law, and while he would argue with them in court he would not mock or embarrass them, as would happen if he encouraged disruption. "I think that over the years we have built up mutual respect among those who litigated against us. By focusing on the issues, trying our cases in court, rather than basing our case or our effort on personal attacks on anyone."[63]

Ferguson's determination to try the case on the facts had the same result that a strategy of theatrical disruption almost certainly would have had in North Carolina in 1972: guilty. (It is nevertheless likely that Ferguson's demeanor earned him some goodwill during the appeals process that geared up almost immediately after the convictions.) That he did not conflate criminal legal defense with protest and movement building was fortuitous. Because he recognized the limitations of courtroom activity in the process of social change, the defense team was able to coordinate with the CRJ and other organizations to build a campaign that demanded freedom for the Wilmington Ten and addressed the systematic oppression of African Americans. This campaign, which will be the subject of the next chapter, grew from the simple act of mobilizing dozens of family, friends, and supporters to observe the trial proceedings into a campaign that managed over the remainder of the decade to capture the attention of the nation and the world.

CHAPTER 4

Alliances and Adversity

U pon their convictions the Wilmington Ten, unable immediately to post appeal bonds, were remanded to the prison system to begin serving their sentences. The United Church of Christ had suffi-cient funds to get only its employee Ben Chavis released, but Chavis chose incarceration as an act of solidarity with his comrades. There he remained until December 1972, when his fear for his safety and questions about his health prompted him to reconsider. On the outside, he threw himself into the work of mounting the campaign to free the Wilmington Ten. It was not until June 1973 that the UCC General Synod amassed the full $400,000 to post bail for the remaining defendants. They remained free pending appeal until February 1976, when the U.S. Supreme Court declined to hear their case. Returning again to prison, they remained behind bars until, their sentences shortened by Governor James Hunt, they were released at different times between June 1978 and December 1979.[1]

The movement to free the Wilmington Ten in all its phases, from the time of their trial in 1972 through their eventual release and reversal of their convictions in 1980, developed along multiple independent but intersecting paths. How interested parties along these paths organized themselves and cooperated and competed tells us much about the African American political landscape in the 1970s. From community-, school-, and church-based associations to political parties built on leftist and nationalist lines to the quickening of a stratum of black elected officials, the manners in which the campaigns to free the Wilmington Ten unfolded reveal the ways power was accrued and spent and lost.

Among the earliest champions of the Wilmington Ten were circles of black nationalists spread across the state of North Carolina. Many of these groups began in response to arrests and campaigns of legal repression, so they were not caught unaware by the events in Wilmington. The most visible nationalist circle in Charlotte was grouped around UNC–Charlotte student Fred Dillahunt, who in 1972 formed the Charlotte Black Political

Prisoners Defense Committee. The organization was able to keep various issues of political repression and police brutality in the public eye with street demonstrations—one in April 1972, led by a man carrying a Viet Cong flag, wended its way from the campus of Johnson C. Smith University to the downtown post office and demanded freedom for Angela Davis, Jim Grant of the Charlotte Three, and Ben Chavis—and public forums. This organization had working relationships with the similarly named but predominantly white-radical North Carolina Committee to Free Political Prisoners and the pan-Africanists of the Student Organization for Black Unity and also provided publicity for the Republic of New Afrika, whose members were being hounded by the FBI. As a sign of tactical flexibility and the gravitational pull of radical politics, Charlotte's black nationalists commanded the attention of rivulets of black discontent associated with traditional electoral politics represented by Dr. Reginald Hawkins and the North Carolina Black Assembly. In December 1972, these groups sponsored a rally to free Angela Davis that drew three thousand people, two-thirds of them black. Davis addressed the meeting via telephone, having been delayed in Atlanta by bad weather. Elizabeth Chavis, Ben's mother, was a featured speaker, as was Owusu Sadauki of the Malcolm X Liberation University, who critiqued imperialism and its impact on Africans and African Americans. He chided the whites in attendance for limiting their organizing to college campuses; if they were serious about interracial solidarity, they would work to promote radical politics in white working-class communities as well.[2]

In Raleigh, St. Augustine's College and Shaw University were the hubs of activity. Helen Othow, Ben Chavis's sister, taught at St. Augustine's and developed a network of activists in the area that worked on prison reform and criminal justice issues and naturally grew into an organization to fight for freedom for the Wilmington Ten. At Shaw University, Harlem transplant John Mendez was beginning a life in the struggle. Influenced by the Reverend Fred Shuttlesworth and other civil rights ministers and the Black Power movement in New York, Mendez soaked up Shaw's history— it was where the Student Nonviolent Coordinating Committee was founded—and also came under the influence of the Malcolm X Liberation University, a Black Power endeavor based first in Durham and then in Greensboro. He became involved with the protests over the murder of Henry "Dickie" Marrow in Oxford and made a strong connection with Ben Chavis. Following Chavis to Wilmington, Mendez helped to establish the Black Messiah church there. He simultaneously grew closer to the Commission for Racial Justice, which for a time employed him as an organizer, and to the pan-Africanist-cum-Marxist circles in the Raleigh–Durham–Chapel Hill area. He was a presence in efforts to radicalize the electoral politics of the Black Assembly and to educate black communities about the connections between the repressive issues they faced and those faced by Africans.[3]

During the trials and until around 1975, the connective tissue of the movement to free the Wilmington Ten was the United Church of Christ's Commission for Racial Justice. Yet despite the CRJ's long history of involvement in criminal justice reform and the fact that one of the accused was a UCC minister and CRJ employee, it was not a foregone conclusion that the church would offer its support. Surprisingly, it took a serious intradenominational dustup to ensure that the UCC fully backed the legal defense and mass struggle of the Ten.

To its credit, the denomination's leadership, including President Robert Moss, did not waver in its support. The General Synod, the church's governing body, regularly adopted resolutions demanding freedom for the Wilmington Ten. The UCC raised bail money in excess of $400,000 for all of the defendants rather than posted bond only for Chavis. And it raised money within the denomination for legal fees and other court costs rather than relied on external fund-raising. As Irv Joyner, who was a staff attorney for the CRJ in the 1970s, explained, by fully funding the campaign to free the Wilmington Ten, the UCC avoided conflicts with allies over money and freed the CRJ to build a united front on common political goals.[4]

The leadership's unwavering commitment met serious opposition from a significant number of predominantly white UCC congregations in the South. The UCC was founded in 1957 by a merger of several Euro-American and African American Protestant Christian traditions. Acknowledgment of fellowship in Christ notwithstanding, racial tensions from the temporal world followed congregants into the new union. The black congregations of the largely rural parts of Virginia and North Carolina that made up the former Christian Church denomination were particularly sensitive to the less-than-perfect racial atmosphere.[5] Despite the establishment of the CRJ as a permanent church organization in 1969, the Reverend Leon White, who spoke for the large number of black UCC members in the South, threatened to lead them out of the church unless the Southern Conference, which included both black and white churches but was white-dominated, changed its "racist posture." Black congregants and their churches were second-class citizens within the conference, he charged. He demanded that the regional body allocate $100,000 to "aid Blacks in North Carolina and Virginia," take affirmative measures to assist the region's black UCC congregations, and otherwise take part in the work of racial reconciliation within the denomination. As Irv Joyner noted at the time, most African American UCC pastors were not recognized by the white conservatives within the Southern Conference.[6]

Upon the conviction of the Ten and the church's posting of their appeal bond, the Southern Conference leadership brayed loudly. James Lightbourne Jr., the conference minister, or superintendent, complained forcefully about the expenditure. He and the majority-white congregations in the Old North State and the Old Dominion believed that the Wilmington Ten were too radical, not legitimately associated with the denomination, and too strident after their convictions to deserve support. He told UCC president Moss that Ben Chavis and Leon White were making matters worse by continuing to agitate against the conviction rather than keeping quiet until the "appeal is heard." They were both "making public statements. . . . This is unfortunate." And even after Moss told him that the UCC had an obligation to defend people who worked at the behest of church bodies like the CRJ, Lightbourne continued to question Chavis's ministerial bona fides.[7] He demanded that the CRJ and Chavis in particular be muzzled:

> The news this morning carries the account of another press conference with Ben Chavis. Once again he is stating his plans for the future. They include traveling around the country raising funds for the defense of political prisoners.
>
> We stand little chance of dealing constructively with the situation in the Southern Conference unless Ben Chavis is stopped from making statements to the press. . . .
>
> Under these circumstances our church people feel that there should be limitations on his activities and that he should not be carrying out the responsibilities that were his when he was arrested.
>
> Something must be done. The situation is urgent.[8]

Letters from local church leaders were even less temperate. The Consistory of the Zion UCC in Lenoir labeled Chavis as "a man who has shown a marked disrespect for the life and property of the community, even though he may eventually be released on a technicality." The officers objected to the use of church funds to post bond because they suspected Chavis would simply continue a pattern of violence and disruption and decided to withhold its contribution to the church's national office. The secretary of the executive council of the Boger UCC in Rockwell in Rowan County opposed bail for Chavis and the church's involvement in the struggle in Wilmington, period. Facilitating Chavis's release on bond would "tear down our good work," she said. Chavis was simply an "outsider, as well as a known instigator of ill feelings and actions in racial matters." And while the treasurer of the Shallow Well UCC in Sanford was supportive of denominational missionary efforts in Africa, he was stunned to see that the CRJ national budget was $700,000 annually, and he asked rhetorically, "What does the Commission for Racial Justice do with $700,000.00? It is being used to support criminals in North Carolina. . . . It is being used to hire Angela Davis, a self-confessed communist, to demonstrate for the United Church of Christ." Members of the First Evangelical and Reformed UCC in Asheboro were unequivocal in their belief that the Ten should be incarcerated.[9]

Winning support for the Wilmington Ten and maintaining it within the UCC at times resembled the street protests, rallies, and conferences designed to build public awareness and force the legal system to act in a just manner. CRJ leaders drafted a plan to publicize the case that included radio publicity, informational picket lines, and an orchestrated campaign to pressure white groups at the meeting of the UCC General Synod. This national ruling body affirmed the decision to support the Wilmington Ten case financially; almost simultaneously and in an effort to calm the backlash in the white UCC congregations in North Carolina, the denomination's president helped to engineer a transfer of Ben Chavis out of the state to the Washington, D.C., office of the CRJ; executive director of the CRJ Charles Cobb secured a commitment from Chavis to modulate his public statements on the case. Still, for years Cobb had to beat back intradenominational opposition.[10]

By itself and in coalition with others, the CRJ was relentless in its work to free the Wilmington Ten. Rejecting the counsel of the white UCC congregations that the case should be allowed to run its course through the legal system, the CRJ developed plans both to create public opinion favorable to radical reform and to directly pressure the legal system to respect the rights of the Ten. And always, the CRJ promoted the view that what happened to the Wilmington Ten was not simply an isolated miscarriage of justice but rather manifested the systematic repression of African Americans. For example, in March 1973, the North Carolina Criminal Justice Task Force, which was formed by the CRJ, sponsored a conference at Raleigh's Shaw University on the topic of criminal justice and political oppression. Representatives of the state Black Assembly, the Southern Christian Leadership Conference, and the Black Independent Union Party participated; Reverend Leon White took the lead and attacked state attorney general Robert Morgan for introducing notorious "no knock" and "stop and frisk" laws, which allowed police intrusion into people's lives without probable cause or a proper warrant.[11]

As it did for the trials of the Wilmington Ten in June and September 1972, the CRJ mobilized to pack the courtroom at subsequent legal proceedings. In preparation for the June 1973 trial of Chavis and Mollie Hicks for accessory after the fact in the murder of Clifton Eugene Wright, the commission noted the history of racist jury selection in the state and called for the people to attend the trial en masse; it also requested several prominent persons to act as court monitors and received commitments from the U.S. Commission on Civil Rights and the offices of U.S. Representatives John Conyers of Michigan, Ronald Dellums of California, and Barbara Jordan of Texas. More, the National Black Assembly, the Congress of African People, the National Conference of Black Lawyers, the Southern Conference Education Fund, the American Civil Liberties Union, and other organizations also agreed to observe the proceedings. The CRJ singled out for criticism Senator Sam Ervin, who was making a national name for himself as the homespun inquisitor of Watergate and Richard Nixon's dirty tricks. Erased by this national adoration was Ervin's historic support for the strategy of Massive Resistance in response to the *Brown v. Board of Education* decision and the Southern Manifesto. The CRJ sought to restore some historical sanity to the lionizing of Ervin. The refusal of this putative "Congressional Civil Liberties expert . . . to send an 'observer' to the trial confuses us. The Civil Liberties of Black people is as important or more so as the truth about the 'Watergate Scandal.'" The Sunday evening before the trial, the CRJ sponsored a united front rally in Wilmington's Robert Strange Park. In ninety-five degrees and high humidity punctuated by rain, four thousand people, overwhelmingly black, listened to Delores Moore, mother of Wayne Moore, who represented the mothers of the Ten; Leon White; revolutionary nationalists Amiri Baraka, Nelson Johnson, and Kojo Nantambu; Winston-Salem Black Panther leader Larry Little; local black politician L. M. Newsome; and headliner Angela Davis as they indicted North Carolina, the U.S. government, and President Nixon and demanded freedom for Chavis and all his codefendants.[12]

The CRJ was not a one-trick pony, and street protests and rallies were not the only tactics it employed. It supported the work of the appeals process, which continued on a pace not dictated by the mass struggle. Yet as Irv Joyner recognized, legal acumen alone would not lead to a successful conclusion of the case; political pressure of different sorts was "a necessity in obtaining a legal victory through the courts." What that pressure consisted of changed over time, and as the 1976 general election approached, Joyner strained to find ways to pressure both presidential candidates and other office seekers to take favorable positions on the case. He advocated a continued direct attack on North Carolina's criminal justice system and bringing into the fold elected officials, community organizations, unions, and churches. And while the CRJ aspired to extend this work nationally, its focus had to be on developing local seminars, conferences, demonstrations, and letter-writing campaigns in North Carolina, supplemented by monthly instances of nonviolent direct action across the state. The CRJ labored in the vineyards, conducting political education and ministering to and visiting the Ten and their families when they were incarcerated. There were moments of exhilaration, as when organizations signaled support or thousands gathered to rally. But as Leon White recollected, they were often met with community indifference, and most days it was like "Jesus being nailed to the cross." The everyday work of the CRJ was grinding, but it was nevertheless accretive. The black Christian Church congregations in North Carolina and eastern Virginia that joined the UCC had been faced with a variety of social justice issues, such as school segregation, racial violence, and environmental degradation, but historically had had no experience organizing around them. Through its work on the Wilmington Ten and linking the various facets of racism, the CRJ brought thousands of black UCC members into a political movement.[13]

The CRJ also offered a locus for the nascent stratum of black political activists who turned their attention to the electoral process. H. M. "Mickey" Michaux Jr. of Durham was a pioneer of North Carolina black electoral politics. He was educated at the Palmer Memorial Institute, the black boarding school in Sedalia, North Carolina, founded and superintended by Charlotte Hawkins Brown, and was thus trained to be a community leader; he graduated from North Carolina Central University in 1952 and its law school in 1964. In 1956, during the time of the Montgomery bus boycott, Michaux, who was working for a black chamber of commerce–type organization, invited Martin Luther King to Durham for a festival that highlighted African American businesses in the Bull City. The invitation blossomed into a lasting friendship. As both an attorney and a participant, Michaux was prominent in local desegregation struggles; he had his share of arrests. King's suggestion to him one night that African Americans would have to extend their reach to grasp the levers of power motivated Michaux to seek elective office, and he ran unsuccessfully for a General Assembly seat in 1964, 1966, and 1968. King's assassination during his last election campaign temporarily drained Michaux of the desire for office, and he refocused his political energy to agitating for a redress of grievances.[14]

After a four-year hiatus, during which he worked with the "forward-thinking" Leon White and others in mass organizing, in 1972 Michaux was elected to the state legislature, culminating one phase of his life in the struggle and commencing another. The third African American elected to the General Assembly in the twentieth century, he joined the first two—Henry Frye and Joy Johnson—in what he termed the "triumvirate." In this troika Frye was the conciliator who sealed legislative bargains, while Johnson and Michaux were hell-raisers who worked comfortably with the Left. The "good cop, bad cop, bad cop" team worked well together and enjoyed major victories such as the establishment of the North Carolina Sickle Cell Syndrome Program, which offers comprehensive treatment and services to the mostly black victims of this disease, and the restoration of felons' franchise and other rights of citizenship. From their perch in the legislature, they not only secured more equitable treatment for African Americans but also helped people to realize that they could facilitate change. But as Michaux acknowledged, the triumvirate's work was made possible by the CRJ. Outside of electoral politics, the CRJ educated African Americans about the workings of the criminal justice system and the intertwined nature of their struggles, whether it was the fight for quality public education, increasing access to higher education, police brutality and the reform of law enforcement, or support for the nascent antiapartheid and African solidarity movements. Because of the egregious nature of the case of the Wilmington Ten, it became the tribune through which most other grievances were expressed. As the CRJ placed local organizing at the center of its work, groups and associations with concerns of their own felt compelled to join ranks with those fighting to free the Wilmington Ten. In 1976, representatives of a cross section of organizations—professional, religious, upper-crust, and grassroots—formed the North Carolina Black Leadership Caucus as an umbrella for all of the state's black organizations. By offering cogent analysis and practical ways to become involved, the CRJ was able to influence the several layers of participants in the black freedom struggle.[15] But it was not the only organization with a national reach to become involved.

ANGELA DAVIS'S APPEARANCE at the June 1973 trial of Ben Chavis and Mollie Hicks signaled the involvement of the National Alliance against Racist and Political Repression (NAARPR) in the campaign to free the Wilmington Ten. Formed in Chicago just a month earlier on the initiative of the Communist Party (CP, or CPUSA), the alliance knit together the party's mass work among racial minorities, against the formation of the carceral state, and in the labor movement. In addition to members from the CPUSA and its Young Workers Liberation League, the founding meeting of the alliance attracted more than six hundred individuals representing around two hundred groups. The FBI's informant at the meeting counted as present local chapters of the Angela Davis Defense Committee, the American Indian Movement, the Republic of New Afrika, the United Farm Workers of America, the National Conference of Black Lawyers, selected chapters of the Black Liberation Army, and the Kentucky Political Prisoners Committee. Representatives from Charlotte's North Carolina Committee to Free Political Prisoners reported the buzz that coursed through the meeting. It was bracing to feel the energy and to know that the Nixon administration had not succeeded in intimidating or pacifying his opposition; likewise, they were heartened to see that the mass movements of the 1960s had not burned themselves out but rather were fortified to take on "domestic repression." They were impressed with the high level of political consciousness and commitment displayed by participants and believed that the multiplicity of local struggles could provide a foundation for a strong national organization dedicated to fighting political repression.[16]

Despite the energy released by both the founding conference and the preliminary work that led to it, during which local groups from across the country were to develop mutually beneficial relationships, in many instances political activists unaffiliated with the Communists declined to join the NAARPR. The Charlotte political prisoner committee had cooperated with the party to sponsor a well-attended rally for Angela Davis in December 1972, and committee members appeared to have a good transactional relationship with NAARPR leader Charlene Mitchell of the CP. But members of the Charlotte group who participated in the founding of the alliance found the leadership "top-down." "Rules of order were used to advantage the conference planners," observed one member; it was obvious to several observers that the shape of the NAARPR had been predetermined by the CP, and local organizations that they encouraged to join would have limited say in the alliance's direction. This self-serving behavior drew criticism from other quarters as well, including the CRJ and others involved in the Wilmington Ten campaign. The alliance publicized—erroneously—that the CRJ had endorsed and participated in its activities. At rallies and demonstrations sponsored by the alliance, speakers who endorsed the CP's point of view were given preference and prominence over those who did not. Decades later, Leon White reflected that a good part of his reservations about the NAARPR was his belief that it placed its sectarian concerns before the needs of the people on whose behalf it campaigned.[17]

A significant casualty of the friction between the alliance and the CRJ was the relationship between Chavis and the CRJ itself. An experienced political operative, Chavis made overtures to Angela Davis and the CP shortly after the June 1972 mistrial. When the NAARPR debuted, it made the general repressive conditions in North Carolina and the specific case of the Wilmington Ten national priorities and named Chavis an organizational vice chairman and treasurer. His acceptance displeased Charles Cobb and Leon White at the CRJ and made building denominational support for the Wilmington Ten more difficult. Chavis's new left-wing connections were grist for the mill operated by the many southern white UCC congregations already hostile to the increasingly uncompromising tenor of the black freedom struggle. But neither did Chavis help his cause by ignoring Cobb's directives to focus on the business of the Washington CRJ office and excuse himself from the intradenominational politics of the Southern Conference of the UCC. Chavis continually inserted himself in North Carolina against Cobb's wishes. And when the alliance formed a North Carolina affiliate in February 1974, which the CRJ opposed, Chavis labeled as "splinter groups" all organizations that fought for the Wilmington Ten but refused to join the alliance. After a series of run-ins with the commission staff, Chavis was suspended from the CRJ for insubordination in June. But while some staff members wanted Chavis fired, Executive Director Cobb demurred. Cobb conceded that Chavis had regularly exercised poor judgment by working closely with the NAARPR and ignoring the wishes of the CRJ and his denomination, but he recognized Chavis's symbolic importance to the world outside of the UCC and lifted the suspension after little more than a month. However, tensions continued to build, and Chavis, a gifted and effective organizer, was gradually earning a reputation as an undisciplined freelancer; ironically, over time the NAARPR began to view Chavis similarly as a seeker of the limelight and a shirker of organizational responsibility.[18]

Nevertheless, the NAARPR was extraordinarily effective in bringing the case of the Wilmington Ten to the attention of the national public, including getting people into the streets for large rallies and building a multiracial and cross-class united front. Like the CRJ, the alliance placed the frame-up of the Wilmington Ten at the center of a vortex of social injustices and repression. Demanding freedom for the Ten was the avenue for agitation and education concerning the other issues swirling around. The alliance was nothing if not methodical, and, recognizing the need for credibility if it was to be a leader in the Wilmington Ten movement, among the first actions it took was to establish a presence in the Tar Heel state.

Planned over several months, the North Carolina Alliance against Racist and Political Repression was led by Ben Chavis's sister Dr. Helen Othow and founded at a two-day conference in Raleigh at the Memorial Auditorium and on the campus of Shaw University on 15–16 February 1974. The opening night rally featured Angela Davis and attracted fifteen hundred people. Breakout sessions included workshops on pending repressive legislation; capital punishment; the suppression of labor unions and the generally hostile southern atmosphere against working-class activity; "behavior modification" programs in prisons, including drugging prisoners as well as subjecting them to sensory deprivation, electroshock, and psychosurgery; legal attacks and jailing of political radicals; and international solidarity. More than three hundred people participated. The program captured the range of liberal and radical causes in which activists were engaged across the state, and representatives from those struggles were included in both the weekend conference and the continuing organization. Members of the National Tenants Organization, the SCLC, the NAACP, the UCC-affiliated Wilmington 10 Defense Committee, and Clergy and Laity Concerned took part in the proceedings. The Reverend W. W. Finlator of Raleigh's Pullen Memorial Baptist Church, one of the most distinguished southern white voices for racial and social equality, shared the stage with Angela Davis, and organized labor was represented by the president of the Asheville local of the Amalgamated Meat Cutters and Butcher Workmen.[19]

Othow recollected that the main component of the work was public education about the Wilmington Ten, with a special emphasis on combating media bias. The North Carolina alliance often picketed the offices of the *News and Observer* after a scurrilous article and wrote letters to the editors of local papers to challenge the pervasive view that the Ten were guilty and fairly convicted. Othow was assisted by Maria Ramos, a non-Communist staff member of the national alliance in New York City. Ramos remembered meeting Chavis on a picket line in front of Manhattan district attorney Frank Hogan's office to protest the frame-up of the Panther Twenty-One in New York, probably around April 1971. (They were acquitted.) They struck up a relationship and became romantically involved with plans to become married. In 1975 she moved into the Chavis family home in Oxford to take charge of organizing hometown support for the Wilmington Ten. (Ben Chavis remained in Washington, D.C., at the CRJ's office.) Although Ramos traveled the state, she was primarily responsible for building support for the Ten and the alliance in her new location. Within short order, she had developed a multiracial core of nearly thirty residents who were available to attend programs and rallies around North Carolina. While black Oxfordites were most receptive to the alliance's work, whites and Native Americans were also receptive, and across the state the alliance had more than one hundred committed members.[20]

The North Carolina affiliate of the NAARPR took the lead in organizing a united front "Stop Racism and Repression" protest in Raleigh on Independence Day 1974. Ten thousand citizens from around the state and nation descended on the state capital to rally for the programmatic elements voiced at the North Carolina alliance's founding meeting the previous February. Drawing on the widespread streams of discontent that produced the protracted campaign to unionize textile giant J. P. Stevens and would soon quicken in support of Joan Little, an African American woman in the Beaufort County jail who killed the jailer who tried to rape her, the rally represented a true united front effort. The Left was represented, including of course the Communist Party, but also the Puerto Rican Socialist Party, the American Indian Movement, and the Black Panther Party. The black nationalist Republic of New Afrika endorsed the coalition, as did the North Carolina Black Assembly. Ralph Abernathy of the civil rights mainstream SCLC marched "with my Communist brothers and sisters, red brothers and sisters, brown brothers and sisters . . . I've come to the march because the same foot of iron that seeks to keep me down as a Black man is seeking to keep us all down, whether we be Christians or Communists." A New York state senator spoke, as did a soldier from Fort Bragg in Fayetteville, North Carolina. Clarence Lightner, Raleigh's first (and, as of 2015, only) African American mayor, joined the march, which was also supported by a city councilman. It was the largest black freedom march in the South since 1968, and it rattled Governor James Holshouser, who mobilized a thousand National Guardsmen and three hundred Highway Patrol officers.[21]

The 4 July protest accelerated opinion and encouraged a variety of people to take public stands favorable to the Ten, and for the next three years the NAARPR was the major voice nationally speaking out against political repression. The North Carolina alliance felt a bounce as disparate organizers came to view it as a viable organization that could amplify their demands. It offered a second home to the state's liberal clergy and laity who had protested the Vietnam War and spoke forcefully for civil rights. Celene Chenier of Durham, who worked on prisoners' rights and prison reform, teamed with Jerry Paul, a well-known defense attorney from Greenville, to organize two hundred people in Jacksonville, the town dominated by the U.S. Marines' Camp Lejeune, to join the state alliance; the alliance also succeeded in making inroads in the cities of Goldsboro and Kinston and had assembled hundreds of other supporters and interested individuals across the state. Of all aspects of the event, the organizers were least satisfied with the participation of the organized labor. So immediately after the march, the NAARPR launched an initiative to support the work of the North Carolina Federation of Labor and unions representing workers in the tobacco, furniture, and textile industries and get them to demand justice for the Wilmington Ten. Michael Myerson, a Communist and NAARPR functionary, reported that officials of the United Furniture Workers were interested in hiring an antiracist activist to organize factories in the state's furniture belt between High Point and Hickory. The Communists lacked a presence in the state's textile mills, but Myerson promised support for the Amalgamated Clothing and Textile Workers Union's fight against brown lung disease; and he appeared to succeed in effecting an entente with Carl Ferris, who headed the labor organizing work for the SCLC.[22]

If the Communist Party did not reap the reward of increased influence among rank-and-file Tar Heel proletarians, its holistic approach of linking different social struggles paid off as the cause of the Wilmington Ten gained sustained national attention. The newly formed Coalition of Labor Union Women and the Coalition of Black Trade Unionists, both of which were only reluctantly recognized by the labor bureaucrats of the AFL-CIO, expressed their solidarity and mobilized their members to take part in public protests. Bert Corona, the Chicano labor organizer, California Democratic Party political insider, and leader of the National Trade Union Organizing Committee for Immigrant Workers, joined the meatcutters' union national president Abraham Feinglass as cochairs of the NAARPR. Local and national officials of the United Electrical Workers also endorsed the alliance's campaign. The St. Louis chapter of the alliance developed strong trade union support for the Wilmington Ten and enjoyed an especially strong relationship with the Amalgamated Clothing and Textile Workers Union. Frank Chapman Jr. was the leader of the chapter and later became a vice chair of the national alliance. Confined in a Missouri prison in 1961 on a sentence of life plus fifty years for murder, he was shipped in 1972 to a Kentucky prison as part of an arrangement to manage prison populations;

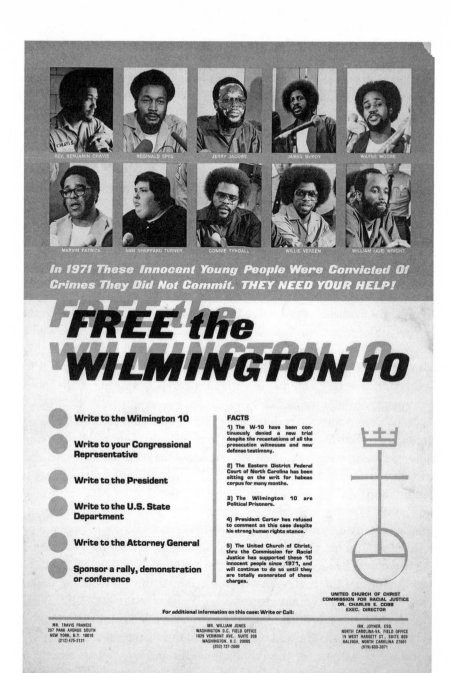

Poster produced by the United Church of Christ's Commission for Racial Justice after North Carolina governor Jim Hunt refused in January 1978 to pardon or release the Wilmington Ten. Courtesy of Kenneth Janken.

in Kentucky he came into contact with Carl and Anne Braden, a fortuitous event that melded his desire for education with political radicalism and awareness. He was returned to Missouri in 1973 and entered a study-release program at the University of Missouri–Rollins, which meant that he was free during the day but returned to custody at night. The St. Louis alliance built support for the Wilmington Ten in coordination with support for prisoners, a campaign against the state's right-to-work law, actions that supported textile workers trying to unionize J. P. Stevens, and international solidarity with the antiapartheid struggle.[23]

As the alliance planned a second national protest in Washington, D.C., for May 1975, other opinion makers awakened and lent their support. On the last day of the month, upwards of four thousand people from around the country marched in the humidity and under a noonday sun past the Justice Department and then to the White House. (A contingent of nearly two hundred from Wilmington organized by Kojo Nantambu, who was then working for the NAARPR, was prepared to travel to the nation's capital, but only one bus showed up, which Nantambu attributed to sabotage by local adversary Golden Frinks of the SCLC; consequently only thirty-five Wilmingtonians participated.) Ben Chavis greeted the crowd in "a colorful dashiki and carrying a long bamboo staff." The Honorable Walter Fauntroy, who served in the House of Representatives as the District of Columbia's nonvoting delegate, on this day also represented the Congressional Black Caucus and gladly received a petition demanding freedom for the Ten with fifty thousand signatures. Marion Barry, the former chairman of the SNCC and future D.C. mayor, brought news that the city council of which he was a member had declared 31 May "Wilmington 10 Day." Shortly thereafter, Representative John Conyers of Michigan read into the *Congressional Record* his concerns about a miscarriage of justice and a continuing pattern of criminalization of political activity. He was followed a couple of months later by Representative Ronald Dellums of California, who offered a scathing critique of the treatment of the Wilmington Ten in comparison to the pardon of disgraced president Richard Nixon. Charles Rangel of New York added his voice, too. And the cause gained advocates in the persons of *Washington Post* and syndicated columnists Colman McCarthy and William Raspberry, whose writings on the subject inflamed liberal opinion against the Ten's unfair treatment and the persecution of Ben Chavis.[24]

WHILE THE NAARPR was relentless and successful in pressing the case of the Wilmington Ten in the court of public opinion, the defendants

The Wilmington Ten held a press conference at Central Prison in Raleigh to denounce Governor Jim Hunt's decision not to pardon them. Left to right: Wayne Moore, Ben Chavis, Wilmington Ten attorney James E. Ferguson, Reginald Epps, Jerry Jacobs, Joe Wright (behind Jacobs), Willie Earl Vereen, and Connie Tindall. Photograph by Steve Murray for the Raleigh News and Observer, *24 January 1978, courtesy of the State Archives of North Carolina, Raleigh.*

continued to suffer defeats at the hands of the legal system in North Carolina. For several years after their conviction at trial, the defendants received nothing but adverse decisions in the North Carolina appellate courts. When the U.S. Supreme Court declined in January 1976 to become involved, a discrete phase of the legal fight was concluded, and the state courts revoked the bond they posted in June 1973. The Ten surrendered to authorities in February 1976 and were returned to prison. Their lives were interrupted—several of them, for example, had used their temporary freedom to pursue college educations—and the movement's most persuasive advocate, Ben Chavis, was muffled behind steel bars. The Wilmington Ten movement was compelled to reconfigure the ways it brought pressure to bear on the authorities.

The first blow in the post-trial legal process was landed on 18 December 1974, when a three-judge panel from the North Carolina Court of Appeals unanimously denied the defendants' appeal.[25] There were many points of contention, but defense attorney James Ferguson distilled the farcical trial down to two major points. First, the jury selection process had been gravely flawed. Second, the trial judge had erred in denying the defense access to Allen Hall's so-called amended statement, which hobbled the defense's ability to adequately confront the prosecution's main witness.

Potential jurors had not been sequestered from each other during questioning, increasing the likelihood that opinions adverse to the defendants, already widely circulating in the region, would become embedded in the jury pool. Judge Robert Martin had forbade the defense from probing jurors' racial attitudes and whether they required the defendants to prove their innocence rather than the state to prove guilt beyond a reasonable doubt; at the same time, the judge allowed the state solicitor wide latitude in his questioning of potential jurors and permitted him to excuse black jurors on account of their race. More, the trial judge had erred in his refusal of the defense's challenge of certain jurors for cause.

The opinion of the court of appeals is an exercise in sophistry. (It deserves mention that Judge Martin at the time of the appeal had recently been appointed by Republican governor James Holshouser to a vacant seat on the court of appeals;[26] though Martin did not participate in the three-judge panel that heard the appeal, it is hard to read the decision and not have the conceit that his fellow jurists were looking out for him.) On the issues raised about jury selection, the court of appeals found that there was no evidence of adverse publicity surrounding the case in eastern North Carolina. The opinion picked out of the trial record bits of exchanges between prosecutors and potential jurors, in which the jurors stated they had an opinion about the case but did not say what it was. Overlooking the dozens of instances in which potential jurors stated emphatically that they believed that at least some of the defendants must have committed the crimes with which they were charged, the appeals court disingenuously concluded that the extant racial polarization that saturated the region at the time was "mere allegation or, at best, a conclusion by counsel."[27]

Issues in the appeal concerning racial bias of potential jurors were treated in a similarly cavalier fashion. The court grudgingly recognized a state supreme court precedent from Reconstruction that allowed attorneys to inquire about jurors' racial bias and qualified its willingness to enforce this right by writing that the need for it "has greatly dissipated and is far less compelling." In negating James Ferguson's attempts to ascertain jurors' racial bias, the three judges criticized his questions as "obviously . . . rambling and confusing. . . . Clearly the trial judge was correct" in stopping him. Ferguson's question to a particular juror about whether he had ever belonged to a club or organization that excluded blacks was labeled by the judges as "bordering upon harassment" and "probably impossible to answer." Judge Martin's refusal to excuse certain jurors because they had made up their minds that the Ten were guilty was upheld as an exercise in judicial discretion. The trial record, as examined in chapter 3, fairly crackles with racial friction; in several instances, jurors who spiritedly clung to their belief in the defendants' guilt were seated anyway after Martin veritably pried from them statements that they would be objective. But appellate judges willfully overlooked racially based tension by saying they were not at the trial and congratulated Martin for his patience and good sense.[28]

The appellate panel contorted itself in its attempt to justify the trial judge's handling of Allen Hall. Without Hall, the state would not have had a case against the Wilmington Ten—or rather, the state would have had to invent someone like him. Hall was the eyewitness who placed all of the Wilmington Ten at the scene of the alleged crimes. The jury had to evaluate Hall's credibility as a witness. When Allen Hall made statements from the witness stand that were substantially different from or contradictory to his signed statement, he explained them away by saying that in subsequent meetings with prosecutor Jay Stroud he had made the corrections and additions and that Stroud had written them on his copy of the signed statement. He testified that he considered the so-called amended statement to be his own. Was this a credible explanation? Did Hall in fact make the corrections and additions, and did Stroud transcribe them? Or was Hall making it up as he went along? The defense team wanted to develop this line of questioning but could not when Judge Martin refused to hand over the so-called amended statement. The court of appeals inspected the statement, gave no weight to Hall's insistence that it reflected his views, and accepted Stroud's contention that what he had written down were his own notes; in any event, the court averred, many of the notes were not complete sentences or were illegible scribbles, so the defense had no right to see it. (The U.S. Department of Justice would later conclude otherwise; it received a copy of the sealed statement and in its analysis found that nearly a dozen of Hall's statements from the stand did not appear in the amended statement.) The judges protected their new colleague and abetted the state's perpetuation of a fraud.

James Ferguson and his colleagues appealed the decision to the supreme court of North Carolina. But because it was not required by law to review unanimous court of appeals decisions, the state's high court in May 1975 simultaneously denied the petition to take the case and allowed the state attorney general's motion to dismiss it "for lack of substantial constitutional question." A petition to the U.S. Supreme Court for it to review Allen Hall's amended statement and take the case out of the hands of the North Carolina judiciary was filed in time for the fall term but was denied in late January 1976.[29] With that, the state superior court revoked the Ten's bail, and they surrendered to authorities in Burgaw, the site of their trial, on 2 February 1976, following a large and boisterous rally and prayer service. They would still be able to pursue legal relief, but it would have to be done from behind prison bars.

The setback caused some active supporters of the cause to rethink their approach to demanding freedom for the Ten. Imani Kazana was among those calling for supporters to adjust their strategies and tactics to build public support. In 1975 Kazana, a Massachusetts native who had previously directed the Harvard-Radcliffe Afro-American Cultural Center, was a resident of the District of Columbia working for the Model Cities program, whose offices were across the street from the CRJ's office. On the invitation of a friend of long standing, she began to volunteer evenings in the CRJ office. There she met Ben Chavis, who had been assigned to Washington, and who remained there until his bail was revoked. (Kazana's political relationship with Chavis grew into a social one as well, as Chavis moved in with her until he surrendered to North Carolina authorities in February 1976.) Kazana was a committed black nationalist; she was a "full participant" in the Republic of New Afrika and a leading member on women's issues in the National Black Political Assembly, which grew out of the Gary convention. While in general she advocated for a broad approach to political education and organizing, she believed that such an approach was ineffective on two levels in the case of the Wilmington Ten, and she set about to remedy the situation.

Despite the major demonstrations in Raleigh and Washington, D.C., Kazana espied what she considered significant and related drawbacks in the organizing work of the NAARPR and the UCC's Commission for Racial Justice. One, as demonstrated by the refusal of the U.S. Supreme Court to hear the appeal, was that neither organization was able to compel the federal government to become involved. Kazana believed that she possessed—not exclusively, of course—a network that could effectively apply such pressure. Shortly after the defendants were once again imprisoned, Kazana brought into being the National Wilmington 10 Defense Committee, comprising ninety members from "all walks of life" but including, significantly, congressional staffers, Representative Ronald Dellums, the District of Columbia's nonvoting congressional delegate

Walter Fauntroy, black elected officials in other parts of the country, and Baltimore Colts running back Lydell Mitchell. The staffers especially were likely helpful in generating the interest of their bosses, including John Conyers of Michigan and Don Edwards of California, who would be instrumental in convincing the Department of Justice to look into the case.[30]

Second, the two existing organizations carried baggage that prevented potential supporters from joining the cause. In the case of the alliance, its connection with the CPUSA was a deterrent; as evidence of this, Kazana pointed to the inability of the alliance to develop much of a presence in Washington, D.C.: "Many people have been unwilling to join the Alliance because of its leftist political image although they have an interest in the Wilmington 10," she explained to Charles Cobb. But the UCC was not blameless, either, she thought. It was clearly supportive, as evidenced by the institutional financial support—$400,000 in bail was not nothing, she rightly said. But the UCC and its commission largely had an inward focus and did not appeal to those who were not church members or church-goers. Kazana said she did not know why this was the case, but it likely had to do with the significant opposition within the denomination itself to aiding the Ten.[31]

Kazana thought the struggle required a new organization unencumbered by the limitations of the alliance and the CRJ. By design it would be complementary, not competitive. Its focus would be on lobbying Congress and publicizing the case, though it could also mobilize people for mass public protests, such as the rally in Raleigh that occurred in February 1976 when the Ten surrendered in Burgaw. (On short notice, the new group sent two buses from Washington.) And unlike the myriad organizations— nationalist, Marxist, Maoist, pan-Africanist, and more—that mushroomed in the 1970s and struggled to formulate a coherent critique of the United States, and for which the Wilmington Ten was but one of many issues, Kazana's creation had a single focus. According to Kazana, she was trying to reach people who, owing to their professions in government, nonprofit agencies, or advocacy, had varying degrees of access to levers of power in Washington. This target audience was put off by theoretical debates, protracted discussions about the "direction" of the movement, and the search for ideological purity, and was not inclined to embrace orthodoxy of any persuasion. The founders of the National Wilmington 10 Defense Committee maintained their own political and ideological commitments but parked them at the door when they came together for the practical work of the new organization, which was a "popular support committee with no particular philosophical lines (religious or political)."[32]

THE NONPARTISAN POLICY of the National Wilmington 10 Defense Committee may not have satisfied either social movement veterans or those newly awakened to political consciousness, but it paid dividends in the new climate brought on by the U.S. Supreme Court's action. As the case was returned to the purview of the North Carolina state courts, it became evident that a strategy based overwhelmingly on domestic pressure was insufficient to get the Ten out of jail. Although from a very early moment, Ben Chavis, Kojo Nantambu, the Youth Organization for Black Unity, and others had invoked Africa and African solidarity in their agitation, it now became imperative to move from rhetoric to an intentional plan to bring global pressure to bear on the state and federal government. In their own ways, the Kazana group, the UCC, and the NAARPR worked to internationalize the struggle and exploit the fissures of the Cold War, but it was the National Wilmington 10 Defense Committee that earned the big prize of convincing Amnesty International to become involved.

Internationalizing the African American freedom struggle had been common currency in the Cold War era—indeed, before then, as well. Arranging it so that the world's attention was focused on particularly outrageous instances of racial injustice frequently checked America's flagrant behavior. Acting in the interests of American hegemony, the U.S. Supreme Court promised the abolition of racially segregated education in the 1954 *Brown* decision, for the country could not maintain its credibility as a beacon of freedom to Africa, Asia, and Latin America if its own black and brown citizens were brazenly subordinated. Fear of a public relations bonanza for the Soviet Union and skeptical attitudes from emerging African nations forced the Kennedy administration to moderate its actions and work to manage a smooth and limited elimination of Jim Crow in the American South, a policy continued in the Johnson administration. But Johnson's intensification of the Vietnam War and the resultant weakened commitment to ameliorating racial inequality (proving that national policy could pursue guns or butter, but not both) served America's international image badly. The savagery exhibited by the Nixon administration in Vietnam, its involvement in the coup in Chile that installed the murderous Augusto Pinochet, its embrace of apartheid and Portuguese colonialism in southern Africa—all this and more infected America's international reputation. With the presidential election season underway in 1976, Wilmington Ten advocates saw an opportunity to press their case in the world arena.

Early that year, the National Wilmington 10 Defense Committee contacted Amnesty International headquarters in London to ask for help. As the premier international human rights organization, Amnesty

International guarded its reputation by carefully vetting cases before taking them up and preventing its affiliates from initiating or participating in campaigns in their own countries, thereby warding off criticisms of politicking. The organization was receptive to the invitation to investigate and signaled more than once that it would like to assist. But it appears as if the organization had some built-in skepticism, because it kept coming back for more information and clarification and demanded more proof of government misconduct and alibi witnesses. Through some fits and starts, Amnesty International moved from an interest in the case to taking it on "an investigatory basis" to finally adopting the Wilmington Ten as "prisoners of conscience" and working for their release from prison and a new trial. Amnesty's West German branch was designated to lead the international campaign, assisted by affiliates in Austria, France, Sweden, Switzerland, Tasmania, Denmark, and the United Kingdom.[33]

Securing Amnesty's assistance was significant. As a candidate and then president, Jimmy Carter strived to patch up America's image abroad by making human rights a centerpiece of his foreign policy; of course, "human rights" also was a convenient cudgel with which to bloody the Soviet Union in the international arena. On the world stage, Amnesty International was not an organization that could be easily dismissed. It was a single-issue organization concerned with freedom for prisoners of conscience and abolishing the death penalty and did not otherwise involve itself with a country's political issues. In cases like the Wilmington Ten, where political actors were persecuted under the veneer of criminal law, Amnesty International was downright reluctant to become involved. In that regard, its single-mindedness was conservative.

Karsten Luethke, one of the more vocal supporters of the Wilmington Ten, was a young German radical living in West Berlin in the 1970s. He recalled that his Amnesty chapter initially took up the case of the Charlotte Three in 1973 and then supported the Wilmington Ten. Using research vetted at the organization's London headquarters, the Berlin chapter circulated petitions, distributed leaflets and pamphlets on the cases, and organized letter-writing campaigns targeting President Jimmy Carter and North Carolina governor Jim Hunt. The chapter also encouraged people to correspond with prisoners of conscience, which Luethke did with Jim Grant. Amnesty International stressed independent work, he said, and urged its chapters to avoid connections with radicals. In the West Berlin chapter, though, there were members who pushed the boundary of what was allowable. They were not so concerned with respectability; rather, they agitated around instances that highlighted a *pattern* of racism in the United States, including the Vietnam War, government repression at Wounded Knee and of the American Indian Movement, and the reinstatement of the death penalty. Luethke believed that his more comprehensive approach to the case of the Wilmington Ten had limited impact in West Germany, but when he visited the United States, Americans close to the case told him that Amnesty's impact was estimable.[34]

The Carter administration was bound to take notice of Amnesty International's findings, as the president treated it as an arbiter of human rights and cited its reports of mistreatment of Soviet dissidents in his furtherance of the Cold War. But international pressure came from other sources, too, as the NAARPR activated its global network to support the cause. As the late historian Kenneth Cmiel argued, the mid-1970s was gold-rush time for human rights politics in the United States and Europe. While in the United States a good deal of that energy was expended on the Soviet Union and its allies, in Europe especially there was great opposition to the United States' violations, both internationally and domestically. In the negotiations surrounding the 1975 Helsinki Conference on Security and Cooperation in Europe, critics of American policy (including the socialist bloc) challenged the primacy of the United States' narrow definition of human rights as being made up almost exclusively of individual freedoms, while they simultaneously raised questions about the country's own domestic human rights record. At the next meeting of the conference in Belgrade, the U.S. delegation was aggressively questioned especially about the Wilmington Ten, and participants received an appeal from Ben Chavis. Chavis recited for the conference the denial of rights of Wilmington's African Americans, the violence against them perpetrated by the Rights of White People group, and the corrupt trial that convicted the Ten, and concluded with a list of political activists who were incarcerated in the United States and the corresponding violations of the Final Act of the Helsinki Conference. Also in 1977, Charlene Mitchell and Michael Myerson of the CPUSA and the NAARPR spent three weeks touring Europe on behalf of the Wilmington Ten. They visited ten countries in West and East Europe, meeting government officials and representatives of political parties, trade unions, and students, who in most instances pledged demonstrations and letter-writing campaigns. The greatest support came from the German Democratic Republic, perhaps facilitated by the presence there of American expatriate Victor Grossman. Grossman remembered frequent articles in the *Junge Welt* newspaper, exhortations to write to U.S. government officials and the Wilmington Ten defendants, and a monster Solidarity Day demonstration held in Berlin's Alexanderplatz.

According to Grossman, it remains largely unknown that American soldiers and officers frequented East Berlin to shop; those who came over on the day of the demonstration "were obviously attracted by the crowd. I asked them in English to sign [a petition]. Not surprisingly, the 2 (?) Black GI's knew immediately of the case, the 2–3 white GIs didn't. But they were all friendly and I think they all signed, with East German TV filming them (they were seen in the news that evening)."[35]

While President Carter began his incumbency saying that the United States' human rights record was unblemished and that in any event he could not intervene in the Wilmington Ten case, which was a state matter, he nevertheless felt the growing international approbation and domestic impatience with his human rights rhetoric. At press conferences, reporters asked him about the Wilmington Ten, drawing comparisons between them and people persecuted in other countries. Awakened to the case by the constant adverse publicity and mass domestic and international pressure, someone in the Carter administration—perhaps the chief of the Justice Department's Civil Rights Division, Drew Days, or Attorney General Griffin Bell himself, or someone in the White House, or some combination of the three—ordered a review of the case. Harvard law professor Lani Guinier, then a Justice Department attorney, and others looked and began to see the troubling patterns of abuse that the defense attorneys had been claiming. Within a month of assuming office, Carter's attorney general expressed a desire for a new trial. In March 1977 the Justice Department ordered the convening of a federal grand jury in Raleigh to investigate possible criminal misconduct on the part of the prosecution. Two months later, in May 1977, in the same Burgaw courtroom in which they were railroaded, a new judge, the Honorable George Fountain, presided over a post-conviction hearing to consider both new information and arguments about the fairness of the 1972 trial. But the state of North Carolina, having won at trial and in every appellate court, felt insulated from public pressure and continued to rationalize its misdeeds. And as will become apparent shortly, Judge Fountain, like the appellate jurists who preceded him, willingly participated in the state's charade.[36]

The state's position, leaky despite being shored up by the appellate courts, began to take on more water when the chief prosecution witness, Allen Hall, recanted his testimony. It was further inundated when reporters from two North Carolina newspapers broke stories that potential witnesses for the defense were intimidated into not testifying and that documents that tended to show Ben Chavis in a pacific role during the events of February 1971 had been "lost" from the offices of the state Good

Neighbor Council. How Hall came to his decision to proclaim that he lied is not entirely clear. Imani Kazana said that owing to her independence from the defense, the CRJ, and the NAARPR, she felt that she had the liberty to act in "unorthodox" ways, and she initiated a correspondence with Hall. They became "pen pals," and during the course of their exchange of letters, he expressed regret for his testimony and asked her what he could do to make things right. She told him he could tell the truth and then handed this bit of intelligence to James Ferguson. Hall, who was out of prison in mid-1976, traveled to Charlotte at Ferguson's expense and recorded a recantation in Ferguson's law office.[37]

The story that Allen Hall was now telling is arresting. In his statement to Ferguson and his grand jury testimony in Raleigh, he said that he lied at the trial when he stated that Chavis and his codefendants had burned Mike's Grocery. He said he lied when he claimed he saw Chavis giving lessons for making Molotov cocktails. He said he lied when he testified that he knew the defendants, for although he knew Joe Wright slightly when they were children, he never hung out with him, and he did not even know the names of the others. He said that contrary to his trial testimony, the only person he had seen with a gun was the murdered Steve Mitchell. At the trial he had said that he decided to tell the truth because his mother had told him to do so; but in his grand jury testimony he said that, too, was a lie, and he had not spoken to his mother about this at all. These were the major lies he said he told, though there were other fabrications. He claimed that he told these lies at the behest of State Solicitor Jay Stroud, who, along with Wilmington police detectives and federal agent Bill Walden of the Bureau of Alcohol, Tobacco, and Firearms, coached him repeatedly. And because Stroud worried that Hall's testimony alone would not be strong enough, the solicitor had called in Jerome Mitchell to corroborate Hall; Stroud brought Hall and Mitchell together at the Cherry state mental hospital in February and March 1972 and again in June and September during the first and second trials so they could develop their stories together. Hall said he lied for several reasons. He received favorable treatment in the form of getting out of prison, enjoying visits with his mother at home and with his girlfriend, and hotel and beach cottage stays while he was preparing to testify. The prosecutor had promised to reduce the sentence he was serving for his guilty plea to burning Mike's. Conversely, the prosecutor had threatened him and his mother if he refused to testify. And he was given money.[38]

Hall's recantation had credibility but was by no means unproblematic. Some of the favorable treatment of him was known to the defense, but the trial judge refused to let the jurors hear that during the trial Hall was in custody but not confined to jail and was allowed to roam the beach; the defense was also aware of the other personal perquisites but was likewise unable to bring them into evidence. A few months after the trial, Jay Stroud intervened in Hall's sentencing for his role in burning Mike's Grocery. He successfully urged a judge to convert the twelve-year sentence as an adult to a one-day-to-twelve-years sentence as a youthful offender, which made it possible for Hall to leave prison after three years. Also after the trial, Stroud visited Hall in prison and gave him money; and although the amounts were nominal from Stroud's perspective, they were more considerable to an incarcerated teen with no means. (For that matter, the same can be said of the other emoluments. A motel room shared with another prisoner and guarded by law enforcement officers, an occasional outdoor excursion, and fast-food fried chicken may have seemed puny to an officer of the court like Stroud, but they were likely powerful inducements to a poor teen facing years of prison time.) Hall's account of rehearsing his testimony with Jerome Mitchell also rings true. Stroud admitted under oath to the grand jury that interviewing witnesses together was unorthodox, but he thought in this case it would help get at the truth. And, as noted in the previous chapter, Stroud's trial notes, which he turned over to the grand jury, strongly suggest that he was telling Hall what to say and what not to say on the stand.

At the same time, Hall's recantation statement and grand jury testimony exhibit some of the same erratic nature that laced earlier statements. His statement to Ferguson in his office was unequivocal, as seen in this exchange:

MR. FERGUSON: Were you there when Mike's Grocery was burned?
ALLEN HALL: Yeah.
MR. FERGUSON: Did you see who burned Mike's Grocery?
ALLEN HALL: Yeah.

Yet when he had a chance to read the interview transcript, he corrected— and partially contradicted—himself:

> ... Where I was asked was I there when Mike's Grocery was burned and I replied, "Yeah," I meant that I was at Reverend Templeton's house and saw Mike's Grocery burning from Reverend Templeton's back yard. When I was asked did I see who burned Mike's Grocery and I replied, "Yeah," I meant to say "No." I did not participate in the burning of Mike's Grocery and I did not see who burned it.[39]

He reversed course again in his grand jury testimony, saying that he, George Kirby, and Steve Mitchell had burned Mike's.[40] When asked to explain the discrepancy, he said he had lied to Ferguson about not knowing who burned Mike's because he was afraid of being arrested for arson.[41] Given that Hall was mentally impaired—his IQ hovered just above 80—it is possible that he feared this, though he had already served time for this crime.

Was Allen Hall lying at the pretrial hearing and trial or in the grand jury room? What if the threats against him and his mother by the prosecutor never occurred? Do his contradictory statements nullify his recantation? If one claims that Hall was so unreliable that his grand jury testimony had no value, then one must reasonably conclude that his trial testimony was also worthless—more so, even, given his outbursts and physical attacks on Ferguson at trial. But if one sets aside Hall's inconsistencies and bizarre behavior, his recantation and grand jury testimony still raise fundamental questions about the fairness of the Wilmington Ten trial and the conduct of the prosecution. Did Hall receive favorable treatment in return for his testimony, which was hidden from the defense? Was Hall coached and told what to say by Solicitor Stroud and BATF agent Walden, among others?

It must have been difficult for Jay Stroud, who was subpoenaed before the grand jury, to sit in the witness box and answer questions about his conduct of the case, which were at the core of the investigation. Usually he was the one to stand before witnesses and make them squirm, but in this instance he was the object of examination. But having given a statement to the FBI and reviewed the case file prior to his grand jury appearance, he presumably was prepared. Yet Stroud's appointment with the grand jury was eerily similar to Allen Hall's time on the witness stand during the trial. With a rehearsed definiteness, Stroud answered some preliminary questions about how he made Hall's acquaintance and came to prosecute the Wilmington Ten. But as the Justice Department attorneys probed how Allen Hall's statement evolved, how the case was prepared against the Ten, and considerations Hall received, Stroud became alternately vague— he utilized Hall's trial mantra that he did not remember—and officious and belligerent, though he did not jump from the stand and assault the attorneys or jurors.

The transcript of the grand jury hearing documents what at best can be described as irregularities and at worst Stroud's attempts to obfuscate the state's misconduct. Stroud flatly denied working closely with the federal BATF and its agent Bill Walden, who was implicated in the framing of the Charlotte Three; Stroud said that the two may have talked briefly about the Wilmington Ten and other matters concerning Ben Chavis but worked largely independently of and separately from each other. He depicted Walden's presence at the interview of Hall and Jerome Mitchell at Cherry Hospital in February 1972 as a matter of convenience. The interview was important in that it produced Allen Hall's statement, which was the basis for his trial testimony. But Stroud had no good explanation for why Walden composed a statement and brought it to Hall to sign, which he did, without the knowledge of Stroud; nor could he explain why the statement that Walden wrote allegedly left out details contained in Stroud's notes, or why he did not compose a statement based on his own notes and bring it to Hall to sign. Improbably, Stroud said he could not remember having conversations with Walden about this. And although Stroud said that Walden was present at other meetings with Hall, including at the Holiday Inn in Wrightsville Beach and/or the cottage at Carolina Beach during the trial, he denied Hall's claim that Walden helped prepare his trial testimony. He also was at a loss to explain why Walden had prepared a trial document that summarized what Hall would testify to.

The interview at Cherry Hospital was important in another respect, too, as it developed a second witness to the crimes allegedly committed by the Wilmington Ten. Jerome Mitchell had previously and consistently denied being at Gregory Congregational Church on the Saturday that Mike's burned. But when the Hall-Mitchell joint interview was over, Mitchell had changed his story. Such joint interviews of witnesses are highly unusual; typically, they are interviewed separately so that they cannot compare stories. But Stroud thought this time it was okay to diverge from protocol; he said he wanted to "confront" Mitchell with Hall in order to get Mitchell to "tell the truth" that he saw the Ten burn Mike's and shoot at emergency personnel, a "truth" that only Hall had stated. To bolster the credibility of this truth, Hall and Mitchell looked at photographs of several of the Ten and identified them as persons who committed the arson; but, Stroud admitted reluctantly and only after prodding, he had shown photographs only of people who were present at Gregory Church and not also a control group of people who the police knew were not there.

Stroud maintained that the case against the Wilmington Ten developed in a straightforward manner, with Hall implicating them after his arrest in May 1971; from there it was a simple matter of finding more evidence and putting them on trial. He denied offering Hall leniency in exchange for his testimony, telling him that he was more interested in "bigger fish" (some of the defendants themselves reported almost identical overtures from the police), or manipulating Hall's anger to get him to testify. But when he was shown his own notes reminding him to do just that—"hold off on some indictments versus big ones and see if this won't make little ones mad"—Stroud's amnesia resurfaced: "I could not begin to tell you what I meant by [this]."[42] Stroud dismissed Hall's more favorable resentencing as a youthful offender as unconnected to his service to the prosecution, even though by his own admission Stroud interceded on Hall's behalf more than once.

At the end of his questioning, a beleaguered Jay Stroud—he must have been a sight, as he apologized for his bleary appearance—disrupted the proceedings by asking a series of questions of the jurors and the Justice Department attorneys. It was not only the type of questions he posed that breached protocol but also the fact that he was asking any questions at all:

> WITNESS: . . . I would like to ask you gentlemen: Has there been a formal civil rights complaint filed in this case?
>
> MR. MARTIN [JUSTICE DEPARTMENT ATTORNEY]: You know as well as I know that I am not at liberty to disclose to witnesses any information about that investigation . . .
>
> WITNESS: Is not a civil complaint, if there has been one, a public document?
>
> MR. MARTIN: I—My job is also not to answer your questions before this Grand Jury. If you have a statement, please proceed with it.
>
> WITNESS: Well, I was trying to determine how this investigation came about—who initiated it.
>
> MR. MARTIN: The role of the Grand Jury is not for you to determine, but to answer the questions that they have of you . . .
>
> WITNESS: I'm not trying to determine the role of the Grand Jury. I know their role, perhaps as well if not better than you do . . . I wanted to be sure that the Grand Jury knew, and as I think they're entitled to know, how this investigation was instigated . . .
>
> MR. MARTIN: Let me say one thing. I resent that remark. You just asked me questions which, as a former employee of the Justice Department, you knew very well I could not answer in your presence, and asking me them in that way, it seems to me rather— knowing—a slight at me.[43]

Stroud then launched a rambling apologia, which amounted to this: the Wilmington Ten were found guilty at trial, the verdict was upheld on appeal, and his conduct was above reproach. Yet when he was done, the question still remained in the minds of the grand jurors: If Allen Hall could testify to one thing at the trial and then recant and further say he had committed perjury at the behest of Jay Stroud, how could he be believed at all, and why did Stroud put so much stock in him?[44]

The Justice Department concluded that there was no basis for filing civil rights charges against Jay Stroud. The primary evidence it had consisted of grand jury testimony of witnesses who either had lied on the stand or had lied in their recantations. But if there was no way to indict Stroud, the U.S. attorney general decided to talk to his North Carolina counterpart, Rufus Edmisten, to persuade him at least to offer a new trial. Edmisten demurred. His boss, the new Democratic governor Jim Hunt, would let the appeals process, of which there was one last step—the post-conviction hearing, in May 1977—conclude before he would press for either a new trial or a pardon.

The principal value of the post-conviction hearing was that, unlike the grand jury, whose proceedings were secret, it was a public affair. Allen Hall once again recanted his trial testimony in all respects in open court. He, along with Jerome Mitchell and Eric Junious, had been the only witnesses to place the Ten at the crimes, and he explained in detail at the post-conviction hearing how Stroud had induced him to commit perjury and how he was coached to testify. The Reverend Eugene Templeton and Donna Templeton testified inter alia that they had not appeared as defense witnesses at the trial because they feared that if they showed up in Burgaw, they would be arrested and charged with conspiracy. The state's attorneys did not dispute this particular assertion, even though on cross-examination they fiercely contested practically all of the rest of their accounts of February 1971. Jay Stroud was obliged to appear as a witness, too; he could not hide behind secrecy, and he was trapped in the webs of his own lies. "I do not recall" and "I don't remember" could not prevent his machinations to convict the Wilmington Ten from coming into public view. Under questioning from James Ferguson, the fabrication of the state's plan was made evident.

Stroud represented himself as a disinterested public servant doing his duty, as opposed to an aggressive prosecutor with a hunger to get the Ten. He had caught this case by a series of coincidences. In May 1971, he said, he had been teaching a night class to police officers when during a break some officers asked him to talk with Allen Hall, who had just been arrested and was talking about the burning of Mike's Grocery and the shooting of Harvey Cumber. Stroud said he obliged the police and spoke with Hall briefly but then turned the matter back to the police to continue their investigation, as per protocol; he did not see Hall again until January 1972, he said, when he was sentenced for his part in the burning of Mike's. But this narrative of happenstance belied a more calculated plan. Ferguson elicited an admission from Stroud that it was irregular for the police to ask a prosecutor to talk with an arrestee before he or she was charged with a crime. The strong implication was that the police knew that Stroud had a keen interest in the events of February 1971. Indeed, Stroud said that he had been on hand at police headquarters during those troubled days advising Wilmington police chief H. E. Williamson, and he felt that someone should pay for the disturbances. He also lied about not talking with Hall after that initial contact in jail. Ferguson confronted Stroud with both his grand jury testimony and his statement to the FBI, which he gave immediately preceding that appearance, in which he said that he had talked to Hall at least four times between May 1971 and January 1972. It was during those months that Hall's story took shape. Stroud admitted—and then quickly recanted—that the notes he took on Hall's statement, which he had claimed at trial was "work product," in fact made up Hall's revised statement and should have been made available to the defense. And he remained stubbornly evasive about the inducements he proffered to Hall in exchange for his testimony. He claimed not to remember Hall's girlfriend and then could not explain why he sent law enforcement officers to Asheville to talk to her and her mother, rather than simply telephoned them. He denied instructing the officers to bring her back to New Hanover County but could not explain the girlfriend's testimony that when the officers arrived at her home her bags were already packed for the trip. He denied intervening right after the Wilmington Ten trial to have Hall's sentence amended to youthful offender status, and when confronted with evidence that he did just that, he said that someone else initiated the process and he was simply doing his part. He continued to insist that there was nothing irregular about having Hall and Mitchell maintained at the beach during the trials or allowing them to visit Hall's mother at her home. When questioned about the security detail, Stroud stated improbably that the guard included agents from the BATF who simply volunteered their time for extended periods. It was hard not to draw a conclusion that implicated federal law enforcement authorities in the persecution of the Wilmington Ten.

But the evisceration of State Solicitor Stroud was of little avail, for it was evident from the beginning that Judge Fountain was forcing the defense to fight from a disadvantaged position. In preparation for the hearing, Ferguson requested that his clients be allowed to attend. He said that with such a sprawling case it was imperative that he be able to confer with them separately and collectively. At the time of the hearing, Chavis and his comrades—except for Ann Shepard, who had already been paroled—were scattered across eight separate prisons in the state. But the judge went along with the state's opposition to the motion. Wrote Ferguson, "Quite frankly, I fail to understand why the respondents oppose petitioners' presence at this crucial hearing and why you have refused to order them present. It has been my experience that almost as a matter of routine, petitioners have been allowed to be present at post-conviction hearings where factual questions are involved." Fountain replied that his decision had nothing to do with the state's objection, but nevertheless he denied the motion.[45]

What played out in the Burgaw courtroom over ten days' time was little more than theater, with starring roles played by Hall, Stroud, and the Templetons; a supporting cast of more than four dozen other witnesses who collectively produced a (tran)script of more than 1,600 pages plus exhibits; and direction by Judge Fountain. At the conclusion of the state's and the petitioners' cases and their closing arguments, the judge commended both parties—Ferguson and his colleagues especially—for their command of the case and the issues involved. After these sympathetic noises and without taking any time to reflect, Fountain issued his ruling straight from the bench: "The only thing, as I understand it, for me to determine is whether there has been or whether there was at the time of the trial in 1972 a substantial denial of constitutional, or any constitutional right of the defendants. And upon the hearing of the evidence I have concluded that my findings would be that there was no such denial and I will prepare an order accordingly with appropriate findings of fact."[46]

Had Judge Fountain been interested, he might have consulted the report prepared by the renowned jurist Luis Rèque of Bolivia, who attended the post-conviction hearing on behalf of Amnesty International. In twenty pithy pages, Rèque summarized the events of February 1971, the two trials and the case against the Wilmington Ten, the denial of appeals, the recantation of the incriminating witnesses, and the post-conviction hearing. Contrary to the ruling of Judge Fountain, this report from an august organization that was cited as the authority on political persecution and human rights violations by the president of the United States found that the Wilmington Ten were not afforded a fair trial, that there was prosecutorial misconduct, that there was considerable evidence of the innocence of the Wilmington Ten, and that therefore Governor Hunt should "grant them a pardon of innocence."[47] Instead, Fountain's order denying post-conviction relief was a wholesale adoption of the state's position.

When he ruled from the bench, the judge said he would file his written order "as soon as I can," citing a full calendar for the anticipated delay.

Unknown to Ferguson, though, Fountain entered into an unorthodox arrangement with the attorney general's office, which agreed to assist him in the preparation of his order. When this became public knowledge, Judge Fountain defended the relationship, saying that as he had no full-time secretary but did have full-time judicial obligations, he requested "clerical and stenographic" help from the attorney general. Yet, as with so much of this case, the reality—as revealed in the exchange of letters among the attorneys and Fountain—was hardly benign.

On 17 June, which was about a month after the post-conviction hearing and two and a half weeks before Fountain filed his order, Assistant Attorney General Richard League sent the judge a "smooth rough of the proposed order on the Wilmington Ten post-conviction hearing. Upon your approval of it, I will be pleased to add the formal parts and type it in smooth and final form." This draft was the foundation of Fountain's final order; though there were minor changes, the ruling that was filed over the judge's signature was substantially identical to League's draft. Not surprisingly, League's concern was presenting as tight an argument as possible, and over the next several days, League returned to the document several times and sent Fountain minor revisions for his approval. In one instance, amendments were made at the judge's request. On 30 June, League sent to Fountain what he considered to be the final copy of the order; he made a few more trivial adjustments and bid the judge to let him know that he approved so that he could print the necessary copies in order for it to be filed.[48]

What is surprising is twofold. First, no copies of League's letters to Fountain nor the proposed findings and order were provided to Ferguson; thus Fountain either solicited or received the legal argument from only one of the adversaries in the proceeding. Such ex parte communications are generally unethical. Second, League contradicted Fountain's claim that the only assistance provided the judge was secretarial in nature and showed how deeply implicated he was in the judge's decision:

In order for us not to have a new hearing in federal court, it is necessary that the factual findings from the state hearing cover all germane points. I have laboriously tried to do this, and I hope you will not delete any of the factual findings I have made unless you recall that they are unsupported by the evidence. . . . Conversely, if I have overlooked something, I hope you will direct me in this regard and I will be pleased to write up some additional findings to add to the order. The same is true of the conclusions of law.[49]

James Ferguson heard about this behind-the-scenes arrangement during a telephone call with League around 1 July, after League had sent off the final order for approval. Ferguson asked for a copy of the proposed order, allowing that his not having received it was "perhaps through an oversight." League fended off the request. In due time, he replied, Ferguson would receive the final order signed by the judge; he saw no need to share the proposed order that he drafted, even while acknowledging that it was a matter of custom to do so: "You were not sent a copy of the order I originally sent in because . . . I simply did not see the need. I am aware that frequently proposed orders are sent to opposing counsel, but I have never understood why this was so in the ordinary case." Ferguson objected to League's implication that the exchange of proposals was mere courtesy; the Wilmington Ten was an active case, and rules demanded that communication between one party and the judge "should be made known to opposing counsel, with or without a request." Still, the attorney general's office would not comply; he checked with Fountain, League wrote, who said that only the filed order represented his judgment, and he did not want the draft orders made public. Only with a formal motion in August to compel the state to produce its proposed findings and a complementary one asking Fountain to recuse himself for appropriating those findings did Fountain and League relent. The judge, while denying both motions, said he did not oppose the release of the state's proposed order, though, in a nod to the trial judge and Jay Stroud, he would not compel the attorney general to do so if he felt that it was work product. Perhaps deciding that this particular skirmish in the public eye was already lost, League sent Ferguson the state's proposed findings, conclusion, and orders as well as League's letters enclosing them.[50]

In this last stop in the North Carolina judicial system, the collusion between the prosecution and the judge was breathtaking. In a case pocked by irregularities, Judge Fountain's order and the process by which it was produced was audacious. While it is not uncommon for judges to request attorneys from both sides to propose various outcomes—for example, during the trial both the prosecution and defense submitted instructions they wanted the judge to issue to the jury—it is practically unheard of for them to request proposals from one side only. Fountain's action was tantamount to failure to perform his duty. As well, Ferguson argued, North Carolina law requires judges "to make appropriate findings of fact and conclusions of law thereon in entering an order upon a post-conviction hearing." The record of the post-conviction hearing strongly suggests that Judge Fountain did not arrive at his findings of fact and conclusions of law independently and after careful consideration. It also suggests that he did not weigh all of the evidence fairly. When Judge Fountain, without the knowledge of Ferguson, requested the material from the attorney general's office and adopted it wholesale as his own, he ceased acting as a jurist and became the prosecution's amanuensis. This, as Ferguson argued, was a violation of the legal profession's code of responsibility.[51]

But none of Ferguson's forensic logic, none of the countless reports of bought witnesses, none of the exposure of judicial malfeasance softened the hard heart of North Carolina justice. Judge George Fountain was upheld, and the Wilmington Ten remained in prison. The legal work had succeeded in revealing the corruption that riddled this political prosecution, but the fact remained that the legal system was fabricated to defend the status quo. Consequently, various appellate courts could blithely dismiss Ferguson's arguments concerning the denial of justice as trivial, inconsequential, or immaterial to the outcome of the case. This is not to say that all was lost—far from it. By the end of 1977, the campaign to free the Wilmington Ten had aroused the nation and summoned the attention of the world. The organizations dedicated to the specific case or to the cause of social justice generally would in the new year take the information generated by the appeals process and redouble their efforts to free the Wilmington Ten in the Cold War arena and in national and local politics, areas in which they could expect far better results than in the courts.

CHAPTER 5

Free the Wilmington Ten at Once!

n January 1976, as political handicappers were trying to predict the upcoming presidential election and African American politicians and partisans debated whether endorsing a major party candidate or supporting a third-party campaign would advance their respective agendas, both the National Alliance against Racist and Political Repression and the Commission for Racial Justice espied a hopeful glimmer for the cause of the Wilmington Ten. Though the organizations adhered to different strategies and might be best described as "frenemies," they both believed that a national election was a big stage on which they could bring their own campaigns to the public's attention. They also thought they could force candidates for president and governor of North Carolina to declare their positions on this miscarriage of justice. Although no candidate expressed such a public opinion, the education, agitation, and action begun in the winter months of the bicentennial year and continuing in the months and years that followed did compel President Jimmy Carter and North Carolina governor James B. Hunt to address the issue. But because both leaders were unwilling to confront honestly and forthrightly the country's and the state's history of racial oppression, their actions only stimulated distrust and further agitation and action. Freedom for the Wilmington Ten was delayed, but ultimately the federal judiciary could not ignore the public's outcry for freedom.[1]

Jimmy Carter and Jim Hunt were white southern Democratic politicians trying, in the post-segregation South, to get out from under the long shadow cast by fire-eaters like George Wallace and Lester Maddox. As the latest iterations of New South politicians, their challenge was to move the needle away from the crude race-baiting of their Democratic Party forebears and to placate newly enfranchised African Americans without alienating their white core constituency. While they were able to change the tone of the rhetoric, they were never able to escape their convictions that gathering whites' votes and support trumped practically all other considerations.

That 85 percent of African American voters marked their ballots for Jimmy Carter in the general election at first blush points to a high level of enthusiasm. But this apparent consensus likely reflected a deep revulsion for Ford-cum-Nixon and the Republican Party's southern strategy. Just below the near unanimity was a palpable anxiety about Carter among many African Americans. For although as Georgia's governor he had plainly stated that it was time for racial discrimination to be over and as a presidential candidate had presented himself as a moral and decent, though flawed, person, he also offered statements that indicated a willingness to conciliate white supremacy. During the Wisconsin primary campaign he endorsed the concept of white "ethnic purity" against federal attempts to desegregate housing in urban neighborhoods. (After repeating his approval, blacks' strong reaction caught up with him, and he issued a retraction.) As a Plains, Georgia, school board chairman he had not opposed segregated education, and as a member of the Georgia legislature he supported an amendment to the U.S. Constitution forbidding the busing of schoolchildren to achieve integration. In his run for Georgia governor in 1970, he presented himself as a defender of the little (white) guy and appealed to the segregationist vote.[2]

Jim Hunt, the son of moderately successful tobacco and dairy farmers, contracted the political bug while enrolled in the agricultural education course of study at North Carolina State College (now University) in Raleigh in the 1950s. He was involved in campus politics and the Young Democrats and in 1960 was seduced by the progressive mystique of Terry Sanford's gubernatorial campaign. Sanford's time as governor was substantial: his legacy includes the North Carolina Fund, which battled to end poverty in the state and supported some organizations in black communities that later joined the ranks of the Black Power movement. But on most matters of race and labor, Sanford's progressive rhetoric was more illusory than manifest. He was committed to the health of the state's low-wage manufacturing industries, and his approach to civil rights was simply incremental. Developing himself into an effective Democratic Party insider, Jim Hunt learned well from Sanford. He extended himself to a black electorate that was expanding significantly as a result of the 1965 Voting Rights Act while in fact offering little of tangible value to it. Working to stanch the exit of white voters from the Democratic Party to the Republicans after 1965, Hunt favored conservative candidates and messages to whites combined with limited overtures to African American elites like the head of the Durham-based Mechanics and Farmers Bank. In April 1968, when he served on the Wilson Human Relations Commission, he participated in a service immediately after Martin Luther King's assassination; when he was criticized by whites for this gesture, he said he went only to make sure that the event remained nonviolent—as if he was the only person who stood in the way of a racial Armageddon.[3]

Candidates Carter and Hunt hoped to sidestep the Wilmington Ten affair by averting their eyes during their campaigns. But the case stubbornly remained in plain view once they assumed office. When the president and the governor began their terms in January 1977, the Wilmington Ten were completing a year behind bars, and organized protest was becoming more than a nuisance—it was creating a national and international venue for public shaming of the United States and North Carolina. For the record, Carter uttered sympathetic noises about his desire to see equal justice for everyone. Hunt, perhaps surprised or annoyed that the case, which had begun two governors before him, still lingered, stonily declared he would not do or say anything until the appeals process was complete, even as he maintained cordial communications with some of the Wilmington Ten's supporters—those who happened to be white, southern, and well placed.[4]

Even before the transition to the Carter administration, the U.S. Department of Justice sensed something was amiss in the Wilmington Ten prosecution. Staff, of course, read the opinion page of the *Washington Post*, which at irregular intervals ran columns on the case by Colman McCarthy and William Raspberry. Just before the election Raspberry alerted his public that the case was again headed to federal court. A young assistant attorney general in the civil rights division, Stan Pottinger, read it and requested an update from his subordinates. While waiting for an answer, Justice officials were visited by emissaries from Brooklyn congresswoman Shirley Chisolm and another member of the Congressional Black Caucus. Sensing something greater than usual brewing, Pottinger consulted with Dan Rinzel, a career attorney in the division, and started to develop a plan to respond, including an investigation of Allen Hall's recantation.[5]

After Ford left office, Pottinger remained as a special assistant to Attorney General Griffin Bell, who, like Carter, was from Georgia. Pottinger's responsibilities apparently remained the same, as he oversaw the Wilmington Ten case until the new assistant attorney general for civil rights, Drew Days, one of the president's last initial appointees, could get through confirmation process and familiarize himself with the case. Until he left in March 1977, Pottinger coordinated the Carter administration's response. He chose to schedule a meeting with Imani Kazana and other National Wilmington 10 Defense Committee leaders and invited the new attorney general to participate. (Bell attended the meeting, though by the account of one civil rights division attorney Bell had a diminished interest in civil rights and believed that it was not evident why there should be civil rights litigation. At the same time, Bell apparently did not interfere with those in his department who were charged with that task.) It was apparently Pottinger's idea—or maybe his and Drew Days's—to convene the grand jury in Raleigh, persuade the attorney general to pressure North Carolina to allow a new trial, and, in the likely event that North Carolina refused, develop options for the federal government to intervene on behalf of the defendants. After reviewing Allen Hall's recantation, he even mulled bringing federal charges against Jay Stroud, though he ultimately demurred due to high hurdles to prosecuting official misconduct.[6]

The daily work in the courts and in the public square was the bedrock of the campaign to free the Wilmington Ten. But pressure on government officials came from elsewhere, too. International public opinion, critical inquiries by members of Congress, and even questions from a stratum of white southerners made the continued persecution of the Wilmington Ten untenable. Having the case and protests in the news interfered with President Carter's human rights foreign policy and the ability of Governor Hunt to project a stable, progressive, and business-friendly image of his state. The result was that over time the Department of Justice discovered a way to intervene in the legal process, while North Carolina's obstinacy stimulated a new round of protest that was guided by a critique that was qualitatively more radical and fundamental than in the past.

Senator Charles Percy of Illinois was the first to speak about the Wilmington Ten from the floor of the Congress in the Carter years. Percy was a moderate Republican who joined with the Congressional Black Caucus, the NAACP, and other civil rights groups in questioning Griffin Bell's fitness for the office of attorney general; he voted against his confirmation, joining twenty other senators, many of whom cited Bell's apparent lack of support for integration. But in March 1977, Percy, on the floor of the Senate, issued an admission that he was partially wrong about Bell and congratulated him for "putting the investigation [of the violation of the Wilmington Ten's civil rights] on a priority basis." In June, Representative Don Edwards, a California Democrat, made his first of many interventions in the case, calling attention to those who "languish in North Carolina jails" and posing this question to House members: "If we are concerned with human rights, what about those here at home?" Edwards became a firm ally of the Wilmington Ten, challenging the attorney general to do more. He organized a special House delegation to travel to North Carolina both to visit the imprisoned Ten and to meet with Governor Hunt to encourage him to pardon the Wilmington Ten or at a minimum to commute their sentences to time served. When Joe Wright was released from prison, Edwards hired him on his staff.[7]

Representative Edwards's reference to the Wilmington Ten and human rights was more than apt given President Carter's emphasis on human rights in U.S. foreign policy. Edwards was not alone in pointing out that this case bared a disjunction between rhetoric and reality, between foreign and domestic policies. The Soviet press pummeled what it considered the United States' double standard of criticizing alleged Soviet violations of human rights while winking at and in many cases abetting repression at home. All aspects of the Wilmington case were narrated in Soviet publications: the racial unrest that led to the school boycott and subsequent violence, the outrageous trial and absurdly long sentences, the conditions behind bars, and how Ben Chavis held up in prison life. "This disgraceful case has become known not only in the US but also beyond its borders, where Washington is making a special effort to present the US as some sort of haven of democracy," read one typically infelicitous article. But while the Wilmington Ten and particularly Chavis were a focus of the Soviet's hammering, the case was never presented as sui generis. Instead, the Soviet press emphasized a pattern of human rights abuses in the United States. There was the matter of political repression, which encompassed not only the Wilmington Ten but also Assata Shakur, Angela Davis, and the Black Panthers, as well as the jailing and beating of nonviolent demonstrators, especially in the South. Prison conditions came in for criticism as well, in which unruly inmates were sent to psychiatric hospitals such as the one in the federal prison in Butner, North Carolina; publications charged that people, especially minorities who expressed political dissent, were liable to be arrested and treated as insane. Soviet news outlets also printed stories critiquing the standard of living in the United States. The socialist countries and much of the rest of the world, but not the United States, considered material security an important measure of human rights. The evidence was very strong that African Americans were living a nightmare in this respect.[8]

The Soviet point was not made subtly, but it was effective. The American public was not the primary audience for Soviet views—the third world and Western Europe were. These were geopolitical areas in which the Soviets were trying to gain influence and diminish America's. Members of Congress had no credible answer to the charges and found that in official forums they had to justify the United States' apparent inaction and make unconvincing distinctions between people in the Soviet Union whom Amnesty International considered political prisoners and the Wilmington Ten and others in the United States whom Amnesty International considered prisoners of conscience.[9]

The regular work of agitation and public relations by the CRJ, the National Wilmington 10 Defense Committee, and the NAARPR, in conjunction with the installation of new administrations in Washington and Raleigh, once again piqued the interest of American journalists. On 6 March 1977, just two days before the federal grand jury convened, the television newsmagazine *60 Minutes*, at the time a pioneer of investigative journalism, broadcast its findings. In an era in which journalists had more opportunity to report the news and interview incarcerated persons unimpeded by official bureaucracy, the story by Morley Safer posed fundamental questions about the fairness of the Wilmington Ten trial and the veracity of Allen Hall's testimony. On camera, Ben Chavis and Eugene and Donna Templeton convincingly explained the circumstances of the events of February 1971, and Allen Hall retold his problematic recantation. Prosecutor Jay Stroud, however, could not successfully explain why he chose a criminal who had admitted being involved in the burning of Mike's Grocery to be his star witness. The segment did not definitively take a stand on the case, but it did convey enough of the recent history of racial violence in Wilmington and the punitive misuse of the North Carolina justice system to provoke a public reconsideration of the case.[10]

With the *60 Minutes* report the American news media rediscovered the story. During the first year of his presidency, President Carter was intently questioned by reporters at his news conferences. In June 1977, a White House correspondent ventured the observation that the president's oft-stated commitment to human rights in foreign countries was in contrast to his silence on the Wilmington Ten. Did the president, the reporter asked, have any words in response to "the Reverend Mr. Chavis and his supporters, including now the NAACP and several prominent business and political and elected leaders in North Carolina, [who] have implored you for your intervention and comments in their behalf[?]" Carter unartfully sidestepped the query. In this controversial case, he "trust[ed] the system in its entirety" and believed "that justice will prevail." But he would not address the issues raised in the legal appeal and the movement to free the Wilmington Ten. He incorrectly stated that "our own system of government" prohibited him from commenting on the case. Perhaps recognizing that his statement lacked substance, he concluded his remark by saying, "But I am not trying to evade the question." A few months later, he was asked more directly, "Mr. President, you said we stand with the unjustly imprisoned. Where do we stand on the Wilmington 10, who have been in jail for over a year on the testimony of witnesses who have recanted?" And then came this point: "I mean it is kind of an international situation now because Brezhnev called in, as I understand, our Ambassador Malcolm Toon at the Soviet Embassy and said, 'What about this? How can you talk about our cases when you have this one?'" The president stood pat. The two politicians at the center of the case were southerners, and Carter would not urge the other to resolve the case, answering "No" to this query: "But you have no inclination to call up Governor Hunt, your fellow southern Governor?"[11]

Indeed, North Carolina was on the receiving end of bad publicity. When the North Carolina Symphony performed before a sold-out audience at New York City's Carnegie Hall in March 1977, newly inaugurated Governor Hunt thought it signified "our coming of age" and was excellent publicity for the state's business climate. Three former governors—Terry Sanford, Robert Scott, and James Holshouser—agreed and accompanied Hunt and many prominent figures from the state's business and political life to the Big Apple. Hunt brought four hundred economic leaders from the Northeast to the event, and promoters marketed the concert heavily to Tar Heel expatriates living in the five boroughs. But they got an earful of an unanticipated sort as concertgoers were greeted by a picket line in front of the auditorium demanding freedom for the Wilmington Ten and the Charlotte Three, organized by the NAARPR. "Tonight's performance is not a concert; it is an industrial advertisement. It is part of a two-day sales campaign by the State of North Carolina to sell northern businessmen on the idea of sending runaway shops to their state," said an alliance spokesperson. The state had also experienced an outbreak of mostly African American motorists concealing the slogan "First in Freedom" on their license plates. The first citation for this violation occurred in 1975 when U.S. Navy veteran James Flowers of Hillsborough put tape over the slogan because "no southern state was first in freedom for blacks." State Attorney General Rufus Edmisten issued a nonbinding opinion that the law prohibiting the act was likely unconstitutional, and the action became a way for North Carolinians, at least partly spurred by the Wilmington Ten, to show their dissatisfaction with the racial status quo. The CRJ broached the idea of organizing a boycott of North Carolina products, although the suggestion aroused the ire of many white members of the Southern Conference of the United Church of Christ and did not evolve beyond a brainstorm session or two.[12]

Jim Hunt felt peer pressure to mitigate the damage done by the persecution of the Wilmington Ten. The Reverend W. W. Finlator of Raleigh's Pullen Memorial Baptist Church, a respected white liberal, outspoken proponent of racial equality, and central figure in the area's social justice initiatives, organized a representative group of white southerners from nine states and the District of Columbia, seventy-one in all, to send an open letter to Governor Hunt asking for freedom of the Wilmington Ten. "We who sign this letter are white," it read.

> We write to you because we believe our future and the future of our region will be seriously affected by the treatment accorded these, our black fellow-citizens. . . .
>
> Their continued imprisonment . . . brings great shame to the state of North Carolina and to the South. We are among the many, many white people in the South who had hoped and believed that our region had moved beyond the day when black people could be persecuted because they worked to achieve full human rights. We do believe in fact that our region *has* moved beyond that point, and we ask you to help us establish that fact by seeing that justice is done in this case.

The letter was followed immediately by a meeting between Hunt and Finlator and three others who initiated the open letter. The four men told Hunt that they purposely chose the medium of a letter signed by a representative group rather than a petition signed by thousands—the implication being that they could have set that as a goal and achieved it. The governor paid close attention to the names of the signers, knew them at least by reputation, and, according to Finlator, was impressed. As Finlator related, he and some of the other signatories counted the governor as a personal friend. He found Hunt generous with his time and attentive to the passion and reason in the letter. And yet Hunt was determined not to act on the matter.[13]

Others also tried quiet persuasion and dialogue unencumbered by street rallies. Charles Cobb and Irv Joyner of the CRJ reported to the UCC's General Synod that the CRJ initiated a series of low-profile meetings with Hunt in August 1977. Groups of church leaders, significant African American politicians from North Carolina, and a delegation of congressmen either had an audience with the governor or met with his aides. The federal Department of Justice tried to reason with the governor and his attorneys, too. Assistant Attorney General Drew Days said that his department encouraged Hunt to give serious consideration to a pardon petition. But as before, Hunt was not moved to correct the wrong. He continued to insist that the court system was the proper venue to address the case, and he implicitly rejected the arguments of well-respected supporters of the Ten that the courts were in fact not adequately equipped to handle the issue and that a political solution was the appropriate one.[14]

Members of the Hunt administration could not evade public interest in the Wilmington Ten, and they worried that they were losing badly in the realm of public opinion. In the first weeks of the Hunt administration, Rufus Edmisten commented publicly that he wished "the Wilmington 10 case would go gentle into that good night." Once his tongue was loosed, it was hard for him to stop. It was the "damnedest case I've ever seen," he said. "I think this case has consumed enough of the time of the people of this state and the federal government to boot . . . I'm getting sick and tired of all these wild allegations." He further castigated the press: "Inflammatory statements are being printed as the truth." The scolding came as part of his announcement that the state would not oppose the post-conviction hearing scheduled for May 1977. In his statement he warned that if the Wilmington Ten's convictions were vacated, the state would likely not retry them, which seemed to be an attempt to influence Judge George Fountain's deliberations.[15]

By the end of 1977 some of Hunt's trusted advisers worried that he might do something they considered unwise just to make the case go away. Richard League, who was an assistant state attorney general and in that capacity was fully involved in the appeals process, was "appalled" by interference in the state's affairs by a congressional delegation and "a timed campaign by national columnists to work up sentiment in favor of relief to the Ten." League believed in the guilt of the Ten and stated that their supporters engaged in "disgraceful acts," including intimidation of witnesses and slandering public officials. He was prepared fully to extend himself to convince the governor to "withstand the pressure."[16]

Hunt had promised some sort of review of the case when the appeals process was concluded, which happened in May when Judge Fountain ruled after the post-conviction hearing that the Ten had received a fair trial and should not be allowed a new one, and the state appeals court agreed. There is some anecdotal evidence that the governor entertained some measure of sympathy for the Wilmington Ten—it is unlikely that Finlator, Dan Pollitt, the University of North Carolina professor of law and well-respected defender of civil liberties, and other white liberals would have been so thoroughly fooled by a political mask. Hunt's victory in the 1976 election owed something significant to the puissance of the nascent black political class and black electorate, which might have tilted him toward finding a compromise that would get the Ten out of prison. And yet as a southern governor—even one of the new breed—Hunt recognized that his ability to remain a viable governor lay largely in the hands of white voters and mainstream white opinion leaders. As a practical matter, he found it impossible to expend his political chits for a cause that was meaningful to blacks and opposed by most whites.

But by January 1978 he could delay a decision no longer, and on the twenty-third of the month he went on statewide television to tell North Carolina what he would do about the Wilmington Ten. His political dilemma was evident in his first utterances: "Thousands of you have written and called my office about it just in recent days. It's a matter that touches deep and conflicting feelings in many people. Much has been said about the case publicly . . . much of it inaccurate." He had devoted "literally hundreds of hours" to the case, including reading the trial record and meeting with prosecutor Jay Stroud and proponents of a pardon. Though he did not explicitly say so, his decision had the potential to define his term in office.[17]

Hunt's review of the events of February 1971 was cursory, mentioning only the fear and tension caused by black teenagers and preteens while omitting the terrorism of the Rights of White People group. He rehearsed the trial as if the proceedings were routine and uncomplicated and emphasized the burning of Mike's Grocery and the armed clashes with firefighters and police who responded to the blaze. He noted that Allen Hall, Jerome Mitchell, and Eric Junious, the state's major witnesses, lied on the witness stand; but by saying no more about this or the serious allegations of prosecutorial misconduct, Hunt in effect discounted these significant issues. With his hand resting on a stack of trial transcripts as on a Bible, Hunt declared, "I have concluded that there was a fair trial, the jury made the right decision and the appellate courts reviewed it properly and ruled correctly. I have confidence in what our courts and judges have done. Accordingly, I cannot and I will not pardon these defendants."

What he would do, he said, was shorten the Ten's sentences by between five and seven years each (except for Ann Shepard, who had completed her imprisonment, and Ben Chavis, who had been sentenced to the longest prison term and whose sentence was reduced by eight years). According to state criminal sentencing guidelines, arson carried a sentence of between five and thirty years, while the charge of conspiring to shoot at emergency personnel carried a sentence of only five years. Hunt then pivoted. He told North Carolinians that shooting at emergency personnel was more serious than arson—even though the Ten were not convicted of shooting, only conspiring to shoot—and so deserved to serve more than the maximum term that the law allowed but less than the stated term for arson. The nine still incarcerated would be eligible for parole in six months to two years. The governor's rationale for reducing the sentences by an arbitrary number of years instead of pardoning them or commuting their sentences to time served was not evident. As the North Carolina Association of Black Lawyers pointed out, Hunt's logic should have dictated a reduction of the total sentence to one for what he considered to be the more serious crime—five years for conspiracy to shoot at emergency personnel.[18]

To rally white North Carolinians to his side, Governor Hunt trotted out the familiar trope of outsiders trying to tell southerners how to conduct their affairs. "I did not make my decision to satisfy . . . those from outside who have criticized North Carolina and our system of justice. I have made the decision that I think is right." Aware that many white North Carolinians would oppose even the very modest move of shortening the Wilmington Ten's sentences, he reminded his audience that he was a governor who was tough on crime. He had proposed legislation that required convicted criminals to pay their victims restitution, restricted judges' discretion in sentencing, and reinstituted the death penalty. Although their sentence reductions meant that they would be eligible for release sometime between June 1978 and December 1979 (depending on the lengths of their original sentences), Hunt emphasized that the Wilmington Ten "are not free to walk out of prison." They would still have to run the gauntlet of parole and, once released, would remain under "close supervision." And, he threatened, if they violated their parole by, among other things, not keeping a job or being unable to support their families or not being in school full time, "they will be returned to prison to finish out their sentences." The barest hint of concession to African Americans was canceled by the governor's law-and-order rhetoric.

Hunt's decision was politically expedient for an elected official who depended on the white electorate and was willing to pander to it rather than lead it. Mickey Michaux, a former state representative from Durham who in 1977 was appointed the U.S. attorney for the Middle District of North Carolina by President Carter and was one of the most influential black politicians in North Carolina, recalled going for a drive with Governor Hunt in late 1977 or early January 1978 and trying to convince him to pardon the Ten. But Hunt had refused the request from one of his most important political supporters. Hunt knew that his decision was not based on the merits of the case, Michaux recalled, but on his fear of losing white support. Nominally progressive, business-friendly Democratic politicians across the state endorsed Hunt's decision, too. So did many Republicans, judging from the letters the governor received. The big exception was the attorney, jurist, and Democratic Party heavyweight I. Beverly Lake Jr., who likened the commutation to giving into outside pressure, but in North Carolina of the late 1970s, his view was considered extreme.[19]

It is reasonable to conclude that Hunt believed that his African American supporters would continue to support him, and the response of African American politicians may reveal the early stages of a process of transformation of some "revolutionaries to race leaders," as the political scientist Cedric Johnson termed it. To be sure, none was happy with the decision, and practically all publicly expressed at least regret. But Mickey Michaux, who had worked his way up from local activist to political power broker, stayed in Hunt's camp, though he said the governor made a "grave error." Howard Lee, the first African American cabinet secretary in North Carolina history, resisted the call to resign in protest of Hunt's decision. After forcefully stating that the governor lost an opportunity to make a humanitarian statement and free the Ten, Joy Johnson accepted an appointment to the state board of parole. Much of the black political class had resigned themselves to the logic of the political system; as one unnamed politician noted of blacks' relationship with Hunt, "right now blacks have nowhere else to turn."[20]

MEANWHILE, PRESIDENT CARTER was not having an easy time, either. While he probably anticipated Soviet broadsides condemning the persecution of the Wilmington Ten and the hypocrisy of his human rights diplomacy, he certainly did not expect his own administration to reinforce that line of attack. And yet that is exactly what occurred that first summer in office when Secretary of State Andrew Young declared while on an official visit to Venezuela that the Wilmington Ten were "very innocent" and that the administration was trying to do something about it. The next year, Young again proclaimed the innocence of the Wilmington Ten, this time adding that the United States had political prisoners—hundreds of them. And like his fellow southerner Jim Hunt, Jimmy Carter also received an open appeal from dozens of prominent white southerners to intervene and lift the "terrible burden of the universal judgment that comes upon us because of the imprisonment of these men." (Ann Shepard, who was convicted only of conspiracy and received the lightest sentence, had been paroled in January 1978, shortly before Hunt's speech.) The president could take issue with each of these actions—he did state publicly that he disagreed with Andrew Young and planned to clear the air with him privately—but it was evident now that the Carter administration would have to try to find a resolution that would end the public embarrassment of the United States.[21]

After Governor Hunt's announcement on the Wilmington Ten, there was renewed and effective pressure on the White House, orchestrated largely by Imani Kazana's National Wilmington 10 Defense Committee. She insisted on meetings with administration officials, and she facilitated the interest of members of Congress in the case. Within two weeks of the governor's abdication of leadership, the defense committee delivered to the White House a petition with forty thousand signatures demanding that Carter intercede with the North Carolina governor. The committee also planned a protest in front of the White House, and Ed Smith, Carter's associate director of public liaison, thought the demonstration was significant enough to agree to meet Kazana and four other leaders beforehand. They demanded the president "make a clear public pronouncement that the Wilmington 10 should at least have a new trial"; instruct the Justice Department to insert itself into the federal appeals process that had been initiated by the attorneys for the Ten; and withhold federal funds to any state that violated human rights.[22]

Here was an opportunity for Carter to make his domestic policy consistent with his foreign policy emphasis on human rights; it would not have been too far of a stretch, given his administration's exploratory intervention during the first days of his presidency. But he did not take it. The White House Office of Legal Counsel advised that administration officials should say only that the president "has formulated no official position with regard to the case." If pressed, they were to concede only "that if there have been 'human rights' violations they will be thoroughly examined," and they were to decline to comment on Hunt's actions. The White House arrived at its strategy using conventional political reasoning. The president's domestic policy staff had concluded that Hunt's decision to reduce the sentences and refuse to issue pardons "was the 'proper political choice to make; a classic compromise. You satisfy your racist constituency and you don't openly inflame blacks.'" Were Carter to voice anything more than a noncommittal bromide about his concern for all instances of human rights violations, he would be violating the "*States Rights*" of North Carolina. Moreover, 1978 was an election year, and "compromises on all fronts would be an important Administration theme."[23]

Some of Carter's advisers thought this was a shallow argument, most particularly Louis Martin, the veteran black journalist and political operative for Presidents Kennedy and Johnson, whom the president brought on as a special assistant in September 1978. Martin had decades of experience straddling the worlds of presidents and political parties, race advancement organizations, and the press and public relations. The administration believed he could help Carter especially with black politicians, whom the president had bypassed in his campaign in favor of securing the blessings of African American clergy. Martin understood that building relationships was the way to make friends out of spurned politicians. He opened the doors of his office to them, requested their expert advice, and at strategic moments introduced them to the president. He also knew that gestures would in this case have to be accompanied by specific concessions. Within the first two weeks of taking the job, he wrote, "The agitation over the Wilmington Ten, at home and abroad, is expected to intensify in the weeks ahead. It is an issue that we do not need. It can be resolved without great difficulty and the time is ripe." He followed with a "Dear Jim" letter to Governor Hunt about "getting some flack on that Ben Chavis case" and asked to have a chat either in Washington or in Raleigh at the governor's convenience.[24]

As large a character as Martin was, however, he was just one person, and on the White House organizational chart, he did not report to the president. Black elected officials knew and liked him, but they viewed his new position as powerless. On the Wilmington Ten, at least, they were right. Carter may have listened to Martin's counsel, but he did not take it; the "classic compromise" held sway, and the president remained mute.

And yet, the president could not completely dither. The agitation that had been accumulating for years and had erupted again with Hunt's announcement grabbed the attention of Drew Days in the Justice Department. In a speech to the Alabama Black Lawyers Association titled "Human Rights, Home Style," Days defended what Carter had done so far about the Wilmington Ten. His administration had ordered an investigation into prosecutorial misconduct and investigative abuses by the Bureau of Alcohol, Tobacco, and Firearms but found no evidence; it then had impaneled a grand jury. In November 1977, the Justice Department was in a watchful, waiting mode. Having been unable to convince North Carolina to show clemency, it mulled an intervention in the Ten's habeas corpus pleadings in federal court, in which their attorneys would ask a judge to overturn their convictions and order a new trial. The National Wilmington 10 Defense Committee's swift action following Hunt's announcement apparently was the stimulation needed for Days to become more engaged. Days ordered his special assistant Lani Guinier, who some years earlier had interned in the Ferguson Chambers law firm, to draft a strategy for addressing the issue. Neither Days nor anyone else in the upper echelons of the Justice Department or in the administration ordered a predetermined outcome, Guinier plainly stated; though the impetus was political and the course of action would be of a lower profile than a presidential statement, "there was absolutely no pressure to do anything about the case except to review it carefully and make a decision on the merits." The work of Justice's legal team clearly pointed toward a flawed prosecution of the Wilmington Ten, a conclusion that Drew Days softened when, in a March 1978 *60 Minutes* update, he said that he was "troubled" by important aspects of the trial and late revelations about the prosecutor's relationship with some of his witnesses. Eventually, the Justice Department decided to file a friend of the court brief in federal district court in North Carolina supporting a new trial for the Wilmington Ten. Days's decision, while significant, was slow to develop.[25]

Hunt and Carter must have thought they could split the difference between their white and black constituents, and for at least two of the Ten, that was, if not optimal, at least acceptable. Wayne Moore and Joe Wright had earlier dissented from Ben Chavis's insistence that the Ten would accept nothing less than a pardon of innocence; they were willing to accept a commutation of their sentences. Wright went further after Hunt's television address. The governor was a good leader, he said, and made a politically motivated decision in a conservative state: "He's good for the state. I'll vote for him if he runs for reelection." Wright counseled patience and restraint in people's response to Hunt, saying that the national media had "blown the case out of proportion." If his remarks seem to contradict the thrust of the campaign to free the Wilmington Ten, who could blame him? He was, after all, the one serving the punishment. He was also the one of the Ten who, according to Wayne Moore, was most attuned to the possibilities of working within the system of electoral politics. It is not without irony but nevertheless possible that Wright's comments about Hunt reflected the developing views of electorally minded black activists.[26]

But from the point of view of ethics and rights and justice, Hunt's craven and Carter's callow actions demanded responses. Within two months of Hunt's televised decision, on 18 March, the NAARPR rallied eight thousand people on the Ellipse in front of the White House. Tireless Elizabeth Chavis, mother of Ben, was there. Angela Davis was center stage, brimming with optimism and trying out a new slogan: "Hey, hey, Mr. Peanut Man. What you gonna do about the Wilmington 10?" A sign of the quickening of the fight, she was joined at the head by Pete Seeger and Ruby Dee, who led the chant of "Human rights begin at home. Free the Wilmington 10!" Two months later, three thousand citizens answered the call of the National Coalition to Support African Liberation to come to Washington. The salient demands of this multiracial and multinational march were cutting diplomatic ties with apartheid South Africa and support for the Wilmington Ten, displaying the tradition of international solidarity and mutuality that had been a part of the campaign to free the Ten from the beginning. Said march organizer Nelson Johnson, the expressed demands concerned not only support for national liberation but also "the day to day struggles in this country."[27]

Petitioning presidents in the form of loud, even disruptive protests is a venerable American tradition; it is mainly in the twenty-first century that presidents have sought to buffer themselves from dissenting voices with the establishment of Orwellian "free-speech zones" far away from presidential motorcades and sightlines. Protesters found a way to capture Jimmy Carter's attention. When he attended the wedding of his nephew in Fayetteville, North Carolina, in December 1977, he was greeted by a small gathering who shouted at him about the Ten and the Charlotte Three. At the same time, the CRJ prepared to deliver a petition with fifteen thousand signatures to Governor Hunt: "We have exhausted every avenue and our voices have not been heard. Gov. Hunt can say the word and these brothers can be home for Christmas," said an exasperated Leon White. "People are becoming very, very impatient with the progress of justice."[28] The day before the NAARPR protest in front of the White House, the president spoke on national defense in Winston-Salem and was met by protesters. Joseph Felmet, a native of Asheville, participant in the 1947 Freedom Ride through North Carolina, pacifist, and candidate for the U.S. Senate, interrupted the president, telling him that he wanted to give him a petition on the Wilmington Ten. Carter tried to ignore him, but Felmet persisted, and the president "quickly ordered an aide to take the petition, promising to read it later."[29] A similar guerrilla action occurred when the president visited the state again in August to shore up his support among the state's tobacco farmers, who were worried about federal antismoking measures. Joined on the podium under the tall oak trees at the Wilson County Public Library by Governor Hunt and former state attorney general Robert Morgan (who had overseen the prosecution of the Wilmington Ten), Carter began his speech to the crowd of six thousand North Carolinians, only to be forced again to address the issue of justice for Chavis and his codefendants. A ruckus in front of him caused by two hundred demonstrators demanding human rights and exposing the administration's hypocrisy on that matter bested Carter, who feebly fell back on a paraphrase of Voltaire: "There is a time in our country to recognize basic human rights. One of those is the right to speak, or even shout, when others are trying to speak." But afterward, Leon White said he wanted the president to address "legitimate issues. The issues are not tobacco. The issues are people's rights."[30]

The ultimate united front organization formed to respond to Hunt's and Carter's pusillanimity was called the North Carolina Coalition to Free the Wilmington Ten. It came into being as a quick response to Hunt's refusal to pardon the Ten, and it planned a massive protest in the state capital on 1 April 1978, among other public actions. The coalition combined the energy and networks of the state's bounty of black nationalists, politically awakened clergy, politicians who grew out of the mass struggles of the 1960s, and organizers from the vigorous black liberation and fragile trade union movements who came to embrace Marxism. The coalition was initiated by the Workers Viewpoint Organization (WVO) and the CRJ; the three co-conveners were Joyce Johnson of the WVO, Leon White of the CRJ, and Jean Linde Wagner of the Women's International League for Peace and Freedom, who had made a lifetime commitment to support women and men imprisoned for their political activities and beliefs. An array of ad hoc organizations, mostly from the Raleigh–Durham–Chapel Hill and Greensboro areas concerned with one or another local issue like a particular case of police brutality, the fate of black colleges in the University of North Carolina system, or the deterioration of public education for poor and minority students, joined as well.

The WVO was a nationwide Communist organization whose roots were in the Asian American and other third world radical student movements that fought for such demands as ethnic studies programs in the university and worked to build campus-community antiracist alliances. Perceiving a lull in these movements in the early 1970s, the WVO and similar organizations immersed themselves in varieties of theory in order to comprehend their current circumstances and map a way forward. Like the Black Panther Party, which formed a half decade earlier, they viewed themselves not simply as racial minorities within the United States but as constituent parts of a third world liberation movement fighting U.S. imperialism around the globe. As they came to conclude that Marxism-Leninism offered the most cogent explanation of the state of the world and prescription for changing it, they aligned with China and Mao Zedong, who seemed to be offering unambiguous material and moral support to the world's anti-imperialist and democratic movements. The WVO, like other New Communist movement organizations, also formed in opposition to the Communist Party, USA. The aversion was based in part on differing international alliances—the CPUSA was firmly oriented toward the Soviet Union—but more so on the CPUSA's neglect of radical and democratic movements based in minority communities. Angela Davis's and Charlene Mitchell's prominence in the party hierarchy notwithstanding, the CP labeled as divisive those insurgent movements inspired by Malcolm X and other black nationalists and radicals.[31]

In North Carolina, the source of WVO membership was twofold. One was college-educated African Americans who arrived at Marxism via the pan-Africanism of the Youth Organization for Black Unity. A second source comprised radical former students—mostly white—from Duke University who were involved in the anti–Vietnam War and women's movements. Many of them were either physicians or other medical professionals long associated with organizing around health-care issues in poor communities. They worked in brown lung clinics for textile workers and in clinics serving poor African American areas of Durham; they also raised money and medical supplies for liberation movements in southern Africa. By 1975 they had concluded that struggles for what amounted to marginally improved care were merely treating symptoms, while what was needed was a cure for the disease of capitalism. These two networks found common ground in making their critique of capitalism and its political system accessible to the industrial working class and the movements of racial minorities, particularly African Americans. To that end, members of the WVO embedded themselves in textile mills, hospitals, and college campuses and organized around everyday issues inside workplaces and communities. Given that the organization was multiracial, it is worth noting that a point of emphasis in its work was combating racism and, through the course of fighting for issues of common concern, educating white workers that their true interests lay in uniting with blacks.[32]

While members of the WVO achieved a modicum of success organizing in trade unions and denting white supremacy in the predominantly white textile mills, they did estimable work in African American communities by championing critical causes like fighting police brutality, racist violence, and inferior educational opportunities and by defending black workers from discrimination. They were capable organizers who also explained their points of view about the economic and political systems. And they consciously deployed white members to work in these campaigns, too, thus putting into practice the multiracial class unity that they valued in principle. In Whitakers, a crossroads hamlet on the Nash–Edgecombe County border, they organized a popular response to the killing of a black agricultural day laborer by a white store owner in April 1977. Charlie Lee complained that he was shortchanged after purchasing items at Joe Judge's grocery and gas station; Judge's response was to shoot him, and initially he faced no repercussions. (The Judge family had a "wild" reputation, and their wealth was said to come from smuggling untaxed cigarettes to northern states.) After a funeral attended by hundreds of angry African Americans, the WVO organized a community coalition to demand that law enforcement and the courts hold Judge accountable. One of the ways they accomplished this in the face of official inaction was to hold a people's trial, at which Judge was arraigned and the capitalist system indicted. The formation of the People's Coalition for Justice forced action, and in September 1977 Judge pleaded no contest to involuntary manslaughter; he was given a ten-year suspended sentence and ordered to pay restitution to Lee's widow in the amount of $25,000. It was by no means perfect justice, but in a geography with rampant racist lawlessness, it was important.

That same month in Greensboro, Gernie Cummings was beaten in a county holding cell by two sheriff's deputies. An organization in which the WVO participated, Concerned Citizens against Police Brutality, gathered evidence, helped Cummings swear out warrants for the deputies' arrests, conducted education, and organized protests that drew upward of one hundred people. Here, too, agitation, education, and organization resulted in affirmative action, as the two deputies were tried in April 1978, convicted of assault, and sentenced to two years in prison with eighteen months suspended. Significantly, neither of these instances of violence was reported in the local press at the times they occurred; friends of the victims approached members of the WVO, which took up the causes and made them news.[33] In different parts of the state, then, the WVO had developed influence in the black freedom struggle and was able to bring it to bear on the once-again high-profile case of the Wilmington Ten.

Likewise, the CRJ brought to bear its protracted history of struggle in the state. The organization that had dedicated itself to prison reform, overhauling the justice system, fighting police brutality, and freeing political prisoners turned its attention to Governor Hunt's outrages. People whose main concern was supporting South Africa's fight against apartheid also joined the coalition. Parents and students opposed to the new high-stakes competency tests, the ancestor of No Child Left Behind, saw the Wilmington Ten as their fight. So, too, did defenders of the state's historically black colleges and universities, who in the 1970s were worried that the UNC Board of Governors was trying to eviscerate them.[34]

Braiding a coalition out of the different strands of local struggles in North Carolina could have been problematic. There were not only the CRJ and the WVO, which seemed to work cooperatively, but also the North Carolina Association of Black Lawyers; clergy and ministerial alliances accustomed to deferential treatment; leftist groups like the NAARPR and the Revolutionary Communist Party; campus-based organizations of black college students, including sororities and fraternities; and local single-issue organizations with their own respective agendas. Additionally, both sectarianism and the opposite tendency to dilute issues in the name of finding common ground were well-known afflictions in the post-1960s Left. The challenge for members of the North Carolina Coalition to Free the Wilmington Ten would be to work cooperatively and engage their political differences in productive ways that might expand people's political acumen. Further, they would have to avoid reducing the new alliance to jockeying for supremacy and squabbling.

This was clearly a concern for the CRJ. At one of the initial meetings of the coalition, Leon White appealed for unity and pleaded for constituent groups to subordinate themselves to the coalition's aims and not get sidetracked by secondary or tertiary disagreements. For Joyce Johnson, it was plainly evident that cooperation was critical and a prerequisite for individual coalition organizations to prosper. "Hunt has done us a favor," she said, for no one could any longer hold any illusions about politicians helping them; standing up for the Wilmington Ten, she said, was standing up for ourselves. Nelson Johnson, Joyce's husband and a member of the WVO, also pitched unity. The railroading of the Wilmington Ten was a concentrated expression of the injustices that drew coalition members to fight for their freedom. On the one hand, the confluence of multiple struggles at the planned 1 April 1978 Raleigh demonstration would make for a powerful expression of mass discontent. On the other hand, the demonstration had to project more than an agglomeration of single issues; it had to establish to the public that the frame-up of the Wilmington Ten and coalition members' specific concerns shared similar systemic causes. The demonstration had to be conducted in such a way as to accurately express the anger and dissatisfaction of the people. All coalition partners agreed that the 1 April action was not a one-off affair. Coalition leaders stressed that they would consider the demonstration a success not based on the numbers of people who came out but on the numbers of people who were energized by the day and returned home to continue the struggle.[35]

In the days leading up to the rally, coalition leaders proclaimed that the event would be much more than a stroll in the park and around town. The Reverend George Gay of the United Church of Christ in Greensboro promised "a militant and spirited" event that upheld the interests of the "black community and working class and poor people." Marie Darr, a 1970 graduate of UNC–Greensboro and a revolutionary-minded textile worker, offered that the day would be "a blow against the capitalist system." Both Leon White and WVO member Paul Bermanzohn, a child of Holocaust survivors and a medical doctor who had a long history of involvement in race and labor issues, said the marchers would abide by the law but that future tactics were open to discussion. Golden Frinks of the Southern Christian Leadership Conference was his usual bombastic self: "I'm tired of saying 'We shall overcome.' [I'm] prepared to violate some laws." Come the day, though, Frinks was more bark than bite.[36]

When their preparatory work was done, the North Carolina Coalition to Free the Wilmington Ten had united on the following overarching demands that reflected its members' common interests: free the Wilmington Ten and provide justice for all oppressed people; stop the competency test and save black schools; support public workers' right to organize and bargain collectively; repeal right-to-work laws and support textile workers at J. P. Stevens; and support African liberation.[37]

The day of the rally, 1 April, was hot. It was nearly eighty degrees when three thousand North Carolinians gathered at Chavis Park (formerly the segregated park for blacks and named for Ben's ancestor John) in downtown Raleigh. Marchers wended their way through African American neighborhoods and stopped in front of Women's Prison and the Governor's Mansion en route to the state capitol. They were joined there by another thousand Raleigh residents as the temperature topped out at eighty-six degrees. A sound truck along the route broadcast short agitational speeches, and marchers kept up their spirited chanting all along the route:

> Fired up! Won't take it no more!
> Hunt, Hunt, you racist dunce! Free the Wilmington Ten at once!
> School discrimination was the Ten's fight. We'll struggle on with all our might
> Hunt and Carter, the rich man's men. It takes the people to free the Ten.
> The courts, the cops, the jails are tools the bosses use to enforce their rules
> Black and white must unite. Justice is our common fight.[38]

The protest remained militant but disciplined. Yet the police saw fit not only to monitor the event but to harass it as well. When the march arrived at the legislative complex for the rally, police stepped in and arrested the person operating the sound truck for allegedly violating a noise ordinance. Nelson Johnson came over to see what was going on, and police swarmed and arrested him too; when a parade marshal tried to intervene, he also was arrested. Both were charged with resisting arrest and assaulting a police officer. Leon White insisted that the arrests were deliberate provocations; James Ferguson called them an attempt to make the demonstration look "non-peaceful." The initial charge of violating a noise ordinance was ridiculous, Ferguson said: "This is not a residential area. The rally was disturbing no one." Nelson Johnson was to be the key-note speaker. As the organizers scrambled to find a replacement for him, Johnson appeared in dramatic fashion after posting bond. "Brothers and sisters," he intoned, "today is a great day"; he then rehearsed the story of the Wilmington Ten and linked their struggle to the necessity for funda-mental social transformation.[39]

The rally was a great success, as organizations went back to press for freedom for the Wilmington Ten *and* to work on their specific local struggles. The North Carolina Coalition to Free the Wilmington Ten took up a "Haunt Hunt" campaign, appearing at the University of North Carolina's May graduation in Chapel Hill, where the governor was the commencement speaker. In early June, he canceled an appear-ance at a High Point high school upon learning that the students were prepared to demonstrate against him and for the Ten. Additionally, the coalition sponsored an April demonstration of four hundred persons in Kinston against poor housing conditions and the continued incarcer-ation of the Ten and participated in a similarly sized rally in Charlotte in June. Keeping in mind the international dimensions of the case, the coalition helped to mobilize more than five hundred North Carolinians to attend the African Liberation Day march that drew thousands to Washington in May.[40]

DESPITE THE DEMONSTRATIONS in the spring of 1978, the legal posi-tion of the Wilmington Ten had not fundamentally changed since they had been convicted five and a half years earlier. In the appeals pro-cess in the North Carolina courts, attorneys for the Ten consistently raised substantive issues about the fairness of the trial, including the farcical jury selection, the judge's rulings about Allen Hall's amended statement, and his limiting the defense attorneys' cross-examination of

On 1 April 1978, the North Carolina Coalition to Free the Wilmington Ten held a massive march and rally through the streets of Raleigh. Pictured in front is Jean Linde Wagner, a co-convener of the coalition. The Reverend Leon White and Joyce Johnson (not pictured) were the other two co-conveners. Photograph courtesy Lucy Lewis.

Hall. When the state court of appeals upheld the convictions, the state supreme court declined to review it, the U.S. Supreme Court decided not to intervene, and the defendants went to prison, Wilmington Ten attorneys raised the same issues in a quick series of federal district court habeas corpus applications in April 1976. The recantations of Hall, Jerome Mitchell, and Eric Junious and the revelations of inducements to testify added another layer to the defendants' claims of state misconduct, and these were included in a second habeas corpus application filed on 23 January 1978, coincidentally the same day as Hunt's decision not to pardon the Ten.[41]

In federal court, the case was assigned to Magistrate Judge Logan Howell, whose task was to prepare a memorandum and set of recommendations for district court judge Franklin Dupree's consideration. Howell faced a case whose record was both voluminous and complex. And as the case accreted more evidence of government misconduct, the Wilmington Ten attorneys filed new briefs on the relevant information, which made Howell's search for findings of fact and conclusions of law more involved. As the issues compounded, defense attorney James Ferguson proposed consolidating the motions from 1976 with later motions. From the perspective of the defendants, the discrete issues raised in their appeals arose from the same set of facts and circumstances, the only difference being they were discovered at different times. It made both common and legal sense for the federal courts to view the case in toto rather than in slices. And to make the case wieldier, Ferguson several times proposed conferences of opposing parties and the court to untangle the issues and propose a schedule for resolving them.[42]

But North Carolina's deputy attorney general Richard League was obdurate in his opposition to practically every one of Ferguson's proposals. There was always some legal hiccup on which League stood, but it was mere pretense. He told Judge Dupree that the different sets of claims were not similar enough to be considered together. He worried that consolidating the claims could lead to delay, which "might be used against us in an argument for bail." There was a court-imposed page limit on "appeal briefing," and combining cases would create "difficulty in comprehending large amounts of material." But in another letter, he seemed to argue just the opposite: it was of little import that unconsolidated cases would lead to a large record, because, he wrote sycophantically, "I feel certain that the Court from its success in the practice of law as a senior partner of an insurance defense firm is perfectly capable of management of voluminous records on its own." Any pre-hearing conference was pointless and burdensome, he wrote. In his own reply, Ferguson observed that the judge could waive the page limit, that the substance of arguments should not be unduly subordinated to form, and that not to join the cases "effectively deprived [his clients] of an opportunity to make a meaningful argument to the effect that they were denied due process *by the cumulative effect of the claimed errors*."[43]

Central to the state's recalcitrant posture was the belief that not only were the convictions proper but the opposition to the verdicts was illegitimate. League pledged whatever "assistance I may to the governor in helping him withstand the pressure being put on him in this regard." Congressional interest in the case "appalled" him; supporters of the Wilmington Ten engaged in "disgraceful acts." Even the UCC participated in "intimidation of witnesses [and] slander of public officials." Attorney James Ferguson, he intimated, was acting unethically in the defense of his clients. Understanding that in the court of public opinion the state was losing, the state's attorneys were poised to wrestle the case to a halt in the federal legal system. It was also important to League to keep Ben Chavis behind bars as long as possible. He opposed allowing Chavis to attend any hearing, and he desired to keep the other nine defendants, who had been paroled at different times in 1978, from observing any court proceedings as well.[44]

With the notable exception of Judge Dupree's inclination to allow the consolidation of the cases, the federal district court seemed unfavorably disposed to an appeal for judicial relief. While Magistrate Judge Howell did most of the court's work on the Wilmington Ten—his boss called him the vice president of all things related to the case—and concluded that the cases should not be joined and considered together, district court judge Dupree was of a different mind, and his word was final. Sometimes that word was inflected with humor. For example, when Ferguson filed a second batch of habeas applications just hours before Hunt announced his refusal to pardon the Ten, Dupree remarked to Howell, "Apparently Ferguson must be privy to the Governor's counsel." He continued that he wished for Howell to prep him to rule on the case as a whole:

He was in my court on other business on yesterday and apparently he took occasion while he was in the building to file nine more habeas petitions. . . . I don't know what these are but it occurred to me that instead of filing nine new lawsuits he should have asked to amend the ones that he already had pending.

I am attaching these things with the request that you take a look at them and if a further hearing is necessary, please conduct the same and when you have everything ready to go so that I can make a decision covering all claims, let me know and I will go to work on it.[45]

Or, as he told Ferguson, "What I had in mind . . . was simply that I did not want to hear this thing piecemeal."[46]

That, however, was practically the only concession the Wilmington Ten got from the Federal District Court of Eastern North Carolina. Logan Howell, for reasons that are not at this remove clear, was slow to act on the Wilmington Ten appeal, a delay that was exacerbated by the case not moving up to Judge Dupree for his attention. Although habeas petitions had been on file in the courthouse since January 1976 and amended briefs since the unsuccessful conclusion of the post-conviction hearing in May 1977, Howell did not make a ruling for Dupree's consideration until September 1977. He rejected all claims under consideration about jury selection, the amended statement, and eyewitness testimony and concluded with this bromide that camouflaged the injustice of affirming a faulty conviction: "No trials are perfect, since they are conducted by mortals. But I am convinced from my painstaking review of this record that these petitioners received a fair trial under the standards embodied in the Constitution as declared by the Supreme Court."[47]

From that point until a hearing was scheduled for April 1979, there was practically no activity in federal court on the part of Howell or Dupree. In fact, Dupree had to cancel a scheduled hearing for December 1978 because Howell had not completed his review of the case, and it therefore "was not ripe" for action. Howell maintained that he had been waiting for months on James Ferguson to designate portions of the record he would use to support his claims—lawyer argot for telling the court what discrete portions of the transcripts and other documents to pay attention to—and claimed that he had never received a response to his request. For his part, Ferguson had always contended that the issues arising from the conviction were so intertwined that he wished to designate the entire record and claimed that he had immediately so informed Howell. When told by the judge just after the Thanksgiving holiday in 1978 that the magistrate was impatient with Ferguson's delay, Ferguson immediately complied while also telling Howell that he had already answered his request. What Judge Dupree called a "breakdown of communications" boiled over into a personal dispute between Howell and Ferguson, who each charged the other with lapsed performance. When, nearly four months later and despite regular prodding from Judge Dupree, the magistrate still had not completed his work, Ferguson publicly chastised Howell's office and filed a motion to bypass him. Howell was furious and accused Ferguson of "a shabby display of dishonesty for the benefit, I suppose, of his backers." When he had finally completed his memorandum and recommendations for Dupree's consideration, Howell dashed off a supplemental report that further accused Ferguson of "a deplorable lack of faithfulness" and "making baseless and derogatory assertions concerning this court" and suggested that Ferguson deserved to be disciplined.[48]

The unfavorable disposition of the court was in marked contrast to the growing interest in the case from the Department of Justice, which in November 1978, in what was described at the time as a highly unusual move, filed an amicus brief in support of the Wilmington Ten that focused on the inconsistencies among Allen Hall's trial testimony, his February 1972 statement, and the so-called amended statement. Why the Justice Department was given a copy of the amended statement is not entirely clear, though it appears as if it was included in a normal exchange of information between agents of the North Carolina State Bureau of Investigation and the Federal Bureau of Investigation in March 1977. It is unlikely that the dissemination of the statement was authorized by state prosecutors, given that Jay Stroud and the state attorney general vigorously opposed revealing it. Lani Guinier remembers that a career Justice Department attorney named Marie Klimesz discovered the copy of the amended statement in a case file. Eventually, Judge Dupree turned over the amended statement to the Wilmington Ten attorneys.[49]

This piece of incriminating evidence convinced the Justice Department to intervene. But some in the department thought that it ought to become involved for more reasons than that it had evidence of prosecutorial misconduct. Lani Guinier believed that the Wilmington Ten raised very good criminal law issues that could warrant a new trial but by themselves did not warrant involvement by the Justice Department. What justified the department's participation in the proceedings was the history of civil rights struggle, of which the Wilmington events were a part. Guinier rehearsed her reasons thus: the case arose out of tensions in the newly desegregated high schools (which process had been mandated by federal courts with the approval of the executive branch); the federal government participated in the investigation and trial of the case as well as in other prosecutions of Ben Chavis; the federal government was interested in prosecuting "known black militants," and certain government agencies—the FBI and the BATF—provided resources for questionable prosecutions; the BATF, however, could not be prosecuted "because they managed to cover their tracks so well." In sum, federal action helped to create the problem, and the government should be accountable to remedy it.[50]

The thrust of the department's brief was unmistakable. Allen Hall committed perjury. His explanations for most of his inconsistent testimony were not true, in that his February 1972 statement was in most instances not amended at all or amended in ways that did not support his testimony. The brief implied that the prosecution knew about Hall's false statements and facilitated them and that the state denied the Wilmington Ten a fair trial.[51]

The amicus brief was of little avail, except as evidence of growing public outrage. When the habeas hearing convened on 6 April 1979 in federal district court in Raleigh, Judge Dupree welcomed the presence of Lani Guinier as the Justice Department's observer and thanked her for the department's contribution to the case. But when Judge Dupree filed his ruling two months later, he denied the defendants' application for relief. Incredibly, he found the inconsistencies between Allen Hall's trial testimony and the amended statement to be of little import. Nor could he understand all the commotion: the prosecutor and trial judge were misguided in trying to keep it from the defense and needlessly brought much of the trial's controversy upon themselves because, as he wrote in a footnote, "there was little, if anything, in this 'amended statement,' even if it can be properly termed as such, which would have been of any benefit to the defense." And with that, he diminished the centrality of Allen Hall's credibility to the outcome of the trial to a sideshow and dismissed as being of no consequence the Justice Department's detailed analysis of the statement and a spreadsheet showing the contradictions among Hall's original statement, the amended statement, and trial testimony. On the other hand, he found that Allen Hall's recantation was false and probably made under pressure. The post-conviction hearing was fair, he ruled, and he had no hesitations whatsoever in adopting all of Judge Fountain's findings—which were not his own but were appropriated from the state's attorney.[52]

Judge Dupree's decision is not surprising given that he leaned heavily on the preparatory work of his magistrate Logan Howell. Dupree's order was all of four pages, in which he adopted Howell's memorandums and recommendations, which in turn had swallowed the earlier decisions of the North Carolina courts. Dupree admitted that following the hearing he had personally reviewed the record only "as time has permitted," so like Judge Fountain, who presided over the state post-conviction hearing, Dupree did not arrive at an independent judgment. And within the extant record of the appeal is a noticeable hostility to the people seeking relief. Judge Dupree referred disparagingly to the "Chavis crowd" and to members of the public interested in the case as a "mob of spectators." Howell and one of the judge's clerks believed that James Ferguson's lawyering was unethical and that he was demagogically appealing to his base. Howell delayed filing his supplemental report that made these charges until after Dupree's order was filed, because he did not want to create an appearance of bias—which he feared Ferguson would opportunistically use. So while Howell avoided the appearance of bias, its existence pervaded his reasoning.[53]

Throughout the time the appeal was in his court, Judge Dupree was the recipient of thousands of pieces of correspondence about the Wilmington Ten: handwritten letters and notes from Americans and residents of France and Germany stating their belief that the defendants were innocent; form letters and telegrams asking him to free the defendants; letters from federal, state, and local elected officials asking for justice for the Ten; and petitions with thousands upon thousands of signatures. Dupree kept each one, it seems, and together they make up about an eight-inch stack of documents in the Franklin T. Dupree Papers in the Southern Historical Collection at the University of North Carolina. To the elected officials, Dupree was polite and gracious in his replies—perhaps he recognized that they were from a coequal branch of government—but he also stated his opinion that they wrote to him because of constituent pressure. To others, he had his clerk send back a form letter, in which he wrote that the judicial code of ethics prevented him from considering their missives in his deliberations. He would rule based on the law and nothing else.

Closer inspection, though, raises questions about the judge's devotion to the exclusion of all but the record before him in his deliberations. He disliked the international reputation his court garnered for foot-dragging on account of the Wilmington Ten and prepared to make rulings in order to blunt those charges. Among his papers is a large file with newspaper clippings about the Wilmington Ten appeals process, many of them highly critical. To the venerable southern antiracist and social justice advocate Anne Braden, who chastised the judge just at the time he canceled a hearing because Magistrate Howell had not finished his review of the case, Dupree let show his feelings about the case:

> For your further information neither your letter and hundreds of other similar communications received by the court from all over the world urging and in many cases demanding favorable action on these petitions . . . will have the slightest effect on this court's decision

when and if the case comes on for hearing before me. . . . At the same time, one cannot but wonder if it has not occurred to the originators of such communications that their effect might be counter-productive if indeed it was not intended to be so.

In his written order denying habeas relief, he took umbrage at the popular belief that the North Carolina courts were "deliberately unfair and oppressive" to the Wilmington Ten. He made a point to reject "out of hand these charges." A native North Carolinian, Judge Dupree was born into a lawyer's family and was intimately connected with the state's judiciary. His affinity for and defense of the rulings of his brethren are not surprising, and his invocation of blind justice was a pose.[54]

AS THE 1970S came to a close, Ben Chavis, the last of the Wilmington Ten to remain in prison, was paroled ten days before Christmas 1979—an early release, said Governor Hunt without a hint of irony, due to his "excellent record" in the Orange County Correctional Facility.[55] During the prior eighteen months, the rest of his codefendants had been paroled and got to the business of reclaiming their lives as best they could. Except for Ben Chavis and Ann Shepard, who remained in politics, the members of the Wilmington Ten shed their collective identity. Some continued their education; others tried to find employment. Until they were released from supervision, however, they would have to bear the additional burden of living in North Carolina, where their notoriety was greatest. The precariousness of their situation was compounded by a scurrilous article by Wayne King in the *New York Times Magazine* that was published in December 1978, around the time that Marvin Patrick and Connie Tindall were paroled. The article disdained any hard reporting into the principal issues of the case, such as the jury selection, Allen Hall's erratic trial testimony, the strong hints that he lied on the stand, and misconduct by the prosecutor. Instead, it highlighted an unidentified source who claimed to have been present when Mike's Grocery was burned on Chavis's orders but not in his presence. The article was allegedly the product of a three-month investigation, but the best that the national paper of record could conclude was that it was

> possible to believe that reasonable judges and juries could have found the Wilmington Ten guilty. . . .
> And it is also possible to believe that, as one [again, unnamed] North Carolina radical has said cynically of the case against Ben Chavis, "they framed a guilty man."[56]

The *Wall Street Journal* piled on three days later with an editorial. Exulting in the conclusion of the *Times*—"not exactly known as a government flunky"—*Wall Street Journal* editors lambasted supporters of the Wilmington Ten, lamented the United States' vulnerability "to this kind of campaign to erode the West's claim to moral superiority," and professed discouragement at "high government officials" who facilitate this "moral myopia." The *Times* had provided cover for the right-wing *Wall Street Journal*.[57]

Decades later the respected journalist and author Mark Pinsky, who in the 1970s as a freelance writer for the *New York Times* assisted Wayne King in reporting this article, reflected on the irresponsible conclusion. At the time Pinsky had a reputation among some North Carolina political activists as being fair-minded and sympathetic to the causes of civil rights and organized labor. Begging the question of whether any Tar Heel radical had in fact related the observation to King that the state framed a guilty man, Pinsky said he argued against ending the article on a snarky note. While the article clearly cast doubt on the innocence of the Wilmington Ten, Pinsky said that he did not mean for the observation quoted above to address the specifics of this case. Rather, he said that he thought the movement to free the Wilmington Ten should not have lionized them and insisted on their innocence; instead, it should have focused entirely and exclusively on the violations of the rule of law and the denial of a fair trial by the trial judge and prosecutor. Pinsky said he argued with King to make the point in a straightforward manner and not insinuate that the Wilmington Ten were guilty, but because King had the byline, he prevailed.[58]

Pinsky's memory calls into question the veracity of the article, a terrible hit job that promoted a view that even the leftists, who brayed at the injustice of the system, believed that the Ten were guilty. One might wonder if the anonymous radical even existed or was simply a fiction through which Wayne King projected prejudices about the movement in North Carolina. It was evident that he believed that the Black Freedom Movement in the state had turned awful and violent and was experiencing the consequences of its actions, if not exactly its just deserts. The *Times'* article cast a long shadow, attenuating opposition to injustice and creating a space in which otherwise well-meaning people could state that the Wilmington Ten must have been guilty of something; but the sentiment was practically no different from the malignant statements of many prospective jurors that required the Wilmington Ten to prove their innocence.

The trope that guilty people were framed and at least some of the Ten must have committed crimes related to the events of February 1971 became the conventional wisdom almost immediately after the U.S. Fourth Circuit Court of Appeals reversed Judge Dupree's decision and overturned the convictions of the Wilmington Ten in December 1980. The convictions were thrown out on a technicality, went the line of reasoning. But even a casual reading of the opinion does not support this smug conclusion. There is no other way to read the decision other than as a denunciation of the state's case and trial judge Robert Martin's conduct.

Justice Harrison Winter, a lifetime Baltimorean who was appointed to the Fourth Circuit bench by Lyndon Johnson in 1966, wrote the published decision, which was joined by John Butzner, who was appointed by Johnson in 1967, and James Sprouse, who had just joined the court the previous year as a Jimmy Carter appointee. The opinion began with a rehearsal of the events of February 1971 and the grounds on which the Wilmington Ten sought to have their convictions thrown out. (It noted that additional arguments had been advanced in an amicus brief from fifty-five members of Congress and adopted by the Ten; interestingly but not surprisingly, given its own record in the case, the state of North Carolina opposed allowing them to file the brief, which the state characterized as "partisan" and "misleading.") The opinion plainly acknowledged that given such a fraught conflict in the streets and the tangled history of litigation, there were bound to be disputes about the facts of the case. Winter illustrated the differences over fact by raising some pointed questions. Was Gregory Congregational Church attacked by white supremacists, or was there violence only in the surrounding neighborhood? Did the introduction of a flurry of photographs at trial, having nothing to do with the crimes for which the Wilmington Ten were charged, inflame the jury? How about the circumstance of Steve Mitchell's death—was its introduction as evidence by the state relevant to the case, or was its value primarily to prejudice the jury? But in the court's opinion, there was no need to sort out all of the facts, because on at least three arguments raised by attorneys for the Ten—the prosecution's withholding of Allen Hall's statement, the prosecution's withholding of Allen Hall's psychiatric record from his time at Cherry state mental hospital, and the judge's restrictions on the cross-examinations of Hall and Jerome Mitchell—there was no disagreement on the factual basis; both sides agreed that the defendants asked for and were denied access to the statement and report and that the defense tried unsuccessfully to extend the cross-examination. This was enough to constitute a fatally unfair trial.[59]

Winter found that as Allen Hall was the primary prosecution witness, a conviction almost certainly depended on the jury believing his testimony.

He listed the inconsistencies between Hall's trial testimony and the statement he gave to prosecutor Jay Stroud and BATF agent Bill Walden; on the stand, Hall had stated several times that he corrected his statement and Stroud recorded his amendments in handwriting on his copy of the statement. But after reviewing the amended statement, Judge Winter concluded that the statement did not corroborate Hall. Hall had lied. But because the prosecutor had not handed over the amended statement to the defense and the trial judge had refused to order it handed over, the jury was denied important information about the chief witness's credibility. Winter clearly contradicted Judge Dupree's finding in federal court that the amended statement had little value and revealed nothing about whether Hall was telling the truth or making up a story.

Similarly, Allen Hall's psychiatric record from his time at Cherry Hospital contained important information bearing on Hall's believability. The defense had asked repeatedly and specifically for records such as this. Two items in the evaluation would have been critical for the jury to hear. First, the report states that Hall said that while he was present at the burning of Mike's Grocery, he did not participate in the arson, whereas at trial he said that he, along with others of the Wilmington Ten, did commit the arson. Second, the evaluation concluded that Hall's IQ was 82, which might very well have had bearing on whether a jury would believe that Hall had the mental capacity to recall the February 1971 events in such great detail.

Keeping relevant information from the jury interfered with a fair trial. But Winter's decision went further. It noted that the defense had made requests for this material numerous times, and the state's response was to misrepresent what evidence it possessed and to stonewall to keep it out of the hands of the defense. On the psychiatric records, for example, Judge Winter concluded that the state had lied when it said that the report was a public record, which the defense must have had, and it was the defense's own fault if it did not use it. The opinion determined that in fact psychiatric records do not become public in North Carolina unless they are introduced into evidence, which the state did not do; it was inconceivable to the appellate court that the defense would have not used it if it had had it.

Regarding both the amended statement and the psychiatric report, the court determined that the prosecution had not simply erred; it had actively worked to suppress these documents. More, the prosecution knew—or should have known—that what its key witnesses were testifying to at trial were lies; prosecutors had an obligation to report the perjury but did not. The facts were, though, that the witnesses' perjuries benefited the state, which was determined to convict Chavis and his codefendants, even if they were in fact not guilty of the crimes they had been charged with. Nor was the trial judge a bystander, for it was he who had limited the defendants' cross-examination of the key eyewitnesses. Sustaining the objections of the prosecutors, trial judge Robert Martin refused to let the jury hear evidence of the favorable treatment afforded Allen Hall, and to a lesser extent Jerome Mitchell; these inducements included living outside of prison while preparing for and testifying at trial, visits to Hall by his girlfriend, visits home for Hall and Mitchell, a shortened prison sentence for Hall, and money deposited into their prison accounts. The court pointed out that the witnesses might have lied about their favorable treatment, but this would have put the prosecutor further in a bind, because he would have then had to report the perjury and Stroud had shown no inclination to do so in other aspects of the trial. The trial judge, the opinion concluded, had worked with prosecutors to deny the Wilmington Ten a fair trial. The jury had convicted them after hearing lies from the prosecution's main witnesses, while the state and trial judge had suppressed evidence that would have helped the defense by showing that Hall and Mitchell had made up their testimony. The trial was a frame-up, and the convictions were overturned.

The state was given thirty days to refile charges, which North Carolina declined to do. The state was grudging. "I do not want to imply that I agree with the Federal appeals court," said Rufus Edmisten, the state attorney general. Other courts had reviewed the case and concluded the trial was fair. However, the Wilmington Ten had served their prison sentences, and a retrial "would serve no useful purpose for the citizens of our state."[60]

Regardless, they were free. It was a great victory and a fitting comeuppance for the political and criminal justice systems that worked in the 1960s and 1970s to criminalize dissent. But it was not a complete victory, as there was no immediate pardon, and as individuals the Wilmington Ten continued to live under a cloud of suspicion. Their pardon did not come until the last days of Governor Beverly Perdue's tenure in office, in 2012. At a distance of four decades, an official of North Carolina could finally see clearly what had plainly been evident: the state's conduct had been outrageous and was a "misappropriation of justice," and she issued pardons of innocence.[61] Unfortunately, it came too late for Joe Wright, Jerry Jacobs, Ann Shepard, and Connie Tindall. But fittingly there was a joyous celebration of the pardons of innocence at Gregory Congregational Church in Wilmington, the headquarters for the 1971 school boycott. Five of the six surviving Wilmington Ten were there, as were their attorneys, comrades in the struggle in the 1970s, and veterans of the black freedom struggle in North Carolina and the South. In 1971, the Rights of White People group had drawn some of its membership from active duty and retired marines from Camp Lejeune. At the pardon celebration was a multiracial contingent of more than a dozen Lejeune marines who had heard of the struggle and wanted to learn more.

Conclusion

The Tragedy of the Ten and the Rise of a New Black Politics

For nearly the entirety of a decade, the people who were known as the Wilmington Ten lived as if nailed to a cross. Outrage compounded outrage. Beginning in February 1971, those of the Wilmington Ten who were still students were expelled from school for their parts in the boycott and had to earn their high school diplomas at the system's continuation, or alternative, school. The next year the Ten were arrested mostly in overnight raids, which seemed to be scheduled at those hours to maximize the frightfulness of the event. Unable to post bond, they spent months in jail awaiting trial. At the same time, the prosecutor allowed Allen Hall, a convicted criminal serving a sentence, a remarkable degree of freedom and privileges in exchange for his lying on the witness stand against the defendants. The prosecutor won a conviction—but only after lying to the court in order to get a new trial, manipulating the jury pool to illegally exclude blacks, improperly withholding evidence from the defense, and knowingly presenting perjured testimony. Found guilty on all counts after a mere few hours of deliberation and sentenced to long terms of imprisonment, the Ten were then scattered to several penitentiaries across the state, where they remained for much of the time their case was on appeal. Doing hard time, they listened with little recourse to a parade of appellate judges pronounce the verdicts fair. Governor James Hunt shortened their sentences but did not free them, sacrificing the Wilmington Ten in order to keep the support of white voters. Finally, the U.S. Court of Appeals for the Fourth Circuit overturned the convictions in 1980, thereby removing the spikes from the hands of the Ten and allowing them to drop down.

But even this litany of wrong and injustice does not fully describe the catastrophe the Wilmington Ten endured. This book has intentionally dealt almost exclusively with the public face of the Wilmington Ten, almost as if the Ten were a single entity. From the vantage point of the political ways the black freedom struggle coagulated around the case and was in turn influenced by it, the individual identities of the Wilmington

Ten were incidental. Individual personalities, passions, and desires mattered little to how the movement was constituted. But those things do matter, intimately so. In the effort to understand the political and social processes at work in the Wilmington Ten, I have consciously chosen in this book to respect their privacy and to let them tell their individual interior tales in their own time and to the extent they see fit to share.

Yet one cannot understand the full measure of the calamity that befell them without at least a mention of the personal disasters each experienced as human beings. On a personal level, even with the vindication of the pardon of innocence, the case of the Wilmington Ten was nothing but a tragedy. For most of the Ten, the effects of the state's ruination of their lives outlasted the years of their imprisonment. Ben Chavis, who returned to work at the Commission for Racial Justice and in various capacities continued his chosen career as a professional revolutionary, was an exception. So, too, was Ann Shepard, who also maintained an active commitment to revolutionary change; she worked with the National Student Coalition against Racism and later with the Greensboro Justice Fund, which was established after the murder of five Communist Workers Party members at an anti-KKK demonstration in Greensboro in 1979. Joe Wright might have broken free. Having graduated from Talladega College in Alabama and worked for U.S. Representative Don Edwards, Wright had found a way to remain involved in civic life in his hometown. He produced a Wilmington public affairs talk radio show and worked with the New Hanover County Human Relations Commission, an organization that failed miserably to stem the Rights of White People violence in February 1971. After more than a decade of persistent effort, in March 1990 he succeeded in getting a superior court judge and the State Bureau of Investigation to expunge his arrest record. Taking a moment to set down his burden, he said, "This stigma has affected me from the day I was arrested, and I dare say that as long as I live in Wilmington or in North Carolina, it will have an effect." He was right: less than four months later, as he was planning to enter law school, he succumbed to sarcoidosis.[1]

But the others who returned to Wilmington lived lives that remained profoundly disrupted. Delores Moore, mother of Wayne Moore, lamented that they were stigmatized as "those convicts," even by black Wilmingtonians. It was difficult for them to find and keep jobs. One of Connie Tindall's sisters, who lived and worked in Wilmington and refused to let her name appear in a newspaper report on the twenty-fifth anniversary of the uprising, commented, "Whatever they have done . . . their whole outlook on life changed after that. It was hard for them to get jobs, I mean everybody had them labeled." Tindall's father earned a living as a longshoreman, and Connie used his connections to find work on the Wilmington docks. But he fell victim to the national war on drugs and served draconian prison sentences and was otherwise ensnared in the criminal justice system for long stretches from the mid-1980s until the first decade of the twenty-first century. Willie Earl Vereen told of working jobs only to have his managers find out who he was and fire him. "A lot of places," he said, "it was like, 'I heard that name somewhere before.' It was always something." "I'm depressed and I'm angry," Vereen said in 1986. Living in Wilmington "is just like in South Africa [under apartheid]. It's no different." Marvin Patrick worked intermittently in construction but reflected that his time in prison and parole had tied him all up and left him unable to do "anything constructive" for himself. Jerry Jacobs, a star tennis player in high school whose aspirations for a professional athletic career were crushed by prison, was pushed into the ranks of the marginally employed. On the fifteenth anniversary of the 1971 uprising, Jacobs was still hurting from his ordeal. A marriage had ended. Another had begun, and he had a young child, but he expressed demoralization at his predicament: "I'm trying to get my life together, and it's hard. I'm not working. I'm married again. I have a little kid. I'm trying to get my life together. I'm trying to get work, and I just have a bunch of problems." He was unemployed when he died of AIDS in 1989. He was eulogized by Joe Wright: "Remember that Jerry was not a bad guy and that Jerry was the victim of this city's insensitivity and bigotry and its unwillingness to face those facts. . . . [A] lot of things killed Jerry Jacobs, not the least of which was the Wilmington 10 case and the people and circumstances that brought it about."[2]

Three kept very low profiles after their paroles, to the point where reporters writing articles about Wilmington Ten anniversaries were unsuccessful in reaching them for comment. James McKoy returned to the Port City and worked a variety of jobs interspersed with periods of unemployment. Reginald Epps studied at Shaw University and graduated from St. Augustine's and remained in Raleigh and out of the public eye. Wayne Moore finished his college education at Shaw University, though his criminal conviction now precluded his dream to become an attorney; he was temporarily caught up in the war on drugs and served additional time in jail. But drawing on the material assistance of the United Church of Christ, he relocated to Ann Arbor, Michigan, where he worked for decades as a unionized electrician.

Practically from the moment they were released from prison and after their convictions were reversed, members of the Wilmington Ten and others involved in the local movement struggled to find their voices and tell their own stories. A little more than a year after he was paroled, Willie Earl Vereen said he had started to write a book about his experiences. Ben Chavis, who had authorial experience, also announced that he was writing a book "on the drama of the Wilmington 10." Neither published his memoirs, though Chavis remained in the public eye and utilized his notoriety to present to audiences his story and analysis of the history of the case. In the first decade of the twenty-first century, Vereen and Connie Tindall teamed with documentary filmmaker Francine DeCoursey on a project titled "The Wilmington Ten: Justice Denied . . . Lives Interrupted," which has so far resulted in a work-in-progress video that prominently features the narratives of these two men and highlights what they endured. The passage of time moved Wayne Moore to tell his story, and with the thirty-fifth anniversary of the uprising in 2006 renewing the public's semi-decennial interest in the case, he was at work committing his experiences to paper. His personally candid and politically engaging memoir, *Triumphant Warrior: A Soul Survivor of the Wilmington Ten*, finally appeared in 2014.[3]

The members of the Wilmington Ten, though, have in general been circumspect in the public retelling of their story. Until they could get their own words and thoughts before the public, they were reluctant to speak to journalists or scholars. One reason was a generally shared feeling that others had benefited in the past or would benefit—pecuniarily, but also in terms of renown—from their story. Robbed of years of their lives, they feared they had been and would be robbed again for someone else's gain. One person associated with the Wilmington Ten would not reveal what he considered to be dramatic details of the warfare around Gregory Congregational Church because he planned to write about it and wanted to benefit from it. Then there was the feeling that the voices belonging to those directly affected should be the ones that are privileged and unmediated. When asked for an interview, Ben Chavis demurred with these words: "I am interested in your research on a subject matter that is inextricably linked to my life's story. The Wilmington Ten is a true story that needs to be told first by the members of The Wilmington Ten and secondly by scholars like yourself who help search and document the truth which benefit all people of the world."[4]

In fact, the Wilmington Ten were created after the fact, and more than one member objected to having his story submerged in this construct. "Wilmington Ten" was shorthand for political repression, but its constant repetition unacceptably sanded down the unique experiences, motivations, struggles, hardships, and desires of the constituent members. There was not only a movement in which the Wilmington Ten were participants to varying degrees; there were also stories of individual dreams stubbed out and of individuals struggling to make their way after a severe blow like incarceration. Stories of compounded loss and stunning resilience are braided in a way that cannot be adequately captured by the synthetic moniker "Wilmington Ten." What happened to them—accident, coincidence, commitment, tragedy, and vindication—belongs to them and is theirs to tell as they see fit.

On a political level, an analysis of the Wilmington Ten case yields a mix of insights into the black freedom struggle in the transitional decade of the 1970s. The civil rights movement of the 1950s and 1960s had a clearly articulated program. It succeeded in dismantling legal segregation and the exclusion of African Americans from political life largely in the South. But with the monumental civil rights legislation of the mid-1960s, there also began a process of incorporation of African American political figures into the electoral system, which had the effect of blunting the more radical and thoroughgoing trends of the freedom struggle. However, this process could not contain, shape, or meliorate the myriad extant discontents. In Wilmington and other parts of North Carolina, dissatisfaction took the form of spontaneous and chronic disruptions in the public schools sparked by continued hostility, disrespect, and exclusion of African American students and parents from these important civic institutions. There were hallway fights and shoving matches between black and white students, walkouts, short-lived boycotts, minor vandalism, and disorganized street protests. African American students demanded fair treatment, including, among other things, official observation of the Martin Luther King birthday holiday, courses in black history, and inclusion of black girls on the cheerleading squads. Raw feelings erupted and just as quickly receded, but they never disappeared and were always at least just below the surface. One cannot not know in advance what particular issue or incident will trip an outpouring of resentment or an uprising, and it is important not to conflate appearance and essence. That is, protests in Wilmington were not only about exclusion of girls and boys from the cheerleading squad and interscholastic sports.

What animated black high school students in Wilmington, North Carolina, was different only in some details from the situations faced by their peers in other locales. Across the region black students faced hostile administrators and school board officials, white students and adults who preferred the racially segregated status quo, and police who were quick to punish and discipline them. Additionally, in Wilmington, they faced African American adults who were haunted by the ghosts of 1898 and whose fear of retaliation was so thick as to preclude their support for their children's grievances. And yet in most other places in North Carolina, the protest movements were evanescent, lasting only days or perhaps a couple of weeks, certainly not more than a couple of months. Pitt County, for example, experienced a school desegregation crisis in the fall of 1971 almost as rough as Wilmington's. The conflict in the schools was layered upon an August 1971 killing of William Murphy, an African American day laborer in the town of Ayden by state trooper Billy Day who shot the man in order to eliminate a witness to the trooper's marital infidelity. For the last half of the summer, African Americans staged frequent street protests, which accelerated protests at Ayden-Grifton High School when it opened in September. When an alleged bomb exploded in the high school boys' lavatory—"alleged," that is, because some witnesses claimed that what occurred was merely a trashcan set on fire—eleven black high school students were arrested. Seventeen-year-old Donald Smith's coerced confession was the only evidence against him, and he was convicted and sentenced to forty years in prison; it was reduced to twenty years on the condition that he not appeal the conviction. With such an example in front of them, ten other teenagers pleaded guilty and were sentenced to an average of thirteen years each. This was the punctuation mark on the movement, and the so-called Ayden Eleven began serving their time, to be remembered by few outside their families. Golden Frinks and the Southern Christian Leadership Conference were an occasional presence in Pitt County during the summer and fall of 1971, and the widespread arrests of protesters and the egregious violations of rights for a time rallied local black moderates to join black nationalists in opposition to local authorities; but neither was capable of sustaining a movement.[5]

What prevented the situation in Wilmington from fading away and being forgotten was the appearance of organizations and individuals who knew how to articulate students' grievances into demands, how to organize students effectively, and how to build alliances. The CRJ and its foremost representative, Ben Chavis, synthesized the grievances of Wilmington's African American high school students into a set of demands that they could act on. During the boycott of February 1971, the organizers were able to receive and absorb assistance from those such as African American soldiers from Ft. Bragg and "brothers off the block" who adhered to the politics and tactics of armed self-defense. Their presence during the height of the uprising likely prevented a rout by the ROWP; the toll they exacted certainly gave the authorities pause and discouraged them from future use of vigilante force.

Beyond the immediate confrontation and crisis, the CRJ and the developing Black Power and black radical-cum-Marxist movements were skilled at broadening the struggle in Wilmington. The Black Youth Builders of the Black Community and the First African Congregation of the Black Messiah offered opportunities to the core of young activists to work through issues of strategy, tactics, and world outlook. The Youth Organization for Black Unity and the *African World* newspaper connected and educated Black Power and pan-African activists across North Carolina and the South. They worked with the Wilmington activists both to publicize the repression and resistance in the Port City and to raise the general level of discourse and political consciousness. Through the efforts of these organizations, what happened in Wilmington became known to and supported by the Black Panther Party, participants in the incipient National Black Political Convention, black high school and college students across the Tar Heel state, and networks of black churches.

It was not just the quantity of support for the situation in Wilmington—and that support increased exponentially after the Wilmington Ten were arrested, tried, and convicted—that was remarkable. Rather, in the efforts to broaden awareness of and support for the Wilmington Ten, the Black Power and leftist black radical advocates and organizations who sustained the movement constructed successful united fronts without compromising their radical and revolutionary beliefs. They sought allies where they could find them: among advocates for reform of the criminal justice system, white liberal clergy and their congregations, people fighting police brutality, parents seeking better education for their children, champions of other political prisoners, revolutionary and national liberation movements around the world, liberal public opinion makers and elected officials in the United States, and politically liberal and moderate members of the public who abjured radical politics but nevertheless were greatly perturbed by the evident railroading of the Wilmington Ten.

For a host of reasons properly outside the scope of this study, the Left-led united front that was exemplified by the Free the Wilmington Ten movement did not survive very far into the 1980s. Michael Dawson's provocative *Blacks in and out of the Left* places a share of the responsibility with the trajectory of the Left in the 1970s. On the one hand, that portion of the Left associated with the Communist Party's National Alliance against Racist and Political Repression, despite its work for the Wilmington Ten, did not fully appreciate the revolutionary potential of the black struggle and was content to allow influential moderates and liberals to direct the united front. Dawson charges that the sector of the black Left that drew its inspiration and analysis from third-world revolutionaries and Mao Zedong and the Chinese Communists tended after the mid-1970s to withdraw from practical organizing in favor of a quest for political clarity and ideological purity—in other words, they tended toward sectarianism, which allowed for the growth of moderate and liberal influence.[6] In North Carolina, such abandonment of the battlefield of practical politics was likely accelerated after the murder of five members of the Communist Workers Party (the successor to the Workers Viewpoint Organization) by members of the Ku Klux Klan and Nazi Party that was organized by an agent of the Bureau of Alcohol, Tobacco, and Firearms in Greensboro in November 1979. As it protested these murders, the Communist Workers Party exhibited a strong tendency to demand that its potential allies adopt the organization's full revolutionary program, thus denying itself both goodwill and a strong united front. It eventually recognized the folly of this approach, but within a few years the organization nationally committed the opposite blunder of diluting its politics in order to gain positional influence among liberals and moderates; it dissolved in 1985.

It did not have to be that way. As Joshua Bloom and Waldo Martin argue in their thorough and considered *Black against Empire: The History and Politics of the Black Panther Party*, the Panthers continued to grow in numbers and cultivate allies and friends domestically and internationally even during the years of its most intense repression. In its steadfastness it was able to win leadership over other circles of the Black Freedom Movement and New Left organizations; similarly, it exercised influence over moderate and liberal political actors who sensed a great danger to the country from the federal government's COINTELPRO and local law enforcement run amok and from the Vietnam War. This united front remained productive and unraveled only when the federal government placed a velvet glove over its iron fist; it offered concessions such as an end to the draft, increased (though still limited) opportunities to black businesses, and modest measures to encourage the incorporation of African American politicians in the system of governance. The net result was that the Black Panthers' moderate and liberal allies no longer felt existentially threatened and turned away from them.[7]

A similar process may very well have been in operation as the Wilmington Ten case reached its denouement in the federal appellate courts. As the Fourth Circuit Court of Appeals organized itself to hear the appeal by issuing instructions to each side about length of briefs

Singing and chanting during the 1 April 1978 march and rally for the Wilmington Ten. The man on the left with the beard is Jim Waller, a member of the Communist Workers Party who was killed at an anti-Klan rally in Greensboro on 3 November 1979. Photograph courtesy Lucy Lewis.

and other submissions and by debating whether to allow a group of U.S. Representatives and the NAARPR to intervene as friends of the court, the circuit's chief judge, Clement Haynsworth, worried about the case. He hesitated to put too severe a limit on the lengths of briefs because the North Carolina attorney general complained that such a restriction would hamper him. It was not that Haynsworth, a conservative judge from South Carolina and one of two unsuccessful Nixon nominees to the U.S. Supreme Court, was solicitous of North Carolina. Rather, he was concerned that, should the court overturn the convictions, the state's attorney general would tarnish the ruling by claiming unfair treatment. When the three-judge panel did in fact reverse the verdict, it was almost as if Haynsworth had expected that course of action all along. Commenting on the decision to its author, Judge Harrison Winter, Haynsworth wrote, "Harm wrought by an overly eager prosecutor can be great. This one seems to have provided a basis for the strident accusations of political motivations in the prosecution."[8] Prosecutor Jay Stroud's misconduct clearly offended the judicial sensibilities of Fourth Circuit Court judges. Coming in the months following the November 1979 Greensboro murders and the national outrage that seemed to be building, it is possible that Haynsworth and his colleagues may also have found it expedient to overturn the Wilmington Ten verdicts, thereby offering proof that justice could be done and simultaneously dividing moderates from the radicals who insisted that justice under the present system was an impossibility. Absent the influence of a vibrant radical Left with a prominent black component, social justice movements were deprived critical insights, and whatever opposition remained to repressive and regressive institutions gradually became incorporated into the political system in a vastly weakened state. There would be no reprise of Representative Joy Johnson's declaration of a united front approach that included revolutionaries in it.

The 1970s in North Carolina was, from the perspective of mass movements, a fluid decade. The state was a petri dish of alternatives to the more staid nonviolent direct action groups that have come to be associated with the civil rights movement. There were black nationalists of both religious and secular varieties; there were groups that embraced Marxism and sought to make the United States a socialist country. There were people who participated in the struggles of the 1960s who tried to grab the levers of power through the ballot box and traditional electoral politics; people like Joy Johnson, Mickey Michaux, Howard Lee, Alma Adams, and Frank Ballance formed the nucleus of a class of black elected officials in the state. These were different trends, markedly different. But in large part because of the extreme repression that was visited on the black freedom struggle in the 1960s and 1970s, those involved in these trends found ways to cooperate, to influence and be influenced by each other. Importantly, the Left offered both valuable social and political critiques and excellent organizing skills. Without these, the movement would not have gone nearly as far as it did. Those headed in the direction of incorporation into the political system were not afraid to be associated with the Left and likely would not have been as successful without the leftist forces.

The case of the Wilmington Ten is memorable not simply because of the excellent lawyering and impressive tactical skills in mass organizing, though the major figures in the struggle possessed these in abundance. The case is edifying because the insurgent political leadership of the 1970s embedded itself in the daily struggles of ordinary people, such as students demanding a quality education, and assisted them in developing an understanding of their circumstances. When the hammer fell, arrests came, and repression was the rule, these same insurgents labored to develop and propagate an understanding that connected different types of popular struggles so that women and men from many walks of life could see what they had in common and act in concert. Flexible in their tactics, they were uncompromising in their analysis that the Wilmington Ten case was not simply unfortunate but symptomatic of systemic repression. They held fast to their belief that through struggle they could achieve a more just society. And for a time in the 1970s, they succeeded in raising the consciousness of the people and instilling in them a sense of possibilities if they dared to struggle.

Notes

ABBREVIATIONS

CRD   Civil Rights Division: Subject Files of Drew Days III, 1977–80, General
        Records of the Department of Justice, RG60, National Archives, College
        Park, Md.
DAP   Department of Administration Papers, Human Relations Council,
        County File, State Archives of North Carolina, Raleigh
DUOHP   Duke University Oral History Program Collection, David M. Rubenstein
        Rare Book and Manuscript Library, Duke University
NA   National Archives, College Park, Md.
NAARPR National Alliance against Racist and Political Repression
NCCFPP North Carolina Committee to Free Political Prisoners FBI Charlotte
        Field Office 157-CE-8777, National Archives, College Park, Md.
SAC   Special Agent in Charge
SANC   State Archives of North Carolina, Raleigh
SCCHC   Southern Conference Church History Collection, Belk Library Archives
        and Special Collections, Elon University, Elon, N.C.
SHC   Southern Historical Collection, Wilson Library, University of North
        Carolina at Chapel Hill
SOHPC   Southern Oral History Program Collection, Southern Historical
        Collection, Wilson Library, University of North Carolina at Chapel Hill

INTRODUCTION

1. Ann Shepard's surname was rendered inconsistently over the course of the history of the Wilmington Ten. Newspaper accounts, campaign publicity, and even some court filings spell the last name variously Shepherd, Shepard and Sheppard. Unless appearing differently in the title of an official document, her name will be spelled "Shepard."

2. Chafe, *Civilities and Civil Rights*; Cecelski and Tyson, *Democracy Betrayed*.

3. Gilmore, *Gender and Jim Crow*.

4. Umfleet, *1898 Wilmington Race Riot Report* .

5. Nash, "Cost of Violence"; Hossfeld, *Narrative, Political Unconscious and Racial Violence*.

6. Tyson, *Radio Free Dixie*; Lewis, *King*. The historiography of nonviolence and armed self-defense has exploded in recent years. Studies to consult include Austin, *Up against the Wall*; Umoja, *We Will Shoot Back*; Hill, *Deacons for Defense*; and Cobb Jr., *This Nonviolent Stuff'll Get You Killed*.

7. P. Jones, *Selma of the North*; Joseph, *Stokely*; Bloom and Martin, *Black against Empire*; Galliard, *Long Dream Deferred*; Cecelski, *Along Freedom Road*.

8. Countryman, *Up South*.

9. Von Eschen, *Race against Empire*; Anderson, *Eyes off the Prize*; Horne, *Black and Red*; Marable, *Race, Reform, and Rebellion*; Janken, *Rayford W. Logan*; Janken, *Walter White*.

CHAPTER 1

1. "5 Students Suspended for Fight," *Wilmington Morning Star*, 26 January 1971, 20; "Black Student Group to Boycott Schools," ibid., 29 January 1971, 2; Eugene Templeton, "Five Questions about Gregory's Involvement in the New Hanover School Crisis—1971" [before June 1971], Heyward C. Bellamy Papers, box 16, folder 1, William M. Randall Library Special Collections, University of North Carolina at Wilmington.

2. On the role of the BATF, see Lani Guinier to Drew S. Days III, memo, 28 April 1978, box 52, and Guinier to Days, memo, 12 May 1978, box 53, CRD. Guinier was the special assistant to Assistant Attorney for Civil Rights Drew Days III; she was charged with reviewing the Wilmington Ten case and making recommendations for intervention by the Justice Department in the appeals process.

3. Applebome, *Dixie Rising*, 210–36; Godwin, *Black Wilmington and the North Carolina Way*, 222–27.

4. Emsley Laney interview, 14 June 1995, Lower Cape Fear Historical Society, Wilmington, N.C.

5. Bertha Todd interview, 13 June 1995, ibid.

6. Ernest Swain interview, 20 June 1995, ibid.

7. Anonymous black male [appended to Walter Bordeaux transcript], interview by Larry Thomas, n.d. [1978], DUOHP; "Barnabus" and Darryl Franks (aka "Daniel Banks"), interview by Larry Thomas, 14 May 1978, ibid.; Timothy Tyson, *Blood Done Sign My Name*.

8. Bertha Todd interview 13 June 1995; anonymous black male [appended to Walter Bordeaux transcript] interview by Larry Thomas, DUOHP; "Barnabus" and Darryl Franks (aka "Daniel Banks") interview by Larry Thomas, DUOHP; "Boycott Set Today," *Wilmington Morning Star*, 3 February 1971, 2.

9. "Barnabus" and Darryl Franks (aka "Daniel Banks") interview by Larry Thomas, DUOHP; "Board Conducts Hearings," *Wilmington Morning Star*, 11 February 1971, 1. On hair and clothing, see Graham, "Flaunting the Freak Flag" and *Young Activists*.

10. Robert Nicholas [director of the Wilmington–New Hanover County Human Relations Commission] to Preston Hill, 13 May 1970, DAP, box 10, folder "New Hanover County, 1970"; "Violence Flames at High Schools," *Wilmington Morning Star*, 8 May 1970, 1; "Quiet Follows in Wake of School Violence," *Wilmington Morning Star*, 9 May 1970, 1; Aaron J. Johnson to Fred Cooper and Preston Hill, 7 May 1970, memo, DAP, box 10, folder "New Hanover County, 1970."

11. Robert T. Nicholas to Boyce Medlin, 16 September 1970, DAP box 10, folder "New Hanover County, 1970." The "Minutes of Sub-Committee of the Education Committee, August 14, 1970," which contains the full list of demands, is attached to this letter.

12. Lani Guinier to Brian Landsberg, memo, 20 March 1978, box 49, CRD; Draft of "Motion of the United States for Leave to File Brief as Amicus Curiae" [August 1978], attached to Drew S. Days III to Wade H. McCree, Benjamin R. Civiletti, and Michael J. Egan, memo, 18 August 1978, box 52, ibid. The history of student unrest and prior federal intervention in Wilmington was omitted from the final version of the government's amicus brief that was submitted in August 1978.

13. "17 Arrested in Wake of Stoning of Cars," *Wilmington Morning Star*, 19 December 1970, 2; "Punishment Meted for Disturbances," ibid, 30 December 1970, 3; "School Principals Act to Punish Disturbers," ibid., 23 January 1971, 15.

14. "Racial Trouble Hits Two Schools," ibid., 2 December 1970, 13. In the Governor Robert Scott Papers, SANC, see Special Incident Report, 24 February 1971, box 332, folder "Highway Patrol Reports IV"; Special Incident Report, 15 January 1971, box 331, folder "Highway Patrol"; and James R. Horton to Gov. Robert Scott, 25 January 1971, box 308, folder "Good Neighbor Council."

15. This paragraph and the next are based on Tyson, *Blood Done Sign My Name*, 130–38 (quote is on 130).

16. Leon White, interview by author, 30 July 2004, Manson, N.C., notes in author's possession; "Troops Called to Keep Curfew in North Carolina Racial Strife," *New York Times*, 8 November 1970, 73; "Racial Trouble Hits Two Schools," 13.

17. "Bladen Students Boycott Two Schools to Protest Student Re-assignment," *Wilmington Morning Star*, 28 December 1970, 1C; "Dynamite Found in East Arcadia High School," ibid., 27 January 1971, 11; "Black Folks' View on High School Unrest," *African World*, 11 December 1971, 11; Chronological Listing of Events, 27 April 1971, Governor Robert Scott Papers, box 332, folder "Highway Patrol Reports IV," SANC; "Officials Probe Arson Cases in Elizabethtown," *Wilmington Morning Star*, 28 April 1971, 1; "ROWP Calls on Scott to Okeh Vigilantes," *Wilmington Morning Star*, 29 April 1971, 2.

18. "Speakers Indict N.C. Integration," *Raleigh News and Observer*, 7 March 1971, sec. 1, p. 9. One of the best overviews of the unequal fashion in which schools were desegregated in North Carolina is Cecelski, *Along Freedom Road*.

19. Charles Jones, interview by author, 16 June 2005, Atlanta, Ga., tape recording and notes in author's possession.

20. George Kirby, interview by author, 5 October 2004, Wrightsville Beach, N.C., tape recording and notes in author's possession; "Young NAACP Commandoes Are 'Task Force' for Freedom," *Chicago Defender*, 3 July 1963, 4; Wayne Moore, interview by author, 9 April 2005, Ann Arbor, Mich., notes in author's possession; Jones interview by author. Daryl Franks also mentioned that he was heavily influence by Cleaver, Malcolm X, Mao, and Marx. "Barnabus" and Darryl Franks (aka "Daniel Banks") interview by Larry Thomas, DUOHP.

21. Templeton, "Five Questions about Gregory's Involvement in the New Hanover School Crisis—1971."

22. Connie Tindall, interview by author, 31 October 2004, Kenansville, N.C., notes in author's possession; Delores Moore, interview by author, 19 July 2004, Wilmington, N.C.; Jeff Portnoy, "Wilmington: A Tale of 3 Cities" [1970], Governor James B. Hunt Papers, Office of General Counsel, Legal Counsel—Files of Jack Cozort

(1977–1984), box 12, folder "Report: 'Wilmington: A Tale of 3 Cities' by Jeff Portnoy (Aug. 1978)," SANC; Bertha Todd, interview by author, 11 November 2004, Wilmington, N.C., tape recording and notes in author's possession.

23. Todd interview by author.

24. Tony Weatherman, telephone interview by author, 2 November 2004, notes in author's possession; Eugene Templeton, interview by author, 27 August 2004, Chapel Hill, N.C., tape recording and notes in author's possession. On the struggle of public housing residents against housing authorities' attempts to control them and deny them their constitutional rights, see Williams, "'Something's Wrong Down Here.'"

25. Eugene Templeton interview by author.

26. Donna Templeton, interview by Larry Thomas, 28 July 1978, interview #B-61, SOHPC (#4007); Eugene Templeton interview by author.

27. Eugene Templeton, interview by Larry Thomas, 1 August 1978, DUOHP; Eugene Templeton interview by author.

28. Eugene Templeton interview by Larry Thomas, DUOHP.

29. Ibid.; Eugene Templeton interview by author; Mac Hulslander, interview by author, 7 June 2007, Raleigh, N.C., tape recording and notes in author's possession. Templeton conceded that the student leaders may have been more familiar with the world and revolutionary organizing than he thought they were, but student leader Charles Jones backed him up. Up until the meetings in the church, there had been no organization; rather, Jones characterized the situation as just high school students trying to confront authority and deal with the racism in the schools. Jones interview by author.

30. Jones interview by author; Todd interview by author.

31. McGeehan, "Getting to the Hospital: An Overview of the Winston-Salem Black Panther Party," 56–57; Tyson, *Blood Done Sign My Name*. SAC, Charlotte, "Non-Prosecutive Summary Report," 29 May 1973, Benjamin Chavis FBI Headquarters 157-HQ-12210, NA, lists Chavis's activities in Charlotte, N.C., in 1968 and 1969.

32. "What We Want: What We Believe" [late January 1971], leaflet, Bellamy Papers, box 3, folder 2.

33. Student boycott leaflet [2 February 1971], ibid., box 16, folder 1; Jim Grant, interview by author, 15 December 2004, Chapel Hill, N.C., tape recording and notes in author's possession.

34. Transcript of Ben Chavis press conference, 2 February 1971, Bellamy Papers, box 16, folder 5.

35. Ibid.

36. "Bellamy Appeals for Community Backing in School Disturbances," *Wilmington Morning Star*, 3 February 1971, 2; New Hanover County School Board, statement responding to student boycotters' demands, 3 February 1971, Bellamy Papers, box 16, folder 1; Heyward Bellamy interview, 19 April 2005, Oral History Collection, William M. Randall Library Special Collections, University of North Carolina at Wilmington, http://library.uncw.edu/web/collections/oralhistories/transcripts/503.html, accessed 1 June 2009; "Amnesty Offered to Boycotting Students," *Wilmington Morning Star*, 3 February 1971, 2; "Commissioners Laud Disorder Handling," *Wilmington Morning Star*, 3 February 1971, 18; "The Reasoned Approach," *Wilmington Morning Star*, 4 February 1971, 6.

37. "Board's Statement Is Ignored by Boycotters: But Schools Will Remain Open," *Wilmington Morning Star*, 4 February 1971, 2; Wilmington P.D. log, 4 February 1971, Bellamy Papers, box 12, folder 8.

38. Aaron Johnson, monthly report of activities [end of February 1971], DAP, box 10, folder "New Hanover County, 1971"; Aaron Johnson, interview by author, 22 September 2004, Fayetteville, N.C., tape recording and notes in author's possession; "Good Neighbor Council Says School Board Derelict in Crisis," *Wilmington Morning Star*, 2 February 1971, B1; "Special Teams Probing Arson, Violence in City," *Wilmington Morning Star*, 5 February 1971, 1; "No Blanketing Blame," editorial, *Wilmington Morning Star*, 5 February 1971, 4.

39. Wilmington P.D. log, 2 February 1971, Bellamy Papers, box 12, folder 8; "Furniture Store Is Fire Bombed," *Wilmington Morning Star*, 4 February 1971, B1; Delores Moore interview by author; Eugene Templeton interview by Larry Thomas, DUOHP; Kirby interview by author; Aaron Johnson interview by author; SAC Charlotte to Director, FBI, 18 May 1971, Wilmington Ten FBI HQ 157-8056, NA.

40. Ben Chavis, remarks at a panel discussion marking the thirty-fifth anniversary of the Wilmington Ten events, 3 February 2006, University of North Carolina at Chapel Hill, notes in author's possession; Kojo Nantambu, remarks at a panel discussion marking the thirty-fifth anniversary of the Wilmington Ten events, 3 February 2006, University of North Carolina at Chapel Hill, notes in author's possession; "Rev. Templeton Suggests Curfew," *Wilmington Morning Star*, 5 February 1971, 2; "Special Teams Probing Arson, Violence in City," 1; "How It All Came to Pass," undated article from an unidentified newspaper, Ben Chavis newspaper clipping file, North Carolina State Library, Raleigh; Wilmington P.D. log, 4 February 1971, Bellamy Papers, box 12, folder 8; Kojo Nantambu, interview by Larry Thomas, 15 May 1978, interview #B-59, SOHPC (#4007).

41. "Blacks March on City Hall, Demand Better Protection," *Wilmington Morning Star*, 6 February 1971, 1; "Claims Wilmington Racial Reports, Lie," *Carolina Times*, 20 February 1971, 1; "Seven Cases of Arson Suspected Wednesday," *Wilmington Morning Star*, 5 February 1971, 3; Templeton, "Five Questions about Gregory's Involvement in the New Hanover School Crisis—1971"; "City Relaxed in Face of Dark Storm Clouds," *Wilmington Morning Star*, 6 February 1971; Nantambu interview by Larry Thomas, SOHPC; Jones interview by author.

42. Jim Grant, interview by Larry Thomas, 10 July 1978, DUOHP; Thomas, *Rabbit! Rabbit! Rabbit!*, 36; C-Man, interview by Larry Thomas, 12 and 16 August 1978, DUOHP; Eugene Templeton interview by author; Grant interview by author; Ben Chavis, remarks at a panel discussion marking the thirty-fifth anniversary of the Wilmington Ten events, 3 February 2006. C-Man described the 1968 riots in Wilmington after King's assassination as being influenced by some college-educated blacks "who had had exposure to community organization and political environment in other cities." For a report on the uprising in Wilmington following the King assassination that highlights points similar to C-Man's, see FBI Charlotte Office, "Racial Disturbances Following Assassination of Martin Luther King, Jr., Wilmington, North Carolina. Racial Matters," memo, 22 April 1968, Classification 157 Field Office Case Files (Charlotte, N.C.), 1957–1978, 157-177-Sub L-3, RG65 Federal Bureau of Investigation, NA.

43. C-Man interview by Larry Thomas, DUOHP; Grant interview by author.

44. Wilmington P.D. log, 6 February 1971, Bellamy Papers, box 12, folder 8; Nantambu interview by Larry Thomas, SOHPC; "One Killed, Three Wounded, as Violence Enters Fourth Day," *Wilmington Sunday Star-News*, 7 February 1971, 1.

45. "Fire Guts NHHS Fieldhouse as Violence Resumes," *Wilmington Morning Star*, 6 February 1971, 2; Wilmington P.D. log, 5 February 1971 and 6 February 1971, Bellamy Papers, box 12, folder 8.

46. Wilmington P.D. log, 4 February 1971, 5 February 1971, 6 February 1971, Bellamy Papers, box 12, folder 8.

47. Eugene Templeton interview by author, 27 August 2004; "Barnabus" and Darryl Franks (aka "Daniel Banks") interview by Larry Thomas, DUOHP; Nantambu interview by Larry Thomas, SOHPC; "Officers Search Church," *Raleigh News and Observer*, 9 February 1971 (source of Wonce observation), clipping in Governor Robert Scott Papers, box 308, folder "Good Neighbor Council," SANC.

48. Wilmington P.D. log, 6 February 1971, Bellamy Papers, box 12, folder 8; "Police Abort White Backlash," *Wilmington Sunday Star-News*, 7 February 1971, 2; "Deaths Follow School Unrest," *Raleigh News and Observer*, 8 February 1971, clipping in Governor Robert Scott Papers, box 308, folder "Good Neighbor Council," SANC.

49. "Disturbance Toll Runs Half Million," *Wilmington Star-News*, 11 February 1971, clipping in Wilmington Movement 1971 clipping file, MS108, William M. Randall Library Special Collections, University of North Carolina at Wilmington; Chronological Listing of Events, 6 February 1971, Governor Robert Scott Papers, box 332, folder "Reports IV," SANC; "One Killed, Three Wounded, as Violence Enters Fourth Day," *Wilmington Sunday Star-News*, 1; "Deaths Follow School Unrest," *Raleigh News and Observer*, 8 February 1971, clipping in Governor Robert Scott Papers, box 308, folder "Good Neighbor Council," SANC. Officer Shaw's trial testimony on the shooting of Steve Mitchell, to which the defense vigorously and repeatedly objected, is in State v. Chavis, 24 N.C. App. 148 (1974), record on appeal, pp. 1781–1801; the defense chose not to cross-examine Shaw.

50. Nantambu interview by Larry Thomas, SOHPC; Grant interview by Larry Thomas, DUOHP; Donna Templeton interview by Larry Thomas, SOHPC; State v. Chavis, 24 N.C. App. 148 (1974), record on appeal, pp. 2090–99; "Chief Williamson Refutes Rights Leader's Charges," *Wilmington Morning Star*, 9 February 1971, 2.

51. "One killed, Three Wounded, as Violence Enters Fourth Day," 1; "Chief Williamson Refutes Rights Leader's Charges," 2; Wilmington P.D. log, 7 February 1971, Bellamy Papers, box 12, folder 8; "Wilmington Strife Marked by Communications Gap," *Raleigh News and Observer*, 9 February 1971, clipping in Governor Robert Scott Papers, box 308, folder "Good Neighbor Council," SANC; Grant interview by Larry Thomas, DUOHP; "Curfew Proclaimed in City and County," *Wilmington Morning Star*, 8 February 1971, 1.

52. "Curfew Proclaimed in City and County," 1; Chronological Listing of Events, 5 February 1971, Governor Robert Scott Papers, box 332, folder "Reports IV," SANC; "Officers Search Church," *Raleigh News and Observer*, 9 February 1971, clipping in Governor Robert Scott Papers, box 308, folder "Good Neighbor Council," SANC; State Bureau of Investigation Incident Log, New Hanover County, 8 February 1971,

Governor Robert Scott Papers, box 323, folder "SBI," SANC; Chronological Listing of Events, 10 and 11 February 1971, Governor Robert Scott Papers, box 332, folder "Reports IV," SANC; Wilmington P.D. log, 8, 9, 10, and 11 February 1971, Bellamy Papers, box 12, folder 8; Ferd L. Davis [adjutant general of the N.C. National Guard] to Harrison Salisbury, 15 February 1971, Governor Robert Scott Papers, box 411, folder "Demonstrations," SANC.

53. "13 Persons Arrested by Wilmington Police," *Wilmington Morning Star*, 18 March 1971, 1; "26 Arrested in Wake of Riots," ibid., 19 March 1971, 1; Ben Franklin to Fred Cooper, Preston Hill, Aaron Johnson, Lynn Martin, Boyce Medlin, and Bud Walker, memo, 17 March 1971, DAP, box 10, folder "New Hanover County, 1971"; "White Student Group Marches on Hemenway Hall in Protests," *Wilmington Morning Star*, 20 March 1971, 2; Chronological Listing of Events, 19 March 1971, Governor Robert Scott Papers, box 332, folder "Highway Patrol Reports IV," SANC; "Schools Closed to Ease Tensions," *Wilmington Morning Star*, 18 March 1971, 1; "Speakers Indict N.C. Integration," *Raleigh News and Observer*, 7 March 1971, 9; "Rights Commission May Act after Look at N.C.," *Raleigh News and Observer*, 7 March 1971, 9.

54. Luther Cromartie to Clyde Fields, 19 February 1971, SCCHC, box "Black Church Dvlp," folder "Wilmington–Gregory," unprocessed manuscript; "The Hoodlums Are Warned," editorial, *Wilmington Morning Star*, 3 March 1971, 4; "The Trouble Must Stop Now!," editorial, *Wilmington Morning Star*, 18 March 1971, 8; "The Portrait of Hate," editorial, *Wilmington Morning Star*, 19 March 1971, 4; "Williamson Resignation Requested," *Wilmington Morning Star*, 22 February 1971, 9; "Council Receives Petition Asking Williamson Ouster," *Wilmington Morning Star*, 23 February 1971, 9; "Commissioners Authorize 12 New Deputy Sheriffs," *Wilmington Morning Star*, 19 March 1971, 19.

55. "Wilmington Chief of Police Criticized by District Judge," *Raleigh News and Observer*, 11 March 1971, clipping in DAP, box 10, folder "New Hanover County, 1971"; "Police Action in Racial Strife Assailed by Judge," *Wilmington Morning Star*, 9 March 1971, 11.

56. Virginia Simkins, letter to the editor, *Wilmington Morning Star*, 10 February 1971, 4; "Hoggard Students Begin Movement for Friendship," ibid., 12 March 1971, 13.

CHAPTER 2

1. There were some exceptions to the isolated nature of the struggles. For example, the Malcolm X Liberation University, which at the time was based in Durham, apparently was teaching high school students in Clinton how to disrupt the beginning of the 1971 school year, and the racial moderates in the state Good Neighbor Council reported in April 1970 that Vietnam veterans were teaching youthful blueberry farm workers the intricacies of guerrilla warfare. See Organized Crime Control Division to Director [State Bureau of Investigation], 30 August 1971, Governor Robert Scott Papers, box 324, folder "SBI reports," SANC; Ben Franklin monthly report, April 1970, Department of Administration Papers, Human Relations Council, Reports File, box 2, folder "Franklin, Ben, Monthly Reports, 1970–1971," SANC.

2. Charles Cobb, "History of the Commission for Racial Justice" [1971], Commission for Racial Justice Collection #2002.21, box 1, unprocessed manuscript, United Church of Christ Archives, Cleveland, Ohio; "'Racist Posture' May Cause Va. and N.C., UCC Pastors' Exodus," *Philadelphia Tribune*, 30 January 1971, clipping in SCCHC, box "Black Church Dvlp," file "Wilmington–Gregory," unprocessed manuscript.

3. "Proposed Wilmington Movement Program—and Demands," 23 May 1971, Bellamy Papers, box 16, file 1.

4. Grant interview by Larry Thomas, DUOHP. For evidence of communication between activists in the orbits of YOBU and the Malcolm X Liberation University and activists in Wilmington, see the following from the BYBBC FBI Charlotte Field Office 157-8263, NA: Crawford Williams, report, 27 July 1971; report received by Crawford Williams, 18 May 1972; and report received by Charles S. Miller, 25 April 1972.

5. Brother Ben Chavis, "How Do You Learn to Be Liberated? (From A Black Perspective)," 2 June 1971, BYBBC FBI Charlotte Field Office 157-8263, NA; Albert Yopp Jr., interview by Timothy Tyson, 15 August 1992, DUOHP; "Klansmen Shot Guards," *SOBU Newsletter*, 24 July 1971, 1. *SOBU Newsletter* later changed its name to the *African World*. Crawford Williams to SAC, Charlotte, 18 January 1972, BYBBC FBI Charlotte Field Office 157-8263, NA; Special Incident Report, 6 October 1971, and Chronological Listing of Events, 4 October 1971, both in Governor Robert Scott Papers, box 332, folder "Highway Patrol Reports II," SANC.

6. Report received by Special Agent James J. Roche Jr., 4 May 1971, BYBBC FBI Charlotte Field Office 157-8263, NA. On the issue of reports of guns, see the following, all in BYBBC FBI Charlotte Field Office 157-8263, NA: Crawford Williams, 27 July 1971; Special Agent James J. Roche Jr. to SAC, Charlotte, 15 September 1971; Crawford Williams, report, 15 November 1971; Crawford Williams to SAC, Charlotte, memo, 12 January 1971; Crawford Williams to NISO, Charleston, S.C. (RM), OSI, Langley AFB (RM), CO 111th MIG, Fayetteville, N.C. (RM), Secret Service, Charlotte (RM), 28 January 1972; Inness Carlson to SAC, Charlotte, 4 April 1972; Crawford Williams to NISO, Charleston, S.C. (RM), OSI, Langley AFB, Va. (RM), CO 111th MIG, Fayetteville, N.C. (RM), Secret Service, Charlotte (RM), memo, 4 April 1972. On Operation SOUL, see "Klansmen Shot Guards," *SOBU Newsletter*, 24 July 1971, 1, and "'Operation SOUL' Project Slated to Start Soon," *Wilmington Morning Star*, 25 June 1971, clipping in BYBBC FBI Charlotte Field Office 157-8263, NA. For the BYBBC's organizational philosophy and principles, see "Philosophy, Black Youth Builders of the Black Community," 1971, leaflet reproduced in Crawford Williams, report, 27 July 1971, BYBBC FBI Charlotte Field Office 157-8263, NA. For the "Three Main Rules of Discipline and the Eight Points for Attention" (1947), see *Quotations from Chairman Mao Tse-tung* (Peking: Foreign Languages Press, 1972), 256–57. Charles Jones, one of the boycott spokespersons, credits the Black Panther Party newspaper for influencing the nascent nationalism in Wilmington; after the uprising, student activists developed connections between their school-based demands and such issues as police brutality, housing, and unemployment in an effort to sustain a broader movement. See Jones interview by author. George Kirby remembered the influence of a variety of Marxist, black nationalist, and Third World revolutionary theorists. See Kirby interview by author.

7. On the Reverend Albert Cleage and the Shrine of the Black Madonna, see Dillard, "Religion and Radicalism," 153–75 (quote is on 170).

8. On the Black Messiah church's desired demographic, see report received by Special Agent James J. Roche Jr., 28 May 1971, and "'Operation SOUL' Project Slated to Start Soon," both items in BYBBC FBI Charlotte Field Office 157-8263, NA; Wayne Moore interview by author; First African Congregation of the Black Messiah prayer service, copy in author's possession. Brother Ben Chavis, "How Do You Learn to Be Liberated? (From a Black Perspective)," 2 June 1971, BYBBC FBI Charlotte Field Office 157-8263, NA, is a short history of the Wilmington uprising and the founding of the BYBBC and the Black Messiah church.

9. See the following from the BYBBC FBI Charlotte Field Office 157-8263, NA: Crawford Williams to SAC, Charlotte, 27 July 1971; Crawford Williams, report, 15 November 1971; Steve Mitchell Week leaflet, February 1972; Crawford Williams, report, 27 July 1971.

10. "'Outside Agitators' Polarize City's Militants," *Greensboro Daily News*, 17 October 1971, clipping attached to B. M. Cullom to Gov. Robert Scott, 10 December 1971, Governor Robert Scott Papers, box 361, folder "New Hanover," SANC; *Wilmington Morning Star* [October 1971], clipping in DAP, box 10, folder "New Hanover County, 1971."

11. On the incident that prompted Kojo Nantambu's arrest, see "Conflict in Wilmington Reaches a New High," *African World*, 16 October 1971, 1; "'I'm the Baddest Man in Wilmington': Kirby," *Wilmington Sunday Star-News*, 3 October 1971, 2, clipping in Wilmington Movement 1971 clipping file, MS108; "Fight Erupts after Ball Game," *Raleigh News and Observer*, 3 October 1971, clipping in Wilmington Movement 1971 clipping file, MS108; untitled article from the *Wilmington Morning Star* [October 1971], clipping in DAP, box 10, folder "New Hanover County, 1971"; and transcript of State of North Carolina v. Roderick Lionel Kirby, No. 725SC489, Fifth District North Carolina Court of Appeals, Spring Session 1972, copy in Office of Attorney General Papers, Education and Corrections Section: Wilmington Ten Case File, unprocessed manuscript, Record Center box 4, SANC. When his appeals were exhausted, Nantambu began serving his sentence in September 1972 and was released after six and a half months.

12. Aaron Johnson interview by author; B. M. Collum to Gov. Robert Scott, 10 December 1971, Governor Robert Scott Papers, box 361, folder "New Hanover," SANC. Clippings attached to this letter identify some of the members of the commission.

13. "Kirby Calling for an End to Area Racial Polarization," *Wilmington Morning Star*, 9 March 1972, 2.

14. Untitled and undated article, *Wilmington Morning-Star* [October 1971], clipping in DAP, box 10, folder "New Hanover County, 1971"; untitled article, *Greensboro Daily News*, 17 October 1971, clipping in DAP, box 10, folder "New Hanover County, 1971"; "Port City's Black Leaders Resent Militants," *Wilmington Morning Star*, 1 December 1971, clipping in BYBBC FBI Charlotte Field Office 157-8263, NA; Crawford Williams, memo, 3 April 1972, BYBBC FBI Charlotte Field Office 157-8263, NA; "Human Relations Group Meet Said 'Most Spirited,'" *Wilmington Morning Star*, 21 March 1972, 13; "Police Chief to Speak at HRC Meet Today," *Wilmington Morning Star*, 6 April 1972, 1C.

15. Ben Chavis, "Where We Are Today as African People Struggling to Be Free," 1 September 1971, attached to Richard Goldberg, memo, 30 November 1971, ROWP FBI Charlotte Field Office 157-7236, NA; "North Carolina–Virginia Committee on Racial Justice Community Organization Programs and Projects" (1972), planning document, in BYBBC FBI Charlotte Field Office 157-8263, NA; "March Is Canceled Frinks Tells Rally," *Greenville (N.C.) Daily Reflector*, 5 September 1971, 1.

16. "Clues Lacking in Wright Death," *Wilmington Morning Star*, 15 March 1971, 6; Kojo Nantambu, interview by Larry Thomas, SOHPC; O. A. Dupree to Governor Robert Scott, telegram, 15 March 1971, Governor Robert Scott Papers, box 411, folder "Demonstrations," SANC; Chronological Listing of Events, 19 March 1971, Governor Robert Scott Papers, box 332, folder "Highway Patrol Reports IV," SANC; "Wilmington Chief: Information Withheld," *Raleigh News and Observer*, 29 March 1971, clipping in DAP, box 10, folder "New Hanover County, 1971"; Ben Franklin to Fred Cooper, Preston Hill, Aaron Johnson, Lynn Martin, Boyce Medlin, and Bud Walker, memo, 17 March 1971, DAP, box 10, folder "New Hanover County, 1971"; Special Incident Report, 16 March 1971, Governor Robert Scott Papers, box 332, folder "Highway Patrol Reports IV," SANC; "Two Teachers, 8 Students Injured in City School Riots," *Wilmington Morning Star*, 18 March 1971, 1; "50 Highway Patrolmen Ordered to Duty Here," *Wilmington Morning Star*, 20 March 1971, 1. Clifton Eugene Wright's shooting is mentioned briefly in Myerson, *Nothing Could Be Finer*, 205, and Godwin, *Black Wilmington and the North Carolina Way*, 239.

17. "Return Williston High to Blacks, Declares Frinks," *Wilmington Morning Star*, 19 March 1971, 1; "Frinks: Blacks Need 'Crash Program' of Education," ibid., 20 March 1971, 1; Du Bois, "Does the Negro Need Separate Schools?"; "SCLC to Form 'Poor Peoples Co-op' in City," *Wilmington Morning Star*, 25 March 1971, 1; Kirby interview by author. For Frinks's background, see Cecelski, *Along Freedom Road*, 83–85. Frinks's pronouncements echoed the Don't-Shop-Where-You-Can't-Work boycotts of the 1920s and 1930s; see August Meier and Elliott Rudwick, "Origins of Nonviolent Direct Action."

18. "SCLC Overrules Good Neighbor Council on School Boycott," *Wilmington Morning Star*, 20 March 1971, 3; Todd interview by author; "All-Black Schools Not a Solution, Says Dr. Eaton," *Wilmington Morning Star*, 20 March 1971, 1. On the ways in which the "outsider" term and an insistence on politeness are used to hamstring protest and demands for equality, see Chafe, *Civilities and Civil Rights*.

19. "150 Students May Boycott Schools Today—Frinks," *Wilmington Morning Star*, 22 March 1971, 1; "School Attendance Down," ibid., 23 March 1971, 11; William H. Hill II to Algernon Butler [federal district court judge], 22 March 1971, Bellamy Papers, box 16, file 6; "US Court Bans Interference with School Operations," *Wilmington Morning Star*, 23 March 1971, 1; "Restraining Order Stays: Judge Butler," *Wilmington Morning Star*, 10 April 1971, 1B. In his testimony in support of making the injunction permanent, schools superintendent Heyward Bellamy stated that Ben Chavis made "inflammatory speeches." Defense attorney Jerry Paul cross-examined Bellamy about this statement, asking him if he was familiar with Judge Walker's comments from the bench that Lieutenant Calley should have been called in to clear out Gregory Congregational Church, if he considered that statement inflammatory, and

why he did not seek an injunction against the judge. Judge Butler put a quick stop to that line of questioning. "US Court Hearing Begins on Injunction," *Wilmington Morning Star*, 8 April 1971, 5A.

20. "NHHS School Faculty Members under Fire," *Wilmington Morning Star*, 19 March 1971, 2 (source of Frinks quote). The reaction of Wilmington activists to Frinks is captured in Delores Moore, interview by author, 19 July 2004, and Leon White, interview by author, 30 July 2004 and 11 June 2007. The demands of the march are discussed in several places, including "Return Williston High to Blacks, Declares Frinks," ibid., 19 March 1971, 1, and "Smithfield Police Halt Black March," ibid., 2 April 1971, 2A.

21. Special Incident Report, 30 March 1971, Governor Robert Scott Papers, box 332, folder "Highway Patrol Reports IV," SANC; "Black Group Reaches Elizabeth-town in 'March against Repression,'" *Wilmington Morning Star*, 31 March 1971, 1; "Smithfield Police Halt Black March," *Wilmington Morning Star*, 2 April 1971, 2A; "SCLC Terminates March on Raleigh; Fitch, Legislative Leaders Confer," *Wilmington Morning Star*, 3 April 1971, 2; Special Incident Report, 5 April 1971, Governor Robert Scott Papers, box 332, folder "Highway Patrol Reports IV," SANC.

22. "Ben Chavis Returns to Port City," *Wilmington Morning Star*, 19 March 1971, 2; "Ex-militant Renounces Violence as a Solution," ibid., 26 March 1971, 2; "SCLC March to Raleigh Set to Start Tuesday," ibid., 29 March 1971, 3.

23. "SCLC to Form 'Poor Peoples Co-op' in City," 1; "Frinks Asks 6 Per Cent Festival Net," *Wilmington Morning Star*, 7 April 1971, 24; "Wilmington Movement, Part II: The SCLC Enters the Picture," *Carolina Times*, 1 May 1971, 6A; Kirby interview by author; Nantambu interview by Larry Thomas, SOHPC; "'Poor Peoples' Store Formed for Profit," *Wilmington Morning Star*, 23 April 1971, 1B; "Frinks Warns on Demands," *Raleigh News and Observer*, 24 May 1971, clipping in Wilmington Movement 1971 clipping file; "200 Join Protest March on City Hall," *Wilmington Morning Star*, 31 May 1971, clipping in DAP, box 10, folder "New Hanover County, 1971"; Intelligence Section to Director [SBI], memo, 10 June 1971, Governor Robert Scott Papers, box 324, folder "SBI reports," SANC; "Riot Charges Case Continued Friday," *Wilmington Sunday Star-News*, 16 June 1971, clipping in Wilmington Movement 1971 clipping file; "Judge Orders Kirby's Background Investigated," *Wilmington Morning Star*, 21 February 1972, 13; "Six Indicted in Connection with 1971 Racial Disorders," *Wilmington Morning Star*, 26 April 1972, 3.

24. The most comprehensive account of the murder of William Murphy by State Trooper Billy Day is "The Truth about the Murder of Bill Murphy," *African World*, special issue, 21 August 1971. On the Pitt County protests, see "Arrested 125 in Ayden for Demonstrating," *Greenville (N.C.) Daily Reflector*, 25 August 1971, 1; "Ayden Shop Damaged by Blast during Demonstrators' Arrest," *Greenville (N.C.) Daily Reflector*, 26 August 1971, 1; Charles Cain to Charles Dunn, 31 August 1971, Governor Robert Scott Papers, box 324, folder "SBI A–Z," SANC; Civil Intelligence Bulletin, 31 August 1971, Governor Robert Scott Papers, box 324, folder "SBI reports," SANC; Civil Intelligence Bulletin, 8 September 1971, Governor Robert Scott Papers, box 324, folder "SBI reports," SANC; "Golden Frinks, 99 Other Demonstrators Sentenced in District Court," *Greenville (N.C.) Daily Reflector*, 10 September 1971, 1; "Terrorism Said Turning Ayden into Armed Camp," *Greenville (N.C.) Daily Reflector*, 10

September 1971, 2; "8 Bombings, 300 Arrests in Ayden," *African World*, 18 September 1971, 3; "Black Student Grievances of Ayden-Grifton," leaflet produced by protesting Ayden-Grifton High School students, 21 September 1971, and the students' undated and untitled explanation of the grievances, attached to Special Incident Report, 28 September 1971, Governor Robert Scott Papers, box 332, folder "Highway Patrol Reports II," SANC; Kirby interview by author. For critical evaluations of Golden Frinks's organizing, see Nantambu interview by Larry Thomas, SOHPC; Delores Moore interview by author; and Leon White interviews by author, 30 July 2004 and 11 June 2007, Manson, N.C., notes in author's possession.

25. Ben Chavis, open letter to the black community of Wilmington, North Carolina [late March or early April 1971], T. J. Reddy Papers, box 2, folder 6, J. Murrey Atkins Library Special Collections, University of North Carolina at Charlotte; Nantambu interview by Larry Thomas, SOHPC; "Klansmen Shot Guards," *SOBU Newsletter*, 24 July 1971, 1.

26. On the Selma campaign, see *Voices of Freedom: An Oral History of the Civil Rights Movement from the 1950s through the 1980s*, ed. Henry Hampton and Steve Fayer (New York: Bantam, 1991), 209–40; *American Experience: Eyes on the Prize* transcript, http://www.pbs.org/wgbh/amex/eyesontheprize/about/pt_106.html, accessed 10 August 2009 (Forman quote); and "Klansmen Shot Guards," *SOBU Newsletter*, 24 July 1971, 1.

27. "Frinks Prepared for Seige [*sic*]," *Wilmington Morning Star*, 21 March 1971, 1; "200 Join Protest March on City Hall," ibid., 31 May 1971, clipping in DAP, box 10, folder "New Hanover County, 1971."

28. "'Operation SOUL' Project Slated to Start Soon," clipping in BYBBC FBI Charlotte Field Office 157-8263, NA; Ben Chavis, open letter to the black community of Wilmington, North Carolina [late March or early April 1971], Reddy Papers, box 2, folder 6; Nantambu interview by Larry Thomas, SOHPC; White interview by author, 11 June 2007. Some of Frinks's ferocity against the CRJ may have originated in the criticisms that those grouped around the commission raised about Frinks's program. They not only questioned the political thrust of the SCLC's work but also accused Frinks of fraud. Frinks had combed the Wilmington black community, selling shares in the poor people's co-op, but it never opened; Frinks, they said, simply pocketed the money.

29. Milton Coleman, telephone interview by author, 16 November 2007, notes in author's possession; report received by Crawford Williams, 18 May 1972, BYBBC FBI Charlotte Field Office 157-8263, NA.

30. "Political Awareness Growing, Anyhow," *African World*, 13 November 1971, 7; "Black Folks' View on High School Unrest," ibid., 11 December 1971, 7; Civil Intelligence Bulletin, 1 October 1971, Governor Robert Scott Papers, box 324, folder "SBI reports," SANC.

31. On Trenton, N.C., see "Unified Black Community Gains Reinstatement," *African World*, 18 March 1972, 11, and "School Violence Continues in Statesville, 2 Schools Close Doors across State," *Wilmington Morning Star*, 18 February 1972, 3. On Cross, S.C., see "Students Educated by Struggling," *African World*, 4 September 1971, 6.

32. "Day of Solidarity to Save Black Schools," *African World*, 13 November 1971, special supplement.

33. Chafe, *Civilities and Civil Rights*, 185–200, recounts the Dudley uprising.

34. Edward Whitfield, interview by Bridgette Burge, 26 February 2006, interview #U-0590, SOHPC (#4007), http://dc.lib.unc.edu/cdm/ref/collection/sohp/id/7980, accessed 20 April 2015.

35. John Mendez, interview by Rob Stephens, 6 February 2008, interview #U-0304, SOHPC (#4007), http://dc.lib.unc.edu/cdm4/document.php?CISOROOT=/ sohp&CISOPTR=5352&REC=7, accessed 31 May 2011; Whitfield interview by Bridgette Burge.

36. "Students' Role in the Struggle," *SOBU Newsletter*, 17 April 1971, 1; "Analyzing the Black Students' Dilemma," ibid., 17 April 1971, 6; Nelson Johnson, "The Struggle in Perspective," ibid., 17 April 1971, 4; Nelson Johnson, "The Question of Unity," ibid., 15 May 1971, 4; Nelson Johnson, "The Nature of the Struggle," ibid., 29 May 1971, 4; Nelson Johnson, "Cleaning Up the Revolution," ibid., 3 April 1971, clipping in SOBU/ YOBU FBI Charlotte Field Office 157-CE-6758, NA.

37. Benjamin Chavis Muhammad, interview by Kieran Taylor, 3 February 2006, interview #U-0332, SOHPC (#4007), http://dc.lib.unc.edu/cgi-bin/showfile.exe? CISOROOT=/sohp&CISOPTR=5805&filename=5847.pdf#search=%22chavis muhammad%22, accessed 31 May 2011. For instances of cooperation between SOBU and Chavis, see, for example, Leon White to Dear Brothers and Sisters, 9 May 1972, Reddy Papers, box 2, folder 3; North Carolina Criminal Justice Task Force newsletter, April 1973, Reddy Papers, box 2, folder 3; "N.C. Independent Black Political Party Formed," *African World*, 11 December 1971, 1; "Day of Solidarity to Save Black Schools," *African World* special supplement, 13 November 1971. This day of solidarity, called to protest the reorganization of the University of North Carolina system, which YOBU felt would irrevocably harm the historically black state colleges, drew five thousand people to Raleigh; one of the speakers was Ben Chavis, who made this statement: "Even though we're in an armed struggle in Wilmington, we have a consciousness about the problems you brothers and sisters are engaged in today. And we are supporting you wholeheartedly." See Mendez interview by Rob Stephens, SOHPC, for another perspective on the cooperation.

38. On the Black Panther Party in Winston-Salem, see Austin, *Up against the Wall*, 266–72, and McGeehan, "Getting to the Hospital"; SAC, Charlotte to FBI Director, 10 March 1971, memo, Black Panther Party—North Carolina, FBI Headquarters File 105-165706-8, Section 10, http://vault.fbi.gov/Black%20Panther%20Party%20/Black%20 Panther%20Party%20Part%2024%20°f%2034/view, accessed 2 June 2011.

39. On the sporadic cooperation between the Black Panther Party and Chavis and the CRJ, see "Frinks Sets Raleigh Trek," *Greenville (N.C.) Daily Reflector*, 31 August 1971, 1, and "Golden Frinks, 99 Other Demonstrators Sentenced in District Court," ibid., 10 September 1971, 1. On the Panthers' push into eastern North Carolina, see Austin, *Up against the Wall*, 270. On Leon White's advice to Chavis, see White interview by author, 30 July 2004.

40. Charles Cobb, "1985 Annual Report of the Executive Director [of the Commission for Racial Justice]," Commission for Racial Justice Collection #2002.21, box 1; French, "Incarcerated Black Female."

41. Leon White to Dear Brothers and Sisters, 9 May 1972, Reddy Papers, box 2, folder 3; "Black Leaders Charge Wilmington 'Racist' City," *Wilmington Sunday*

Star-News, 13 June 1972, 2A; "The Wilmington Report," prepared by members of the North Carolina Criminal Justice Task Force from testimony presented at public hearings on 19 August 1972 at the First African Congregation of the Black Messiah, Commission for Racial Justice Collection #2002.21, box 79.

42. Nelson Johnson, "Political Prisoners," *African World*, 5 August 1972, 6.

43. Ibid.

44. Nelson Johnson, "Consciousness and Revolution," *African World*, 18 September 1971, 4; report prepared by Special Agent James Roche Jr., 9 March 1971 (date prepared), SOBU/YOBU FBI Charlotte Field Office 157-CE-6758, NA.

45. "A Black Presidential Candidate—for What?," *SOBU Newsletter*, 12 June 1971, 5; report received by Special Agent James J. Roche Jr., 19 August 1971, Wilmington Ten FBI HQ 157-8056, NA; Special Agent James J. Roche Jr. to SAC Charlotte, memo, 15 September 1971, BYBBC FBI Charlotte Field Office 157-8263, NA; "N.C. Independent Black Political Party Formed," *African World*, 11 December 1971, 1.

46. For an excellent contemporary account of the Gary convention, see Jim Grant, "A Black Beginning in Gary," *African World*, 1 April 1972, 1. On the history and legacy of the Gary convention, see C. Johnson, *Revolutionaries to Race Leaders*, and Smith, *We Have No Leaders*.

47. Resolution on Wilmington, February 1972, BYBBC FBI Charlotte Field Office 157-8263, NA; "Blacks Issue Plea on Wilmington," *Raleigh News and Observer*, 27 February 1972, clipping in Committee of Racial Justice [*sic*] FBI Charlotte Field Office 157-8527, NA; "Black People's Position Outlined at Conference," *African World*, 18 March 1972, 3.

48. Report received by Special Agent Charles S. Miller, 25 April 1972, BYBBC FBI Charlotte Field Office 157-8263, NA.

49. "What Happened to the Black Political Agenda?" *African World*, 22 July 1972, 6; "Black Agenda," *African World*, undated clipping attached to report to Special Agent John Willis, 6 November 1972 [date prepared], NCCFPP.

50. Report received by Special Agent Robert S. Shields, 8 June 1972, Committee of Racial Justice [*sic*] FBI Charlotte Field Office 157-8527, NA.

51. Det. R. K. Carroll and Det. D. L. Dickerson to Maj. Edgar C. Duke (of the Raleigh Police Dept.), 25 July 1972, Committee of Racial Justice [*sic*] FBI Charlotte Field Office 157-8527, NA; "North Carolina Holds 2nd Black Political Convention," *African World*, 5 August 1972, 1; "Building the Black Assembly," *African World*, undated clipping from September or October 1972, attached to report sent to Special Agent John Willis, 6 November 1972 [date prepared], NCCFPP; "NC Black Assembly Convenes in Rocky Mt.," *African World*, 28 October 1972, 12.

52. "Building the Black Assembly," undated clipping from September or October 1972; "NC Black Assembly Convenes in Rocky Mt.," 12.

CHAPTER 3

1. Special Incident Report, 2 September 1971, Governor Robert Scott Papers, box 332, folder "Highway Patrol Reports III," SANC; Special Agent William Pearson, report, 7 September 1971, ROWP FBI Charlotte Field Office 157-7236, NA; Special

Agent Inness Carlson to SAC Charlotte, 17 September 1971, ROWP FBI Charlotte Field Office 157-7236, NA; Special Agent James Underhill, report on ROWP, 29 October 1971, ROWP FBI Charlotte Field Office 157-7236, NA; Chronological Listing of Events, 7 October 1971, Governor Robert Scott Papers, box 332, folder "Highway Patrol Reports II," SANC; Charlotte Field Office to Director, FBI, 4 October 1971, ROWP FBI Charlotte Field Office 157-7236, NA; "Chavis Arrested on Traffic Charge," *Wilmington Morning Star*, 7 October 1971, clipping in ROWP FBI Charlotte Field Office 157-7236, NA; *Wilmington Morning Star*, untitled and undated clipping, DAP, box 10, folder "New Hanover County, 1971"; Special Agent Inness Carlson to SAC Charlotte, 12 October 1971, ROWP FBI Charlotte Field Office 157-7236, NA; "Reporter Says Police, KKK Rode in Same Cars during N.C. Trouble," *Baltimore Afro-American*, 30 October 1971, clipping in ROWP FBI Charlotte Field Office 157-7236, NA.

2. Chronological Listing of Events, 7 October 1971, Governor Robert Scott Papers, box 332, folder "Highway Patrol Reports II," SANC; Fred Cooper to Preston Hill and Aaron Johnson, 7 October 1971, DAP, box 10, folder "New Hanover County, 1971"; Aaron Johnson to Preston Hill, 7 October 1971, DAP, box 10, folder "New Hanover County, 1971"; "Chavis Arrested on Traffic Charge," clipping in ROWP FBI Charlotte Field Office 157-7236, NA; Ben Chavis, interview by Blackside, Inc., for *Eyes on the Prize II: America at the Racial Crossroads 1965 to 1985*, 18 April 1989, Henry Hampton Collection, Film and Media Archive, Washington University Libraries, St. Louis, Mo., available at http://digital.wustl.edu/cgi/t/text/text-idx?c=eop;cc=eop;rgn=main;view=text;idno=cha5427.0149.030, accessed 29 May 2012. The discussion of the arrests and petty harassment of Chavis is discussed in his answer to question 6. Other examples of such harassment are recounted in Myerson, *Nothing Could Be Finer*, 109–15.

3. O'Reilly, *"Racial Matters,"* 267–69, 276, 281, 283, 287–89, 291–92; SAC Charlotte to Director, FBI, 27 August 1969, Benjamin Chavis FBI Headquarters 157-HQ-12210, NA.

4. Tyson, *Blood Done Sign My Name*, 146–48; "Government Witnesses, in Return for Immunity, Link Chavis to Plot," *Baltimore Afro-American*, 29 April 1972, 16; "Chavis Innocent, Grant Convicted," *Baltimore Afro-American*, 6 May 1972, 3. For an extensive discussion of Hood and Washington, see Schutz, "'Going to Hell to Get the Devil,'" chap. 5.

5. Nantambu interview by Larry Thomas, SOHPC. Nantambu is mistaken about the number of teenage males who were present with Wright. He identified three: Don Nixon, Donald Rheddick, and Jerome McClain. But in fact Don Nixon is an alias for Rheddick, and only two persons were charged in the shooting of Wright—Nixon and McClain. "13 Persons Arrested by Wilmington Police," *Wilmington Morning Star*, 18 March 1971, 1; "Two Teachers, 8 Students Injured in City School Riots," *Wilmington Morning Star*, 18 March 1971, 1; Ben Franklin to Fred Cooper and others, 17 March 1971, memo, DAP, box 10, folder "New Hanover County, 1971"; O. A. Dupree to Robert Scott, 15 March 1971, telegram, Governor Robert Scott Papers, box 411, folder "Demonstrations," SANC; "Clues Lacking in Wright Death," *Wilmington Morning Star*, 15 March 1971, 6; Chronological Listing of Events, 19 March 1971, Governor Robert Scott Papers, box 332, folder "Highway Patrol Reports IV," SANC;

"Wilmington Chief: Information Withheld," *Raleigh News and Observer*, 29 March 1971, clipping in DAP, box 10, folder "New Hanover County, 1971"; "City Police Seek Killer of Wright," *Wilmington Morning Star*, 20 March 1971, 1.

6. Nantambu interview by Larry Thomas, SOHPC; Don Nixon offender record, http://webapps6.doc.state.nc.us/opi/viewoffender.do?method=view&offenderID=03 41098&searchLastName=nixon&searchFirstName=don&searchSoundex=Y&search Gender=M&listurl=pagelistoffendersearchresults&listpage=1, accessed 7 June 2012; State of North Carolina vs. Donald Jerome Nixon, 71-CR-17668, and State of North Carolina vs. Donald Jerome Nixon, 71-CR-17685, both in microfilm reel no. 73-16-151, copy in author's possession.

7. Nantambu interview by Larry Thomas, SOHPC.

8. "Clues Lacking in Wright Death," 6; Chronological Listing of Events, 19 March 1971, Governor Robert Scott Papers, box 332, folder "Highway Patrol Reports IV," SANC; "50 Highway Patrolmen Ordered to Duty Here," *Wilmington Morning Star*, 20 March 1971, 1; Ben Chavis to the Black Community of Wilmington, North Carolina [end of March 1971], Reddy Papers, box 2, folder 6; "17-Year-Old Brother's Head Blown off by Ku Klux Klan," *Black Panther*, 3 April 1971, clipping in Black Panther Party—North Carolina, FBI Headquarters File 105-165706-8, Section 11, http://nara-wayback-001.us.archive.org/peth04/20041019151532/http://foia.fbi.gov/ bpanther/bpanther12.pdf, accessed 8 June 2012; the article is on p. 132.

9. "Talk about Africa Trip Boosts Bail," *Baltimore Afro-American*, 29 February 1972, 1; "Chavis' Bond Is Reduced to $15,000," *Wilmington Morning Star*, 2 March 1972, 1; Ben Chavis, "From the New Hanover Jail," *African World*, 18 March 1972, 4; W. D. Oxendine to Fred Cooper and Preston Hill, 18 June 1973, DAP, box 10, folder "New Hanover County, 1971"; "Molly Hicks Convicted," *African World*, 30 June 1973, 2; Inness Carlson to SAC, Charlotte, 10 July 1973, BYBBC FBI Charlotte Field Office 157-8263, NA. See also Gilbert H. Burnett interview, 4 October 2002, Oral History Collection, William M. Randall Library Special Collections, University of North Carolina at Wilmington, http://randal13.uncw.edu/ascod/?p=digitallibrary/ digitalcontent&id=200, accessed 11 June 2012.

10. Discharge summary from Cherry Hospital, North Carolina Department of Mental Health, Goldsboro, 29 November 1971, contained in State of North Carolina vs. Allen R. Hall, 71-CR-8195, microfilm reel no. 72-18-264, copy in author's possession; "US Court Bans Interference with School Operations," *Wilmington Morning Star*, 23 March 1971, 1.

11. Complaint for arrest—simple assault and assault and battery, 11 March 1971, contained in State of North Carolina vs. Allen Hall, 71-CR-7269, microfilm reel no. 72-18-266, copy in author's possession; complaint for arrest—assault with a deadly weapon, 9 March 1971, contained in State of North Carolina vs. Allen Hall, 71-CR-7270, microfilm reel no. 72-18-265, copy in author's possession; discharge summary from Cherry Hospital, North Carolina Department of Mental Health, Goldsboro, 29 November 1971; Nantambu interview by Larry Thomas, SOHPC.

12. State of North Carolina vs. Tommy Atwood, James Bunting, Benjamin F. Chavis, Carnell E. Flowers, Jerry Jacobs (Alias Scarface), James McKoy, Marvin Patrick, Ann Shepherd, Connie Tindall, Willie E. Vereen, and Michael Peterson,

Original Transcript of Probable Cause Hearing, 30 March 1972, pp. 22–23, 24–27, 41, 42, 46, 47, http://www.justice.gov/crt/foia/readingroom/wilmington/, accessed 18 June 2012; Frank R. Cherry to the Honorable Judge of the September 20th Criminal Session of the Superior Court of New Hanover County, motion, 22 September 1971, contained in State of North Carolina vs. Allen Hall, 71-CR-8195, copy in author's possession; Judge Joshua James, order, 22 September 1971, contained in State of North Carolina vs. Allen Hall, 71-CR-8195, copy in author's possession; discharge summary from Cherry Hospital, North Carolina Department of Mental Health, Goldsboro, 29 November 1971; State v. Chavis, 24 N.C. App. 148 (1974), record on appeal, pp. 1433ff.; SAC Charlotte to Director, FBI, 16 March 1972, Wilmington Ten FBI HQ 157-8056, NA (on interest of FBI and BATF in this case). The transcripts of the probable cause hearing; the jury selection in the first Wilmington Ten trial in June 1972, which ended in a mistrial; and the second trial, which ended in convictions, are available at http://www.justice.gov/crt/foia/readingroom/wilmington/, accessed 18 June 2012. When I began research on this book, the only official record of the trial was in State v. Chavis, 24 N.C. App. 148 (1974), record on appeal, which does not contain much by way of the June 1972 trial; I have found it useful to use the record on appeal and the transcripts available on the Department of Justice's Freedom of Information Act website in tandem.

13. SAC Charlotte to Director, FBI, 24 February 1972, Wilmington Ten FBI HQ 157-8056, NA; SAC Charlotte to Director, FBI, 6 March 1972, Wilmington Ten FBI Charlotte Field Office 176-37, NA; SAC Charlotte to Director, FBI, 16 March 1972, Wilmington Ten FBI HQ 157-8056, NA; "Chavis, 9 Others Arrested in Wake of '71 Violence," *Wilmington Morning Star*, 17 March 1972, 1; "Arrests Grow to 12 in Wake of 1971 Civil Disturbances," *Wilmington Morning Star*, 22 March 1972, 1; SAC Charlotte to Director, FBI, 23 March 1972, Wilmington Ten FBI HQ 157-8056, NA; "Six Indicted in Connection with 1971 Racial Disorders," *Wilmington Morning Star*, 26 April 1972, 3; "Port City '13' now up to '14,'" *Wilmington Morning Star*, 28 April 1972, 1D; "Additional Arrest Made in Racial Disorder Case," *Wilmington Morning Star*, 3 May 1972, 5; SAC Charlotte to Director, FBI, 3 May 1972, Wilmington Ten FBI HQ 157-8056, NA.

14. "Chavis, 9 Others Arrested in Wake of '71 Violence," 1; Ben Chavis to Leon White, 17 March 1972, transcribed in SAC, Charlotte to Director, FBI, 20 March 1972, Wilmington Ten FBI HQ 157-8056, NA; "Picketing of Jail Goes into 2d Day," *Wilmington Morning Star*, 21 March 1972, 2; "Disorder Hearing Changed to Mon.," *Wilmington Morning Star*, 24 March 1972, 1D; "Blacks Protest Chavis' Jailing in Raleigh March," *Wilmington Morning Star*, 26 March 1972, 3; "Kirby: Chavis, Others Will Go Free 'One Way or the Other,'" *Wilmington Morning Star*, 25 March 1972, 17.

15. "Kirby: Chavis, Others Will Go Free 'One Way or the Other,'" 17; "Vigilante Ultimatum Led to Arrest," *African World*, 1 April 1972, 7. How this educational point was used by religious organizations and labor advocates will be discussed below. On the white supremacy campaign and Wilmington riot of 1898, see Umfleet, *1898 Wilmington Race Riot Report*, http://www.history.ncdcr.gov/1898-wrrc/report/report.htm, accessed 25 June 2012.

16. Ben Chavis, "From the New Hanover Jail," *African World*, 18 March 1972, 4; "Letter from the Wilmington 11," ibid., 15 April 1972, 17.

17. Kojo Nantambu's statement, contained in Crawford Williams, letterhead memo, 3 April 1972, BYBBC FBI Charlotte Field Office 157-8263, NA; "Human Relations Group Meet Said 'Most Spirited,'" *Wilmington Morning Star*, 21 March 1972, 13; "Resolution on Wilmington" [February 1972], BYBBC FBI Charlotte Field Office 157-8263, NA; "Blacks Issue Plea on Wilmington," *Raleigh News and Observer*, 27 February 1972, clipping in Committee of Racial Justice [*sic*] FBI Charlotte Field Office 157-8527, NA; "Chaos Created by Coverage of White Media," *African World*, 1 April 1972, 8; "Black People's Position Outlined at Conference," *African World*, 18 March 1972, 3; memo [concerning meetings in April and May 1972 of the North Carolina Black Caucus] received by Special Agent Robert S. Shields, 8 June 1972, Committee of Racial Justice [*sic*] FBI Charlotte Field Office 157-8527, NA; report received by Special Agent Charles S. Miller, 25 April 1972, BYBBC FBI Charlotte Field Office 157-8263, NA.

18. Irv Joyner, statement at press conference, 18 March 1972, contained in Crawford Williams, letterhead memo, 3 April 1972; Irv Joyner, interview by author, 1 December 2006, Durham, N.C., notes in author's possession. In the beginning of their ordeal, the group of defendants was sometimes referred to as Ben Chavis and the Wilmington 9, but fairly quickly it became simply the Wilmington Ten, with Chavis incorporated into the group.

19. "Hearings Open for Chavis, 11 Others Here," *Wilmington Morning Star*, 31 March 1972, 2; "Justice Absent from Wilmington Hearing," *African World*, 15 April 1972, 3.

20. Gilbert Burnett interview.

21. Ibid.

22. State of North Carolina vs. Tommy Atwood et al., 30 March 1972, 2–3; "Finlator Raps Port City," *Wilmington Morning Star*, 14 April 1972, 1; "Burnett Answers Finlator," *Wilmington Morning Star*, 15 April 1972, 1; "Burnett: More Violence in Recent Court Cases," *Wilmington Morning Star*, 3 May 1972, 21.

23. "Hearings Open for Chavis, 11 Others Here," 2.

24. State of North Carolina vs. Tommy Atwood et al., 30 March 1972, 14–18.

25. Ibid., 38, 64, 53ff., 74–83.

26. Ibid., 42, 48–49, 67, 87–92, 172–82.

27. Ibid., 198–99; "Deputies Avert Physical Attack on Ben Chavis by Witness Allen Hall," *Wilmington Morning Star*, 1 April 1972, 3.

28. State of North Carolina vs. Tommy Atwood et al., 30 March 1972, 41, 46, 47.

29. Ibid., 18–37, 183–91, 125–26; "Justice Absent from Wilmington Hearing," *African World*, 15 April 1972, 3.

30. "Special Session to Try Disorder Cases Monday," *Wilmington Morning Star*, 1 May 1972, 22.

31. State of North Carolina vs. Benjamin Franklin Chavis, Marvin Patrick, Connie Tyndall [*sic*], Jerry Jacobs, Willie Earl Vereen, James McKoy, Reginald Epps, Wayne Moore, Joe Wright, George Kirby, and Ann Shepard, Transcript of Testimony [of first trial], 5 June 1972, 29–31, 34, 41–43, http://www.justice.gov/crt/foia/readingroom/wilmington/, accessed 18 June 2012.

32. "Defendants Seek Move to US Court," *Wilmington Morning Star*, 2 May 1972, 15; "Federal Judge Remands Chavis Trial to State," ibid., 31 May 1972, 15.

33. "Joshua James: A Just and Proud Man," *Wilmington Sunday Star-News*, 2 July 1972, 13C.

34. State of North Carolina vs. Benjamin Franklin Chavis et al., Transcript of Testimony [of first trial], 5 June 1972, 44–46, ; "Jury Selection Nears End in Burgaw Trial," *Wilmington Morning Star*, 9 June 1972, 2; "Mistrial Declared Due to Illness of Prosecutor," *Wilmington Morning Star*, 13 June 1972, 1.

35. James Ferguson, interview by author, 27 June 2007, Charlotte, N.C., notes in author's possession; James E. Ferguson, interview by Rudolph Acree Jr., 3 March 1992 and 17 March 1992 (#J-0004), SOHPC (#4007), http://dc.lib.unc.edu/cdm/ref/collection/sohp/id/1277, accessed 18 July 2012.

36. Ferguson interview by author; Ferguson, interview by Rudolph Acree Jr., 3 March 1992 and 17 March 1992, SOHPC.

37. State of North Carolina vs. Benjamin Franklin Chavis et al., Transcript of Testimony [of first trial], 5 June 1972, 154, 200, 237, 260, 263, 313, 323, 340, 390, 392, 532, ; "Jury Selection Nears End in Burgaw Trial," *Wilmington Morning Star*, 9 June 1972, 2. On the composition of the jury pool, see "Only Three OKd for '11' Trial Jury," *Charlotte Observer*, 14 September 1972, clipping in Reddy Papers, box 2, folder 4.

38. State of North Carolina vs. Benjamin Franklin Chavis et al., Transcript of Testimony [of first trial], 9 June 1972, 534–87.

39. Ibid., 588–95, ; State of North Carolina vs. Benjamin Franklin Chavis, Marvin Patrick, Connie Tyndall [*sic*], Jerry Jacobs, Willie Earl Vereen, James McKoy, Reginald Epps, Wayne Moore, Joe Wright, George Kirby, and Ann Shepard, Transcript of Testimony [of second trial], 11 September 1972, 26–30, http://www.justice.gov/crt/foia/readingroom/wilmington/, accessed 18 June 2012.

40. State of North Carolina vs. Benjamin Franklin Chavis et al., Transcript of Testimony [of first trial], 5 June 1972, 596–99.

41. "Wilmington 10 Prosecutor Sought 'KKK' Jury," *Wilmington Journal*, 12 September 2012, http://wilmingtonjournal.com/wilmington-10-prosecutor-sought-kkk-jury/, accessed 14 September 2012.

42. Jay Stroud's handwritten notes about a mistrial [June 1972] included in ibid. These and other related notes by Stroud are deposited in Timothy B. Tyson Papers, box 7, folder 63, SHC.

43. On the state's motion for a jury from a county other than Pender, see "Chavis, 10 Others Go on Trial Today in Arson, Assault," *Charlotte Observer*, 11 September 1972, clipping in Reddy Papers, box 2, folder 5.

44. Ibid.; "Chavis Trial Witness Contradicts Himself," *Charlotte Observer*, 30 September 1972, clipping in Reddy Papers, box 2, folder 5; Dale Johnson, telephone interview by author, 15 August 2012, notes in author's possession.

45. Judge Robert McKinney Martin Jr., interview by Tom McLean, 28 October 1996 and 14 November 1996 (#J-0043), SOHPC (#4007), http://dc.lib.unc.edu/cdm/ref/collection/sohp/id/1292, accessed 15 August 2012; Tyson, *Blood Done Sign My Name*, chap. 10 (characterization of the trial as a "sham and mockery" is on 245).

46. State v. Chavis, 24 N.C. App. 148 (1974), record on appeal, 324–26, 374–83, 392–96, 505–12.

47. Jay Stroud's handwritten notes about jury selection [September 1972] included in "Wilmington 10 Prosecutor Sought 'KKK' Jury." These and other related notes by Stroud are deposited in Timothy B. Tyson Papers, box 7, folder 63, SHC.

48. State v. Chavis, 24 N.C. App. 148 (1974), record on appeal, 392–96, 412–22, 428, 451, 470, 483; see also 582–93, 620.

49. Ibid., 531–33, 555, 1026–27.

50. Ibid., 1127–29, 1244–46.

51. Ibid., 1128–29.

52. Ibid., 1345–46.

53. Ibid., 1054–1108, 1112–14, 1117–2000, 1203–17, 1232–35, 1154–56.

54. Ibid., 1344, 1345, 1290–98; "Chavis Trial Witness Contradicts Himself"; Statement of Allen Hall, 18 February 1972, Dan Pollitt Wilmington Ten Collection, copy in author's possession.

55. State v. Chavis, 24 N.C. App. 148 (1974), record on appeal, 1308–11, 1317–19.

56. Statement of Allen Hall, 7 June 1971, 18 February 1972, Hall CE & Rebuttal, n.d., all in Dan Pollitt Wilmington Ten Collection.

57. State v. Chavis, 24 N.C. App. 148 (1974), record on appeal, 1284, 1367; State of North Carolina vs. Benjamin Franklin Chavis et al., Transcript of Testimony [of second trial], 624–25, 426–32, 1897, 1949–52.

58. Lahav, "Theater in the Courtroom," 393.

59. Ferguson interview by author.

60. "Chavis Found Guilty," *Wilmington Morning Star*, 18 October 1972, 1; "Violence Trial Defendants All Given Prison Sentences," ibid., 19 October 1972, 2A.

61. Barkan, "Political Trials and the 'Pro Se' Defendant in the Adversary System," 334.

62. Ferguson interview by author.

63. Ferguson interview by Rudolph Acree Jr., 3 March 1992 and 17 March 1992, SOHPC.

CHAPTER 4

1. James Lightbourne Jr., to Ministers of the Southern Conference, 20 December 1972, SCCHC, box "Social Justice CRJ," folder "Correspondence—Wilmington Ten"; Moore, *Triumphant Warrior*, 294; Dr. [Charles] Cobb, Gloria Dandridge, Leon White, Ben Chavis, and Irv Joyner, "Mobilization around Trial of Ben Chavis and General Synod Campaign around Securing Bail for the Wilmington 9" [May 1973], Commission for Racial Justice Collection #2002.21, box 79, unprocessed mss.; James Lightbourne to Karl Vercourteren, 4 September 1973, SCCHC, box "Social Justice CRJ," folder "Correspondence—Wilmington Ten."

2. SAC, Charlotte to Director, FBI, 28 April 1972, memo, Benjamin Chavis FBI Headquarters 157-HQ-12210, NA; [FBI Field Office] Charlotte to Director, 29 April 1972, ibid. ; Special Agent Guy Cox to SAC, Charlotte, 25 July 1972, NCCFPP; [FBI Field Office] Charlotte to Acting Director, FBI, 27 July 1972, NCCFPP; [FBI Field Office] Charlotte to Acting Director, FBI, 28 July 1972, NCCFPP; report to Special Agent John Willis, 5 September 1972, NCCFPP; report to Special Agent John Willis,

6 November 1972, NCCFPP; report to Special Agent John Willis, 12 December 1972, NCCFPP; "Sponsors of Angela Davis Concerned over Impact," *Charlotte Observer*, 8 December 1972, clipping in NCCFPP.

Some of the nationalists aspired to form a revolutionary pan-African party and were at least nominally influenced by the ideas of Ghana's Kwame Nkrumah and Guinea's Sékou Touré. For these circles, the main task was revolutionary national-ist change in Africa and across the Atlantic African diaspora, and taking up issues like defending political prisoners or combating political repression were primarily means to that end. These groups were not single-issue organizations. Among the first efforts to unite these circles occurred in late March 1971, when Kwame Ture (Stokely Carmichael) gathered leaders from nationalist strongholds in the eastern half of the United States in Greensboro to lay plans for a party. That the meeting was convened in North Carolina was testament to the development of revolutionary nationalism in the state, which was represented by the SOBU and the Malcolm X Liberation University. Revolutionaries from Boston; Washington, D.C.; New York; Chicago; Atlanta; St. Petersburg; and Houston also attended. According to Ture, whose senti-ments were echoed by Nelson Johnson of SOBU, the chief obstacle to the movement's progress was of its own creation: the substitution of rhetoric and sloganeering for study and analysis, action, and organizing. Participants in the meeting promoted a mélange of theorists and strategists for mapping the movement, including the classical Russian Marxists Georgi Plekhanov and Nikolai Bukharin, Malcolm X, and Frantz Fanon, and they began a debate, which would intensify in the coming years, over the relative merits of Marxism and pan-Africanism as a guiding ideology. To promote clarity, Carmichael proposed opening a pan-Africanist bookstore. (Financial straits prevented it from coming to pass.) And recognizing that, in the words of one of the meeting's rapporteurs, "most of the political juice has been squeezed out of integration as an issue," the assembled leaders adumbrated plans for unifying likeminded groups and building alliances with organizations with which they shared more limited common goals. Their discussion produced a good survey of the topog-raphy, with initiatives to build an African liberation solidarity movement, work to influence a number of black nationalist collectives, develop ties with black workers' organizations like the Dodge Revolutionary Union Movement and the Black Workers Congress, and establish a liaison with religious organizations like the CRJ. Partici-pants in the meeting considered the SOBU to be the most developed organization; it made plans to extend beyond the college campus, where it was strong, and into communities such as Rocky Mount and the black GI coffeehouses in Fayetteville. See Charlotte Field Office to FBI Headquarters, 8 April 1971, letterhead memo, SOBU/ YOBU FBI Charlotte Field Office 157-CE-6758, NA; report received by G. Dargan Frierson, 11 March 1971, SOBU/YOBU FBI Charlotte Field Office 157-CE-6758, NA; Frank Williams to Brothers and Sisters, 26 January 1971, SOBU/YOBU FBI Charlotte Field Office 157-CE-6758, NA.

3. Dr. Helen Othow, telephone interview by author, 5 June 2007, notes in author's possession; "Ben Chavis–Wilmington 9 Legal Defense Committee," North Carolina Criminal Justice Task Force newsletter, April 1973, in Reddy Papers, box 2, folder 3; Helen Othow, "Here's to Jay Stroud," *Criminal Justice News*, October 1973, in Reddy

Papers, box 2, folder 3; report received by Special Agent Robert S. Shields, 15 January 1974, Committee of Racial Justice [*sic*] FBI Charlotte Field Office 157-8527, NA; Mendez interview by Rob Stephens, SOHPC.

4. Joyner interview by author.

5. Denominational histories of the UCC can be found at http://www.ucc.org/about-us/short-course/, accessed 22 May 2013, and http://www.ucc.org/about-us/hidden-histories/, accessed 22 May 2013.

6. "'Racist Posture' May Cause Va. and N.C., UCC Pastors' Exodus," *Philadelphia Tribune*, 30 January 1971, clipping in SCCHC, box "Black Church Dvlp," folder "Wilmington—Gregory"; "Chavis Sentenced to 25–29 Years," *Charlotte Observer*, 19 October 1972, clipping in Reddy Papers, box 2, folder 5.

7. James Lightbourne to Robert Moss, 13 December 1972, SCCHC, box "Social Justice CRJ," folder "Correspondence—Wilmington Ten"; James Lightbourne Jr. to Ministers of the Southern Conference, 20 December 1972, ibid.

8. James Lightbourne to Robert Moss, 22 December 1972, ibid.

9. Consistory, Zion UCC, Lenoir, N.C., to Robert Moss, 28 January 1973, ibid.; Shelbia Mullis to Secretary, Executive Council, United Church of Christ, 9 February 1973, ibid. The predominantly white Community UCC in Raleigh was notable for its support of the Wilmington Ten and the position of the national church hierarchy. See Richard King to Robert Moss, 28 February 1973, ibid.; Dudley O'Connell to James Lightbourne, 30 January 1976, ibid.; members of the First Evangelical and Reformed UCC, Asheboro, to Robert Moss, 16 March 1976, ibid. Russell Rollin, who succeeded James Lightbourne as conference minister, also recalled the intradenominational racial friction, and in particular the CRJ speaking on behalf of the UCC, when it was a principle that local congregations speak for themselves. Russell Rollin, interview by author, 14 May 2007, Hillsborough, N.C., notes in author's possession.

10. Dr. [Charles] Cobb, Gloria Dandridge, Leon White, Ben Chavis, and Irv Joyner, "Mobilization around Trial of Ben Chavis and General Synod Campaign around Securing Bail for the Wilmington 9" [May 1973]; Irv Joyner to Charles Cobb, 9 May 1973, memo, Commission for Racial Justice Collection #2002.21, box 79; Robert Moss to James Lightbourne, 2 January 1973, SCCHC, box "Social Justice CRJ," folder "Correspondence—Wilmington Ten"; Charles Cobb to Executive Council of the UCC, memo, 20 June 1975, SCCHC, box "Social Justice CRJ," folder "Correspondence—Wilmington Ten."

11. Commission for Racial Justice press release, March 1973, Commission for Racial Justice Collection #2002.21, box 1.

12. Commission for Racial Justice press release, 13 June 1973, leaflet announcing rally on 17 June 1973, and "Rally in Wilmington," *Criminal Justice News*, July 1973, all in Commission for Racial Justice Collection #2002.21, box 79; Inness Carlson to SAC, Charlotte, 10 July 1973, BYBBC FBI Charlotte Field Office 157-8263, NA; "'Watergate' Justice Seen Here," *Wilmington Star-News*, 18 June 1973, 1.

13. Irv Joyner to Ben Chavis, Bill Land, and Leon White, 29 January 1976, NAARPR Papers, box 14, folder "Memo: WM-10 work, UCC & WM-10 Comm," unprocessed ms., Schomburg Center for Research in Black Culture, New York Public Library; White interview by author, 11 June 2007.

14. H. M. "Mickey" Michaux Jr., interview by author, 6 June 2013, Raleigh, N.C., notes in author's possession.

15. Ibid.; H. M. "Mickey" Michaux Jr., interview by Joseph Mosnier, 23 June 1995 (#A-0392), SOHPC (#4007); Jordan, "Black Legislators"; Finger, "Minorities Get the Squeeze."

16. Report to Special Agent Richard Eisgruber, 20 June 1973, NCCFPP; "Report on the National Conference," *NC Political Prisoners Committee Newsletter* #9 [1972], ibid.

17. "Report on the National Conference," *NC Political Prisoners Committee Newsletter* #9 [1972], NCCFPP; Statement by the Reverend Dr. Everett C. Parker, Director, Office of Communication, United Church of Christ, 20 June 1974, Commission for Racial Justice Collection #2002.21, box 78; Marilyn Moore [assistant to executive director of CRJ] to Charles Cobb [executive director of CRJ], memo, 27 July 1976, Commission for Racial Justice Collection #2002.21, box 79; Coordinating Committee of the National Wilmington Ten Defense Committee to Charlene Mitchell, 13 September 1976, box 13, folder "Natl. Wm 10 Def. Comm," NAARPR Papers; Charlene Mitchell to Coordinating Committee of the National Wilmington Ten Defense Committee, 18 October 1976, box 13, folder "Natl. Wm 10 Def. Comm," NAARPR Papers; White interview by author, 11 June 2007.

18. "Chavis Says Coalition Will Fight Repression," *Raleigh News and Observer*, 6 February 1972, clipping in NCCFPP; Charles Cobb to Staff Members, CRJ, 26 July 1974, Commission for Racial Justice Collection #2002.21, box 79; Charles Cobb to Ben Chavis, 6 July 1981, Commission for Racial Justice Collection #2002.21, box 79; Charlene Mitchell to Ben Chavis, 8 September 1980, NAARPR Papers, box 11, folder "Ben Chavis."

19. "Chavis Says Coalition Will Fight Repression"; "A Call to a Founding Conference for a North Carolina Alliance against Racist & Political Repression, February 15–16, 1974," NCCFPP; "North Carolina Alliance Founding Conference Declares State a 'Disaster Area,'" *The Organizer* [newsletter of the NAARPR], March/April 1974, Reddy Papers, box 2, folder 2; report received by Special Agent Robert S. Shields, 15 February 1974, Committee of Racial Justice [*sic*] FBI Charlotte Field Office 157-8527, NA. On behavior modification programs in prisons in the 1960s and 1970s, see Cobb, "'Behavior Modification' in the Prison System."

20. Othow interview by author; Maria Ramos, telephone interview by author, 17 September 2010, notes in author's possession.

21. Othow interview by author; Ramos interview by author; "Unity Is Our Weapon" [July 1974], NAARPR Papers, box 36, folder "July 4, 1974"; "Effective Protest to Be 'Life or Death' for 31 on Death Row in N.C.," *The Organizer*, March/April 1974, in Reddy Papers, box 2, folder 2; "10,000 in N.C. Protest March," *Chicago Defender*, 9 July 1974, 4; "March in Raleigh against N.C. Racism," *Carolina Peacemaker*, 6 July 1974, 1; "4,000 March Here in Peaceful Protest," *Raleigh News and Observer*, 5 July 1974, 1; "Police, Patrol Keep Close Eye on March," *Raleigh News and Observer*, 5 July 1974, 1; "Marchers Hear Abernathy, Davis," *Raleigh News and Observer*, 5 July 1974, 7. For Joan Little, see McNeil, "'Joanne Is You and Joanne Is Me'"; and McGuire, *At the Dark End of the Street*, 246–78.

22. Report to Special Agent Goldberg, 13 August 1974, NCCFPP; Members and Friends Directory, North Carolina Alliance against Racist and Political Repression [October 1974], NAARPR Papers, box 36, folder "Directory—NC Alliance—Members and Friends"; Minutes of NAARPR Executive Board meeting, 5 July 1974, Reddy Papers, box 2, folder 2; Mike Myerson to W. W. Finlator, 22 July 1974, NAARPR Papers, box 36, folder "North Carolina Follow-up"; Michael Myerson to Carl Ferris, 25 July 1974, NAARPR Papers, box 30, folder "North Carolina Corres. Re: July 4th."

23. Minnie Brown to the Wilmington 10 Defense Committee, 15 May 1975, Reddy Papers, box 2, folder 5; William Lucy to Charlene Mitchell, 10 June 1975, ibid.; NAARPR letterhead from February 1976 listing national officers, NAARPR Papers, box 14, folder "W-10 Rally and Press Stmt, 2/2/76"; Frank Rosen and Frank Banks Jr. to Rufus Edmisten, 28 August 1975, NAARPR Papers, box 14, folder "W-10 Rally and Press Stmt, 2/2/76"; Frank E. Chapman Jr., telephone interview by author, 16 and 18 November 2010, notes in author's possession; Chapman, "Pages from the Life of a Black Prisoner, No. 4, 1971"; Chapman, "Black Prisoner Speaks Out."

24. "1,000 Rally Here, Protest Conviction of Wilmington 10," *Washington Post*, 1 June 1975, 3; "Joan Little Addresses Washington, D.C. Rally," *Wilmington Morning Star*, 1 June 1975, clipping in Wilmington Ten FBI Charlotte Field Office 176-37, NA; report received by SA Richard Goldberg, 2 June 1975, Wilmington Ten FBI Charlotte Field Office 176-37, NA; Crawford Williams to SAC (100–11890), 6 June 1975, Wilmington Ten FBI Charlotte Field Office 176-37, NA. Estimates of the number of attendees varied widely, with the *Post* counting 1,000, the *Morning Star* counting 1,200, and the FBI counting 4,000. Cong. Rec. 20162–163 (20 June 1975); Cong. Rec. 31509–510 (2 October 1975); Cong. Rec. 37002 (17 November 1975). For a good overview of the acceleration of support in 1975, see Eric Dreyer, "Vengeance and Justice in North Carolina," *Encore American and Worldwide News*, 21 June 1976, 10, 13–18.

25. State v. Chavis, 24 N.C. App. 148 (1974). All quotes in the discussion of the appeal are from this document.

26. Martin interview by Tom McLean, 28 October and 14 November 1996, pp. 110–111, SOHPC.

27. State v. Chavis, 24 N.C. App. 148 (1974).

28. Ibid.

29. State v. Chavis, 287 N.C. 261 (1975); Chavis v. North Carolina, 423 U.S. 1080 (1976).

30. Imani Kazana, interview by author, 19 May 2008, Hyattsville, Md., notes in author's possession; Imani Kazana to author, 27 May 2008, e-mail in author's possession; Imani Kazana to Charles Cobb, 9 March 1976, Commission for Racial Justice Collection #2002.21, box 1.

31. Imani Kazana to Charles Cobb, 9 March 1976, National Wilmington 10 Defense Committee Papers, box 448, folder "Letters to & from CRJ-NY & Alliance," unprocessed mss., Moorland-Spingarn Research Center, Howard University, Washington, D.C.; Kazana interview by author; Irv Joyner to Ben Chavis, Bill Land, and Leon White, 29 January 1976, NAARPR Papers, box 14, folder "Memo: WM-10 work, UCC & WM-10 Comm." The CRJ found it almost impossible to puncture the

suspicion of the white UCC congregations, which likely accounts for its inward focus; see Irv Joyner, "Proposal for National Education and Mobilization Campaign in Support of the Wilmington 10," 15 September 1976, SCCHC, box "Social Justice CRJ," folder "Correspondence—Wilmington Ten."

32. Imani Kazana to Charles Cobb, 9 March 1976, Commission for Racial Justice Collection #2002.21, box 1; Kazana interview by author. For an example of how larger and unrelated ideological and political differences tended to disrupt the agenda of the National Wilmington 10 Defense Committee, see The People [a Washington, D.C., black nationalist collective] to Imani Kazana, 25 February 1978; and Imani Kazana to The People, 7 March 1978, both in National Wilmington 10 Defense Committee Papers, box 447, folder "1978 Correspondence."

33. See the following in the National Wilmington 10 Defense Committee Papers, box 448, folder "Amnesty International": Angela Meentzen to Wilmington 10 Defense Committee, 11 March 1976; [Carolyn Moody] to Amnesty International International Secretariat, 26 July 1976; Anne Burley to Carolyn Moody, 12 August 1976; Imani Kazana to Carolyn Moody, 28 September 1976; Imani Kazana to Anne Burley, 28 September 1976; Imani Kazana to Anne Burley, 29 January 1977; Anne Burley to Imani Kazana, 4 March 1977.

34. Karsten Luethke [in Berlin], telephone interview by author, 26 June 2013, notes in author's possession.

35. Cmiel, "Emergence of Human Rights Politics in the United States"; Michael Myerson to Victor Grossman, 11 March 1976, NAARPR Papers, box 13, folder "Wilmington 10: Correspondence since 3/7/76"; Rev. Benjamin F. Chavis Jr., "Public Appeal to Belgrade Conference," *Peace Courier* [October 1977], copy in National Wilmington 10 Defense Committee Papers, box 448, folder "Correspondence to & from Ben"; Victor Grossman to author, 22 May 2013, e-mail in author's possession.

36. Stan Pottinger to Dan Rinzel, 25 February 1977, memo, box 49, CRD; Transcript of the President's News Conference, 13 June 1977, http://www.presidency .ucsb.edu/ws/?pid=7670, accessed 27 July 2013; Daniel Rinzel to Drew S. Days III, 1 March 1977, memo, box 49, CRD; Lani Guinier, telephone interview by author, 12 December 2007, notes in author's possession; Lani Guinier to author, 14 May 2008, e-mail in author's possession. Guinier was certain that though political considerations may have stimulated the decision to look into the case, neither she nor other staff attorneys working on the case were ordered to come to particular conclusions, which she said were arrived at solely on the case's merits.

37. Petition for Post-conviction Relief, State of North Carolina v. Benjamin F. Chavis, et al., 4 February 1977, Dan Pollitt Wilmington Ten Collection. Exhibit A of this petition is Hall's recantation, which is dated 4 August 1976. "The Untold Story of the Wilmington 10," *Greensboro Daily News*, 14 November 1976, reprinted in *Criminal Justice Issues*, November 1976, in Reddy Papers, box 2, folder 3; Kazana interview by author, 19 May 2008.

38. Transcript of Grand Jury Investigation in the Matter of the Wilmington Ten (1977), pt. 1, pp. 85–167, Dan Pollitt Wilmington Ten Collection.

39. Allen Hall recantation, 4 August 1976, included in Petition for Post-conviction Relief, 4 February 1977, Dan Pollitt Wilmington Ten Collection.

40. Transcript of Grand Jury Investigation in the Matter of the Wilmington Ten (1977), pt. 1, pp. 90–93.

41. Ibid., pt. 1, p. 143.

42. Ibid., pt. 2, p. 38.

43. Ibid., pt. 2, pp. 155–58.

44. Ibid., pt. 2, pp. 193–95.

45. James E. Ferguson to the Hon. George Fountain, 26 April 1977, and Fountain to Ferguson, 27 April 1977, Office of Attorney General Papers, Education and Corrections Section: Wilmington Ten Case File, Record Center box 1, folder "Cert. Pet & Pet. for Mandamus," SANC.

46. Transcript of Post-conviction Hearing, State of North Carolina v. Chavis (1977), p. 1662, Dan Pollitt Wilmington Ten Collection.

47. Luis Rèque, "The Wilmington Ten Case," 25 July 1977, Governor James B. Hunt Jr. Papers, General Correspondence, box 126.2, SANC.

48. "Rough Draft" of Order on Post-conviction Hearing, enclosed in Richard N. League to Honorable George M. Fountain, 17 June 1977; League to Fountain, 20 June 1977; League to Fountain, 21 June 1977; League to Fountain, 30 June 1977; all in Dan Pollitt Wilmington Ten Collection.

49. League to Fountain, 17 June 1977, Dan Pollitt Wilmington Ten Collection.

50. Motion for Production of State's Proposed Findings, Conclusions and Order, 23 August 1977; James E. Ferguson II to Richard N. League, 6 July 1977; League to Ferguson, 8 July 1977; Ferguson to League, 13 July 1977; League to Ferguson, 18 July 1977; Motion to Recuse, 23 August 1977; all in Judge George M. Fountain's Wilmington Ten Case File, 1971–1978, folder 6 (J. Ferg. corres & encl. motions), SANC; Order denying Motion for Production of State's Proposed Findings, Conclusions and Order, 13 September 1977, and Richard N. League to Frances Futch, Clerk, Superior Court of Pender County, 21 September 1977, both in Dan Pollitt Wilmington Ten Collection.

51. Motion for Production of State's Proposed Findings, Conclusions and Order, 23 August 1977, and Petition for Writ of Mandamus to the Superior Court of Pender County to Forthwith Order Petitioners' Discharge from Custody, 29 October 1977, both in Dan Pollitt Wilmington Ten Collection.

CHAPTER 5

1. Irv Joyner to Ben Chavis, Bill Land, and Leon White, 29 January 1976, NAARPR Papers, box 14, folder "Memo: WM-10 work, UCC & WM-10 Comm." On the recurring debate over the merits of black political organizing within the two-party system, see C. Johnson, *Revolutionaries to Race Leaders*, especially 195–202, which concerns the 1976 presidential election; and Dawson, *Blacks in and out of the Left*.

2. Amaker, "Faithfulness of the Carter Administration in Enforcing Civil Rights," 737–38; Sanders, "'Sad Duty of Politics.'"

3. On the North Carolina Fund, see Korstad and Leloudis, *To Right These Wrongs*; and Grimsley, *James B. Hunt*. See also Chafe, *Civilities and Civil Rights*.

4. W. W. Finlator to Fr. Charles Mulholland, Prof. Daniel Pollitt, and Rev. Collins Kilburn, 15 August 1977; W. W. Finlator to Signers of Open Letter to N.C. Gov. James B. Hunt, 19 September 1977, both in Dan Pollitt Wilmington Ten collection.

5. Stan Pottinger to Dan Rinzel, 1 November 1976, memo, Day Book, 15 November 1976, Stanley Pottinger Papers, box 111, folder "534—Wilmington Ten," Gerald R. Ford Library, Ann Arbor, Mich.

6. J. Stanley Pottinger, Memorandum for the Attorney General, 31 January 1977; Fay Cain, attorney general's secretary, appointment note [n.d.]; Stan Pottinger to Dan Rinzel, 25 February 1977; Brian Landesberg to Daniel Rinzel, re: Mr. Pottinger's memorandum, 25 February 1977; all in Pottinger Papers, box 111, folder "534—Wilmington Ten." On Griffin Bell's approach to civil rights during his tenure as attorney general, see "Discussant: Frank R. Parker," 751–53, and "Discussant: Drew S. Days III," 747–50, both in Rosenbaum and Urginsky, *Presidency and Domestic Policies of Jimmy Carter*.

7. "Senate Backs Bell as Attorney General," *New York Times*, 26 January 1977, A15; Cong. Rec. 7225–7226 (10 March 1977); Cong. Rec. 17463 (3 June 1977); Don Edwards to Griffin Bell, 7 June 1977, Ike Andrews Papers #4404, ser. 3, folder 221, SHC; Charles Cobb to John R. Deckenbeck, 7 April 1981, Commission for Racial Justice Collection #2002.21, box 79, unprocessed mss.

8. See, for example, the following works in *Current Digest of the Soviet Press*: I. Andronov, "If You Criticize—Off to the Madhouse!," 3 November 1976, 16–17, http://dlib.eastview.com/browse/doc/13635950, accessed 22 May 2014 (on psychiatric hospitals); V. Kobysh, "'Human Rights': For Export and at Home—American Political Prisoner Ben Chavis Talks with an Izvestia Correspondent," 22 June 1977, 7, http://dlib.eastview.com/browse/doc/13632158, accessed 22 May 2014 ("This disgraceful case"); Andrei Tolkunov, "Virus of McCarthyism," 12 April 1978, 17, http://dlib.eastview.com/browse/doc/13630522, accessed 22 May 2014; S. Kondrashov, "Observer's Notes: About a Certain American Anniversary," 3 May 1978, 15–16, http://dlib.eastview.com/browse/doc/13630092, accessed 22 May 2014; "In Defense of Human Rights," 14 June 1978, 3–4, http://dlib.eastview.com/browse/doc/13629535, accessed 22 May 2014; "The Capitalist World: Thousands of Political Prisoners," 9 August 1978, 4, http://dlib.eastview.com/browse/doc/13629656, accessed 22 May 2014; "Belated Admission," 13 December 1978, 20–21, http://dlib.eastview.com/browse/doc/13631330, accessed 22 May 2014; and Aleksandr Chakovsky, "An Open Letter to U.S. President J. Carter," 12 March 1980, 1–19, http://dlib.eastview.com/browse/doc/13625656, accessed 22 May 2014.

9. Cong. Rec. 22970–971 (26 July 1978); Cong. Rec. 23534–535 (31 July 1978).

10. "60 Minutes," 6 March 1977, transcript in Governor James B. Hunt Papers, Office of General Counsel, Legal Counsel—Files of Jack Cozort (1977–1984), box 12, folder "'60 Minutes' CBS Transcript (March 6, 1977)," SANC.

11. The President's News Conference, 13 June 1977, http://www.presidency.ucsb.edu/ws/index.php?pid=7670, accessed 29 May 2014; The President's News Conference, 15 December 1977, http://www.presidency.ucsb.edu/ws/index.php?pid=7016, accessed 29 May 2014.

12. [Article, missing a title, on the Carnegie Hall protest], [*Greensboro Daily News*], 10 March 1977, clipping in SCCHC, box "Social Justice CRJ," folder "Wilmington Ten"; "Symphony Heading for Carnegie to Bolster 'New Image' of South," *New York Times*, 8 March 1977, 22; "Concert: Disciplined North Carolina Symphony Comes to Town," *New York Times*, 12 March 1977, 24; "N.C. Case Provokes Allegations," *Daily Tar Heel*, 16 March 1977, 1; "N.C. License Plate Decision Is Expected," *Lewiston (Maine) Daily Sun*, 10 April 1975, 29, http://news.google.com/newspapers?nid=1928&dat=19750410&id=_Q8gAAAAIBAJ&sjid=CmYFAAAAIBAJ&pg=2264,1511092, accessed 30 May 2014; "License Decision Delights Edmisten," *Wilmington Morning Star*, 22 April 1977, 1D, http://news.google.com/newspapers?nid=1454&dat=19770422&id=YhtOAAAAIBAJ&sjid=GBMEAAAAIBAJ&pg=3588,4081603, accessed 30 May 2014; "Boycott Splits '10' Backers," *Raleigh News and Observer*, 23 December 1977, clipping in SCCHC, box "Social Justice CRJ," folder "Wilmington Ten"; Southern Conference, United Church of Christ press statement, n.d., SCCHC, box "Social Justice CRJ," folder "Wilmington Ten."

13. Open Letter to Governor Hunt, [1 September 1977], Dan Pollitt Wilmington Ten Collection; W. W. Finlator to Signers of Open Letter to N.C. Gov. James B. Hunt, 19 September 1977, ibid.

14. Charles Cobb and Irv Joyner, Wilmington Ten Mobilization and Education Report—1977–78, delivered to the 12th General Synod of the United Church of Christ, 20 April 1979, Commission for Racial Justice Collection #2002.21, box 1, unprocessed mss.; "Pardon for '10' Discussed Again," *Raleigh News and Observer*, 19 October 1977, clipping in Dan Pollitt Wilmington Ten Collection; "Letter Asking Pardon for '10' Present to Governor Hunt," *Raleigh News and Observer*, 2 September 1977, clipping in Dan Pollitt Wilmington Ten Collection.

15. "Edmisten Meets with Bell on Wilmington 10 Case, Seeks to Have Case Resolved," *Hendersonville (N.C.) Times-News*, 24 March 1977, http://news.google.com/newspapers?nid=1665&dat=19770324&id=4aojAAAAIBAJ&sjid=dSQEAAAAIBAJ&pg=5408,2409836, accessed 4 June 2014; Rufus Edmisten, quoted in "The Attorney General Has Left His Job," *The Carolinian*, March 31, 1977, reprinted in *The Wilmington 10 Editorials and Cartoons* ([New York?]: United Church of Christ, Commission for Racial Justice, 1977); "Attorney General Stepped Out of Line," *Wilmington Morning Star*, 21 May 1977, http://news.google.com/newspapers?nid=1454&dat=19770521&id=sLUsAAAAIBAJ&sjid=KBMEAAAAIBAJ&pg=4081,3916667, accessed 4 June 2014; "Wilmington 10," letter to the editor, *Wilmington Morning Star*, 3 June 1977, http://news.google.com/newspapers?nid=1454&dat=19770603&id=erosAAAAIBAJ&sjid=JRMEAAAAIBAJ&pg=2112,451872, accessed 4 June 2014.

16. Richard League to Jack Cozart, 16 December 1977, Office of Attorney General Papers, Education and Corrections Section: Wilmington Ten Case File, Record Center box 2, "Chavis Post Conviction Hearing File #2," SANC.

17. Text of governor's statement on Wilmington 10, *Raleigh News and Observer*, 24 January 1978, 5A; Grimsley, *James B. Hunt*, chap. 10. All quotes from Hunt's statement in this and the next three paragraphs are from the *Raleigh News and Observer*.

18. North Carolina Association of Black Lawyers, "The Wilmington 10 Decision: Governor Hunt's Abdication of Leadership," background briefing paper, 28 January 1978, Dan Pollitt Wilmington Ten Collection.

19. Michaux interview by author; Grimsley, *James B. Hunt*, 146. For a survey of white opinion in North Carolina on Hunt's decision, see "Hunt Gets Praise, Criticism," *Raleigh News and Observer*, 25 January 1978, 1.

20. "NC Reaction on 10 Varies," *Raleigh News and Observer*, 24 January 1978, 1; "Political Aftermath of Decision Unclear," ibid., 25 January 1978, 5A; "Ten Supporter Named to Commission," *Chapel Hill Newspaper*, 31 January 1978, clipping in Dan Pollitt Wilmington Ten Collection. This configuration may have looked more pronounced in North Carolina because of the perceived practical considerations in delineating friends and allies in the home state of the Wilmington Ten. It may be that similar configurations occurred in other localities and for similar considerations. For example, black activists-cum-electoral politicians may have remained on the side of Atlanta's black mayor Maynard Jackson when he foiled a strike by sanitation workers in order to grasp levers of power. But such a timorous approach was not the only one by the black political figures inside and outside the state. The Commission for Racial Justice, of course, maintained its steadfast critique of Tar Heel politics; because it kept faith with its permanent interests and avoided permanent allies, it was free to dissent from politicians who took black votes for granted. Affiliates of the NAARPR, too, stirred up officials in different locations to confront Hunt and Carter; according to Ben Chavis, the national alliance was particularly skilled at developing favorable opinion among elected officials. And separately, the District of Columbia's city council, the Congressional Black Caucus, and the National Conference of Black Mayors bucked their local, state, and national Democratic establishments. On alternatives to falling into line with leading elected politicians and examples thereof, see Reed, "A Critique of Neoprogressivism in Theorizing about Local Development Policy: A Case from Atlanta," in *Stirrings in the Jug*, 163–77; "Orlinski Asks U.S. to Support Wilmington 10," *Baltimore Afro-American*, 22 October 1977, http://news.google.com/newspapers?nid=1715&dat=19771022&id=ELpjAAAAI BAJ&sjid=sioMAAAAIBAJ&pg=2092,10782197, accessed 11 June 2014; Ben Chavis to All National, Regional, and Local Organizations Working in Defense of The Wilmington, N.C., Ten, 21 June 1976, Commission for Racial Justice Collection #2002.21, box 78, unprocessed mss.; "D.C. Panel Considers Boycott of North Carolina Products," *Lexington (N.C.) Dispatch*, 24 May 1978, 12, http://news.google.com/newspapers? nid=1734&dat=19780524&id=R-EbAAAAIBAJ&sjid=klEEAAAAIBAJ&pg= 5569,2309495, accessed 11 June 2014; "Black Caucus Leader Critical of Carter," *Spokane Spokesman-Review*, 13 February 1979, 5, http://news.google.com/ newspapers?nid=1314&dat=19790213&id=7D10AAAAIBAJ&sjid=B-4DAAAA IBAJ&pg=7366,6423182, accessed 11 June 2014; "Black Mayors Hit at Carter," *Tuscaloosa News*, 21 July 1978, 19, http://news.google.com/newspapers?nid=1817& dat=19780721&id=6QgdAAAAIBAJ&sjid=5Z4EAAAAIBAJ&pg=6560,4618528, accessed 11 June 2014.

21. "Young Declares 'Wilmington 10' Were Innocent," *Washington Star*, 14 August 1977, clipping in SCCHC, box "Social Justice CRJ," file "Wilmington Ten"; "Young Says 'Wilmington 10' Are Innocent," *Los Angeles Times*, 14 August 1977,

A11; Transcript of President's News Conference on Foreign and Domestic Matters, 21 July 1978, http://query.nytimes.com/mem/archive/pdf?res=F30A13F 8345513728DDDA80A94DF405B888BF1D3, accessed 20 January 2014; draft of open letter to Jimmy Carter, [September 1978], Dan Pollitt Wilmington Ten Collection; on Ann Shepard's release from prison, see "Sentence Was 34 Years, *New York Times*, 15 December 1979, 10.

22. Ed [Smith] to Seymour [Wishman], 2 February 1978, memo; Ed [Smith] to Midge [Costanza], 3 February 1978, memo; Margaret Costanza to the President, 10 February 1978, memo; all in Public Liaison Files, box 35, Seymour Wishman series, folder "Wilmington 10 [North Carolina Civil rights] 1/78/2/78 [O/A 4495]," Jimmy Carter Library, Atlanta.

23. Ed [Smith] to Midge [Costanza], 3 February 1978, memo; Ed [Smith] to Midge [Costanza], 10 February 1978, memo (*"States Rights"*); Robert J. Lipshutz (Counsel to the President) to Imani Kazana, 22 February 1978; all in ibid.

24. Louis Martin to Anne Wexler, 13 September 1978, memo; Louis Martin to ~~Dear Governor~~ Jim [Hunt], 20 September 1978, Special Assistant to the President Files, box 107, Louis Martin series, folder "Wilmington Ten [1]," Jimmy Carter Library, Atlanta. Alex Poinsett's *Walking with Presidents* is an insightful biography of Martin; chapter 8 pays special attention to his years in the Carter administration and offers the observation about Carter's relationships with black churches and politicians.

25. Drew Days, "Human Rights, Home Style," speech to the Alabama Black Lawyers Association, 11 November 1977; Drew Days to Terry Adamson, 18 January 1978, memo; Lani Guinier to Brian Landsberg, 20 March 1978, memo; Lani Guinier to Drew Days III, 3 March 1978, memo, all in box 49, CRD; Guinier interview by author; Lani Guinier to author, 14 May 2008, e-mail in author's possession; "60 minutes," 19 March 1978, transcript in North Carolina Collection, University of North Carolina Library, Chapel Hill.

26. Daniel F. Rinzel to Files, 24 June 1977, box 49, CRD; "1 of '10' Praises Hunt, Says He'd Vote for Him," *Charlotte Observer*, 28 January 1978, clipping in Reddy Papers, box 2, folder 6; for comments on Joe Wright, see Moore, *Triumphant Warrior*, 206–8; and Thomas Wright, interview by author, 21 September 2004, Raleigh, N.C., notes in author's possession.

27. "8,000 Rally at White House," *Washington Post*, 19 March 1978, B1; "The Gentle Protester Elizabeth Chavis, Is Up Front Now," ibid., 18 March 1978, C1; "3,000 Marchers Protest U.S.–South African Ties," ibid., 21 May 1978, C2. (The North Carolina Coalition to Free the Wilmington Ten—discussed below—estimated the May rally's attendance at 10,000.)

28. "Carter Arrives in Fayetteville for Wedding; Avoiding Public Eye" and "Hunt Receives Petition Asking for '10's' Release," both in *Hendersonville (N.C.) Times-News*, 17 December 1977, http://news.google.com/newspapers?nid=1665&dat=19771217&id= Az5PAAAAIBAJ&sjid=LiQEAAAAIBAJ&pg=6881,6481281, accessed 11 June 2014.

29. "President Carter Tries to Soothe Tar Heels," *Spartanburg Herald-Journal*, 18 March 1978, http://news.google.com/newspapers?nid=1876&dat=19780317&id=RYI sAAAAIBAJ&sjid=ps0EAAAAIBAJ&pg=6818,4082570, accessed 11 June 2014; a

brief biographical sketch of Joseph Felmet is at http://www2.1ib.unc.edu/mss/inv/f/
Felmet,Joseph.html#d1e146.

30. "Delegation Wants Carter's ear," *Wilmington Morning Star*, 29 July 1978, 1B;
"Carter Praises Tobacco . . . ," *Wilmington Sunday Star-News*, 6 August 1978, 1A; ". . .
As Supporters of '10' Jeer Him," *Wilmington Sunday Star-News*, 6 August 1978, 1A;
Helen Thomas, "Carter 'Managing' the News," *Lodi News-Sentinel*, 14 August 1978, 6,
http://news.google.com/newspapers?nid=2245&dat=19780814&id=NOAzAAAAIBA
J&sjid=bDIHAAAAIBAJ&pg=5112,4586855, accessed 11 June 2014.

31. Dawson, *Blacks in and out of the Left*, 98–100; Dawson, *Black Visions*, 196–98.

32. Bermanzohn, *Through Survivors' Eyes*, parts 1 and 2; Waller, *Love and
Revolution*, part 1.

33. "Suspended Term Given in Slaying," *Raleigh News and Observer*, 20 September
1977, 1; Bermanzohn, *Through Survivors' Eyes*, 139–43; Waller, *Love and Revolution*,
118–20; "Protesters Ask Justice in Cummings, Ten Cases," *Carolina Peacemaker*, 11
February 1978, clipping courtesy Signe Waller; "Two Deputies Will Serve Six Months,"
Greensboro Record, 7 April 1978, clipping courtesy Signe Waller. The characterization
of the Judge family as "wild" and the source of their wealth circa 1977 is from a telephone conversation with Whitakers town administrator Gwen Parker, 18 June 2014.

34. A comprehensive overview of the North Carolina Coalition to Free the
Wilmington Ten can be found in "Wilmington 10: Broad Struggle Serves to Build the
Party," *Workers Viewpoint*, April 1978, 1, 23–26.

35. Handwritten notes of the meeting of the North Carolina Coalition to Free
the Wilmington Ten, [18 February 1978 or 18 March 1978], John Kenyon Chapman
Papers, box 1, folder 1, SHC.

36. "10 Civil Disobedience Hinted," *Greensboro Daily News*, 24 March 1978, clipping courtesy Signe Waller; "Frustrated '10' Backers Promise Rougher Tactics," ibid.,
24 March 1978, clipping courtesy Signe Waller.

37. Leaflet publicizing the 1 April 1978 rally to free the Wilmington Ten, John
Kenyon Chapman Papers, box 1, folder 1, SHC.

38. "Two Local Rallies Herald 'Ten' March," *Carolina Peacemaker*, 1 April 1978,
clipping courtesy Signe Waller; chant sheet for the 1 April 1978 rally to free the
Wilmington Ten, John Kenyon Chapman Papers, box 1, folder 1, SHC.

39. "Nelson Johnson Arrested," *Carolina Peacemaker*, 8 April 1978, clipping courtesy Signe Waller; "10 Rally Marred by Arrests on Assault, Noise Charges," *Greensboro
Daily News*, 2 April 1978, clipping courtesy Signe Waller; "1,500 Backers of '10' March
on State Capitol," *Raleigh News and Observer*, 2 April 1978, 8; "Wilmington 10: Broad
Struggle Serves to Build the Party," *Workers Viewpoint*, April 1978, 1, 23–26.

40. North Carolina Coalition to Free the Wilmington Ten to Brothers and Sisters,
14 March 1978, John Kenyon Chapman Papers, box 1, folder 1, SHC.

41. Application for writ of habeas corpus, 1 April 1976, Chavis v. State of North
Carolina 637 F.2d 213 (4th Cir. 1980), record on appeal, pp. 291–95; petitioners' reply
to respondents' answer and petitioners' response to respondents' motion to dismiss,
22 July 1976, ibid., record on appeal, pp. 328–43; application for writ of habeas
corpus, 23 January 1978, ibid., record on appeal, pp. 677–81; answer to petition and
motion to dismiss, 6 March 1978, ibid., record on appeal, pp. 682–99.

42. Motion for emergency relief and to amend original petition for a writ of habeas corpus, 31 October 1977, copy in Dan Pollitt Wilmington Ten Collection; order on motion for joinder and consolidation and memorandum and recommendation on one habeas corpus claim, 7 July 1978, Chavis v. State of North Carolina 637 F.2d 213 (4th Cir. 1980), record on appeal, pp. 802–5; James Ferguson to Franklin Dupree, 20 February 1978, and John T. Redmond to Franklin Dupree, 1 March 1978, Franklin T. Dupree Papers, #4806, subseries 3.2, box 74, folder 1275, SHC.

43. Richard League to Franklin Dupree, 5 December 1977; League to Dupree, 23 February 1978; James Ferguson to Franklin Dupree, 20 February 1978 (emphasis added), all in Dupree Papers, subseries 3.2, box 74, folder 1275, SHC.

44. Richard League to Jack Cozart, 16 December 1977, and Richard League to Andrew Vanore, 7 February 1978, memo, Office of Attorney General Papers, Education and Corrections Section: Wilmington Ten Case File, Record Center box 2, "Chavis Post Conviction Hearing File #2," SANC; Richard League to Franklin Dupree, 5 January 1979, Dupree Papers, subseries 3.2, box 74, folder 1275, SHC.

45. Franklin Dupree to Logan Howell, 24 January 1978, memo, Dupree Papers, subseries 3.2, box 74, folder 1275, SHC.

46. Franklin Dupree to James Ferguson, 24 November 1978, ibid.

47. Memorandum and Recommendation (Logan D. Howell), 9 September 1977, Chavis v. State of North Carolina 637 F.2d 213 (4th Cir. 1980), record on appeal, pp. 599–669 (quote is on 669).

48. Franklin Dupree to James Ferguson, 21 November 1978; James Ferguson to Logan Howell, 22 November 1978; James Ferguson to Logan Howell, 4 December 1978; Logan Howell to James Ferguson, 30 November 1978; Franklin Dupree to James Ferguson, 24 November 1978; Franklin Dupree to Logan Howell, 5 February 1979, memo; Logan Howell to Franklin Dupree, 6 February 1979; Franklin Dupree to Rufus Stark, 22 March 1979, all in Dupree Papers, subseries 3.2, box 74, folder 1275, SHC; "Lawyer Says '10' Delayed by Magistrate," *Wilmington Morning Star*, 19 March 1979. See the following in the Dupree Papers, subseries 3.2, box 74, folder 1275, SHC: Logan Howell to Franklin Dupree, 30 March 1979; Logan Howell, draft addendum to memorandum and recommendation, 30 March 1979; James Ferguson to Logan Howell, 19 July 1979.

49. See Motion of the United States for leave to file brief as amicus curiae, [November 1978], copy in author's possession courtesy Brian Landesberg; motion of the United States for leave to file appendix analyzing Allen Hall's amended statement, 14 November 1978, Chavis v. State of North Carolina 637 F.2d 213 (4th Cir. 1980), record on appeal, pp. 815–18; appendix E to motion of United States, Chavis v. State of North Carolina 637 F.2d 213 (4th Cir. 1980), record on appeal, pp. 819–33; Guinier interview by author; Order of F. T. Dupree, 1 December 1978, Chavis v. State of North Carolina 637 F.2d 213 (4th Cir. 1980), record on appeal, p. 840.

50. Lani Guinier to Drew Days, 28 April 1978, box 52, CRD.

51. Brief for the United States as Amicus Curiae, Chavis v. State of North Carolina, copy in Office of Attorney General Papers, Education and Corrections Section: Wilmington Ten Case File, Record Center box 2, "United States Amicus Brief, etc.," SANC.

52. Memorandum of decision and order, 19 June 1979, Chavis v. State of North Carolina 637 F.2d 213 (4th Cir. 1980), record on appeal, pp. 1097–1100.

53. Dupree to Howell, 24 January 1978; Dupree to Howell, 23 March 1979; Bill Pappas to Franklin Dupree, 2 April 1979, all in Dupree Papers, subseries 3.2, box 74, folder 1275, SHC.

54. Dupree to Howell, 23 March 1979; Franklin Dupree to Anne Braden, 22 November 1978, both in Dupree Papers, subseries 3.2, box 74, folder 1275, SHC; memorandum of decision and order, Chavis v. State of North Carolina 637 F.2d 213 (4th Cir. 1980), record on appeal, pp. 1097–1100.

55. "Last Defendant in a Firebombing Is Released from Carolina Prison," *New York Times*, 15 December 1979, 10.

56. Wayne King, "The Case against the Wilmington Ten," *New York Times Magazine*, 3 December 1978, 60ff.

57. "The Wilmington One," *Wall Street Journal*, 6 December 1978, clipping attached to Charles E. Cobb to Frederick Taylor, 8 December 1978, Commission for Racial Justice Collection #2002.21, box 79.

58. Mark Pinsky, telephone interview by author, 24 May 2012, notes in author's possession. Pinsky contends that the same mistake has plagued other attempts to redress judicial wrongs, including Sacco and Vanzetti and Julius and Ethel Rosenberg.

59. Chavis v. State of North Carolina 637 F.2d 213 (4th Cir. 1980); Response in Opposition to Motion for Leave to File Brief as Amici Curiae, 1 February 1980, ibid., record on appeal, no page.

60. "No Appeal Planned in Race Strife Case," *New York Times*, 19 December 1980, D19.

61. "Former Gov. Bev Perdue Talks about the Wilmington 10," 6 February 2013, http://www.wncn.com/video?clipId=8332400, accessed 19 December 2013.

CONCLUSION

1. "Judge Clears 'Wilmington 10' Defendant," *Wilmington Sunday Star-News*, 4 March 1990, 1C; "Friends, Family Remember Wright," *Wilmington Morning Star*, 20 June 1990, 1A; "Joe Wright's Legacy," *Wilmington Morning Star*, 19 June 1990, letter to the editor, 8A.

2. "'10' Member Sees Very Little Change in Racist Attitudes," *Wilmington Morning Star*, 27 December 1979, 1A; "Free at Last? Not Yet," ibid., 11 March 1979, 4D; "The Wilmington 10," *Wilmington Sunday Star-News*, 18 February 1996, 1D; "The Wilmington 10 Case: Trial and Prison," *Wilmington Morning Star*, 10 February 1986, 1; "Jacobs' Death Brought End to a Tormented Life," *Wilmington Morning Star*, 21 March 1989, 1A.

3. "'10' Member Sees Very Little Change in Racist Attitudes," 1A; "The Wilmington 10 Case: Trial and Prison," 1; "The Wilmington 10 (Part 4): Forty Years Later with Francine DeCoursey," http://whqr.org/post/wilmington-10-part-4-forty-years-later-francine-decoursey, accessed 18 July 2014; Moore, *Triumphant Warrior*.

4. Ben Chavis to author, 3 February 2006, e-mail in author's possession.

5. Myerson, *Nothing Could Be Finer*, 56–57. For a small but representative sample of reporting on the conflict in Ayden and Pitt County, see "This Has Got to Stop!," *African World*, 21 August 1971, 1; "8 Bombings, 300 Arrests in Ayden," *African World*, 18 September 1971, 3; "Arrest 33 Marchers in Ayden for Parading without Permit," *Greenville (N.C.) Daily Reflector*, 22 September 1971, 1; and "Terrorism Said Turning Ayden into Armed Camp," *Greenville (N.C.) Daily Reflector*, 10 September 1971, 2. See also the analysis of the Human Relations Commission in Leonard Wiggins to Fred Cooper and Preston Hill, 1 October 1971, DAP, box 14, folder "Pitt County, 1971." See as well documents related to Pitt County in Governor Robert Scott Papers, box 332, folders "Highway Patrol, Reports I" and "Highway Patrol, Reports II," and box 324, folder "SBI reports," SANC.

6. Dawson, *Blacks in and out of the Left*.

7. Bloom and Martin, *Black against Empire*.

8. Clement Haynsworth to Judge Bryan and Judge Winter, 29 April 1980, and Clement Haynsworth to Harrison Winter, 10 November 1980, Harrison L. Winter Papers, Ms. 195, box 2.83, folder "Case #80-8064," Milton Eisenhower Library, Johns Hopkins University, Baltimore.

Bibliography

PRIMARY SOURCES

Court and Legal Records

Chavis v. North Carolina, 423 U.S. 1080 (1976).

Chavis v. State of North Carolina 637 F.2d 213 (4th Cir. 1980).

State v. Chavis, 24 N.C. App. 148 (1974).

State v. Chavis, 287 N.C. 261 (1975).

State of North Carolina vs. Tommy Atwood, James Bunting, Benjamin F. Chavis, Carnell E. Flowers, Jerry Jacobs (Alias Scarface), James McKoy, Marvin Patrick, Ann Shepherd, Connie Tindall, Willie E. Vereen, and Michael Peterson, Original Transcript of Probable Cause Hearing, 30 March 1972, http://www.justice.gov/crt/foia/readingroom/wilmington/, accessed 18 June 2012.

State of North Carolina vs. Benjamin Franklin Chavis, Marvin Patrick, Connie Tyndall [*sic*], Jerry Jacobs, Willie Earl Vereen, James McKoy, Reginald Epps, Wayne Moore, Joe Wright, George Kirby, and Ann Shepard, Transcript of Testimony [of first trial], http://www.justice.gov/crt/foia/readingroom/wilmington/, accessed 18 June 2012.

State of North Carolina vs. Benjamin Franklin Chavis, Marvin Patrick, Connie Tyndall [*sic*], Jerry Jacobs, Willie Earl Vereen, James McKoy, Reginald Epps, Wayne Moore, Joe Wright, George Kirby, and Ann Shepard, Transcript of Testimony [of second trial], http://www.justice.gov/crt/foia/readingroom/wilmington/, accessed 18 June 2012.

State of North Carolina vs. Allen Hall, 71-CR-7269, microfilm reel no. 72-18-266, Office of the Clerk of Superior Court of New Hanover County, Wilmington, N.C.

State of North Carolina vs. Allen Hall, 71-CR-7270, microfilm reel no. 72-18-265, Office of the Clerk of Superior Court of New Hanover County, Wilmington, N.C.

State of North Carolina vs. Allen R. Hall, 71-CR-8195, microfilm reel no. 72-18-264, Office of the Clerk of Superior Court of New Hanover County, Wilmington, N.C.

State of North Carolina vs. Donald Jerome Nixon, 71-CR-17668, microfilm reel no. 73-16-151, Office of the Clerk of Superior Court of New Hanover County, Wilmington, N.C.

State of North Carolina vs. Donald Jerome Nixon, 71-CR-17685, microfilm reel no. 73-16-151, Office of the Clerk of Superior Court of New Hanover County, Wilmington, N.C.

Interviews Conducted by Author

Ballance, Frank, 20 December 2008, Butner, N.C.

Chapman, Frank E., Jr., 16 and 18 November 2010, by telephone.

Coleman, Milton, 16 November 2007, by telephone.

Ferguson, James, 27 June 2007, Charlotte, N.C.

Grant, Jim, 15 December 2004, Chapel Hill, N.C.

Grossman, Victor, 22 May 2013, by e-mail.

Guinier, Lani, 12 December 2007, by telephone.

Hankins, Lethia, 11 November 2004, Wilmington, N.C.

Hulslander, Mac, 7 June 2007, Raleigh, N.C.

Hunoval, Mathias [in Belize], 25 April 2014, by telephone.

Jennings, Harvard, 16 August 2006, by telephone.

Johnson, Aaron, 22 September 2004, Fayetteville, N.C.

Johnson, Dale, 15 August 2012, by telephone.

Jones, Charles, 16 June 2005, Atlanta, Ga.

Joyner, Irv, 1 December 2006, Durham, N.C.

Kazana, Imani, 19 May 2008, Hyattsville, Md.

Kirby, George, 5 October 2004, Wrightsville Beach, N.C.

Landsberg, Brian, 3 June 2008, by telephone.

Luethke, Karsten [in Berlin], 26 June 2013, by telephone.

Michaux, H. M. "Mickey," Jr., 6 June 2013, Raleigh, N.C.

Moore, Delores, 19 July 2004, Wilmington, N.C.

Moore, Wayne, 9 April 2005, Ann Arbor, Mich.

Othow, Helen, 5 June 2007, by telephone.

Parker, Gwen [Whitakers, N.C., town administrator],
    18 June 2014, by telephone.

Pinsky, Mark, 24 May 2012, by telephone.

Ramos, Maria, 17 September 2010, by telephone.

Rollin, Russell, 14 May 2007, Hillsborough, N.C.

Templeton, Donna, 24 August 2004, by telephone.

Templeton, Eugene, 27 August 2004, Chapel Hill, N.C.

Tindall, Connie, 31 October 2004, Kenansville, N.C.

Todd, Bertha, 11 November 2004, Wilmington, N.C.

Weatherman, Tony, 2 November 2004, by telephone.

White, Leon, 30 July 2004 and 11 June 2007, Manson, N.C.

Wonce, Benjamin, 14 August 2011, Wilmington, N.C.

Wright, Thomas, 21 September 2004, Raleigh, N.C.

Interviews Conducted by Larry Thomas, Deposited in the Duke University Oral History Program Collection, David M. Rubenstein Rare Book and Manuscript Library, Duke University

Anonymous black male [appended to Walter Bordeaux transcript], n.d. [1978].

"Barnabus" and Darryl Franks (aka "Daniel Banks"), 14 May 1978.

C-Man, 12 and 16 August 1978.

Grant, Jim, 10 July 1978

Templeton, Eugene, 1 August 1978.

Interviews Deposited at the Lower Cape Fear Historical Society,
Wilmington, N.C.

Laney, Emsley, 14 June 1995.

Todd, Bertha, 13 June 1995.

Swain, Ernest, 20 June 1995.

Interviews Deposited in the Oral History Collection, William M. Randall Library
Special Collections, University of North Carolina at Wilmington

Bellamy, Heyward, 19 April 2005.

Burnett, Gilbert H., 4 October 2002.

Moore, Wayne, and Benjamin Wonce, 17 April 2009.

Interviews Deposited in the Southern Oral History Program Collection,
Southern Historical Collection, Wilson Library, University of North Carolina
at Chapel Hill

Ferguson, James E., interview by Rudolph Acree Jr., 3 March 1992 and 17 March
1992, interview #J-0004.

Martin, Judge Robert McKinney, Jr., interview by Tom McLean, 28 October 1996 and
14 November 1996, interview #J-0043.

Mendez, John, interview by Rob Stephens, 6 February 2008, interview #U-0304.

Michaux, H. M. "Mickey," Jr., interview by Joseph Mosnier, 23 June 1995, interview
#A-0392.

Muhammad, Benjamin Chavis, interview by Kieran Taylor, 3 February 2006,
interview #U-0332.

Nantambu, Kojo, interview by Larry Thomas, 15 May 1978, interview #B-59.

Templeton, Donna, interview by Larry Thomas, 28 July 1978, interview #B-61.

Whitfield, Edward, interview by Bridgette Burge, 26 February 2006, interview
#U-0590.

Interviews Conducted by Others

Chavis, Ben, interview by Blackside, Inc., for *Eyes on the Prize II: America at the*
Racial Crossroads 1965 to 1985, 18 April 1989, Henry Hampton Collection, Film
and Media Archive, Washington University Libraries, St. Louis, Mo.

Yopp, Albert, Jr., interview by Timothy Tyson, 15 August 1992, Duke University Oral
History Program Collection, David M. Rubenstein Rare Book and Manuscript
Library, Duke University, Durham, N.C.

Manuscript Collections

Black Panther Party—North Carolina, FBI Headquarters File 105-165706-8, Section 10, http://vault.fbi.gov/Black%20Panther%20Party%20/Black%20Panther%20 Party%20Part%2024%20°f%2034/view.

Black Panther Party—North Carolina, FBI Headquarters File 105-165706-8, Section 11, http://nara-wayback-001.us.archive.org/peth04/20041019151532/http://foia .fbi.gov/bpanther/bpanther12.pdf.

Heyward C. Bellamy Papers, William M. Randall Library Special Collections, University of North Carolina at Wilmington.

Commission for Racial Justice Collection #2002.21, unprocessed manuscript, United Church of Christ Archives, Cleveland, Ohio.

National Alliance against Racist and Political Repression Papers, unprocessed manuscript, Schomburg Center for Research in Black Culture, New York Public Library, New York.

National Wilmington 10 Defense Committee Papers, unprocessed manuscript, Moorland-Spingarn Research Center, Howard University, Washington, D.C.

Dan Pollitt Wilmington Ten Collection, unprocessed manuscript, in author's possession.

Stanley Pottinger Papers, Gerald R. Ford Library, Ann Arbor, Mich.

Public Liaison Files, Jimmy Carter Library, Atlanta, Ga.

T. J. Reddy Papers, J. Murrey Atkins Library Special Collections, University of North Carolina at Charlotte.

Southern Conference Church History Collection, unprocessed manuscript, Belk Library Archives and Special Collections, Elon University, Elon, N.C.

Special Assistant to the President Files, Jimmy Carter Library, Atlanta, Ga.

Signe Waller Wilmington Ten Collection, unprocessed manuscript, privately held.

Wilmington Movement 1971 clipping file, MS108, William M. Randall Library Special Collections, University of North Carolina at Wilmington.

Harrison L. Winter Papers, Milton Eisenhower Library, Johns Hopkins University, Baltimore, Md.

National Archives, College Park, Md.

BYBBC FBI Charlotte Field Office 157-8263.

Benjamin Chavis FBI Headquarters 157-HQ-12210.

Civil Rights Division: Subject Files of Drew Days III, 1977–80. General Records of the Department of Justice, RG60.

Classification 157 Field Office Case Files (Charlotte, N.C.), 1957–1978, 157-177-Sub L-3, RG65 Federal Bureau of Investigation.

Committee of Racial Justice [*sic*] FBI Charlotte Field Office 157-8527.

North Carolina Committee to Free Political Prisoners FBI Charlotte Field Office 157-CE-8777.

ROWP FBI Charlotte Field Office 157-7236.

SOBU/YOBU FBI Charlotte Field Office 157-CE-6758.

Wilmington Ten FBI Charlotte Field Office 176–37.
Wilmington Ten FBI HQ 157-8056.

Newspapers and Collections of Newspaper Articles

African World

Baltimore Afro-American

Black Panther

Carolina Peacemaker

Carolina Times

Chicago Defender

Current Digest of the Soviet Press.

Daily Tar Heel

Greenville (N.C.) Daily Reflector

Hendersonville (N.C.) Times-News

Lewiston (Maine) Daily Sun

Lexington (N.C.) Dispatch

Lodi (California) News-Sentinel

Los Angeles Times

New York Times

Raleigh News and Observer

SOBU Newsletter

Spartanburg Herald-Journal

Spokane Spokesman-Review

Tuscaloosa News

Washington Post

Wilmington Morning Star

Wilmington Sunday Star-News

The Wilmington 10 Editorials and
    Cartoons. [New York?]: United
    Church of Christ, Commission for
    Racial Justice, 1977.

Workers Viewpoint

*Southern Historical Collection, Wilson Library, University of
North Carolina at Chapel Hill*

Ike Andrews Papers.

John Kenyon Chapman Papers.

Franklin T. Dupree Papers.

Timothy B. Tyson Papers.

State Archives of North Carolina, Raleigh

Department of Administration Papers, Human Relations Council, County File.

———, Human Relations Council, Reports File.

Judge George M. Fountain's Wilmington Ten Case File, 1971–1978.

Governor James B. Hunt Jr. Papers.

———, Office of General Counsel, Legal Counsel—Files of Jack Cozort (1977–1984).

Office of Attorney General Papers, Education and Corrections Section: Wilmington
    Ten Case File, unprocessed manuscript.

Governor Robert Scott Papers.

SECONDARY SOURCES

Amaker, Norman C. "The Faithfulness of the Carter Administration in Enforcing
    Civil Rights." In *The Presidency and Domestic Policies of Jimmy Carter*, edited
    by Herbert D. Rosenbaum and Alexej Urginsky, 737–60. Westport, Conn.:
    Greenwood Press, 1994.

Anderson, Carol. *Eyes off the Prize: The United Nations and the African American Struggle for Human Rights, 1944–1955*. New York: Cambridge University Press, 2003.

Applebome, Peter. *Dixie Rising: How the South Is Shaping American Values, Politics and Culture*. New York: Times Books, 1996.

Austin, Curtis J. *Up against the Wall: Violence in the Making and Unmaking of the Black Panther Party*. Fayetteville: University of Arkansas Press, 2006.

Barkan, Steven E. "Political Trials and the 'Pro Se' Defendant in the Adversary System." *Social Problems* 24 (1977): 324–36.

Bermanzohn, Sally Avery. *Through Survivors' Eyes: From the Sixties to the Greensboro Massacre*. Nashville: Vanderbilt University Press, 2003.

Bloom, Joshua, and Waldo E. Martin Jr. *Black against Empire: The History and Politics of the Black Panther Party*. Berkeley: University of California Press, 2013.

CBS News. "The Wilmington Ten." *60 Minutes*, 6 March 1977.

———. "The Wilmington Ten." *60 Minutes*,19 March 1978.

Cecelski, David. *Along Freedom Road: Hyde County, North Carolina, and the Fate of Black Schools in the South*. Chapel Hill: University of North Carolina Press, 1994.

Cecelski, David S., and Timothy B. Tyson, eds. *Democracy Betrayed: The Wilmington Race Riot of 1898 and Its Legacy*. Chapel Hill: University of North Carolina Press, 1998.

Chafe, William H. *Civilities and Civil Rights: Greensboro, North Carolina, and the Black Struggle for Freedom*. New York: Oxford University Press, 1981.

Cha-Jua, Sundiata Keita, and Clarence Lang. "The 'Long Movement' as Vampire: Temporal and Spatial Fallacies in Recent Black Freedom Studies." *Journal of African American History* 92 (2007): 265–88.

Chapman, Frank E., Jr. "A Black Prisoner Speaks Out." *Equity and Excellence in Education* 12 (1974): 17–18.

———. "Pages from the Life of a Black Prisoner, No. 4, 1971." In *Freedomways Reader*, edited by Esther Cooper Jackson, 259–61. Boulder, Colo.: Westview Press, 2000.

Cmiel, Kenneth. "The Emergence of Human Rights Politics in the United States." *Journal of American History* 86 (1999): 1231–50.

Cobb, Charles E. "'Behavior Modification' in the Prison System." *Black Scholar* 5 (May 1974): 41–44.

Cobb, Charles E., Jr. *This Nonviolent Stuff'll Get You Killed: How Guns Made the Civil Rights Movement Possible*. New York: Basic Books, 2014.

Countryman, Matthew J. *Up South: Civil Rights and Black Power in Philadelphia*. Philadelphia: University of Pennsylvania Press, 2006.

Dawson, Michael C. *Blacks in and out of the Left*. Cambridge, Mass.: Harvard University Press, 2013.

———. *Black Visions: The Roots of Contemporary African-American Political Thought*. Chicago: University of Chicago Press, 2001.

Dillard, Angela D. "Religion and Radicalism: The Reverend Albert B. Cleage, Jr., and the Rise of Black Christian Nationalism in Detroit." In *Freedom North: Black Freedom Struggles outside the South, 1940–1980*, edited by Komozi Woodard and Jeanne F. Theoharis, 153–75. Gordonsville, Va.: Palgrave, 2003.

Dreyer, Eric. "Vengeance and Justice in North Carolina." *Encore American and Worldwide News*, 21 June 1976, 10, 13–18.

Du Bois, W. E. B. "Does the Negro Need Separate Schools?" *Journal of Negro Education* 4 (1935): 328–35.

Elbaum, Max. *Revolution in the Air: Sixties Radicals Turn to Lenin, Mao and Che.* London: Verso, 2002.

Fascell, Dante B. "Did Human Rights Survive Belgrade?" *Foreign Policy* 31 (1978): 104–18.

Fergus, Devin. *Liberalism, Black Power, and the Making of American Politics, 1965–1980.* Athens: University of Georgia Press, 2009.

Finger, Bill. "Minorities Get the Squeeze." *North Carolina Insight*, Summer 1980, http://www.nccppr.org/drupal/content/insightarticle/944/minorities-get-the-squeeze, accessed 5 June 2013.

Frazier, Robeson Taj P. "The Congress of African People: Baraka, Brother Mao, and the Year of '74." *Souls* 8 (2006): 142–59.

French, Laurence. "The Incarcerated Black Female: The Case of Social Double Jeopardy." *Journal of Black Studies* 8 (1978): 321–35.

Galliard, Frye. *The Long Dream Deferred: The Landmark Struggle for Desegregation in Charlotte, North Carolina.* 3rd ed. Columbia: University of South Carolina Press, 2006.

Gilmore, Glenda Elizabeth. *Gender and Jim Crow: Women and the Politics of White Supremacy in North Carolina, 1896–1920.* Chapel Hill: University of North Carolina Press, 1996.

Godwin, John L. *Black Wilmington and the North Carolina Way: Portrait of a Community in the Era of Civil Rights Protest.* Lanham, Md.: University Press of America, 2000.

Graham, Gael. "Flaunting the Freak Flag: *Karr v. Schmitt* and the Great Hair Debate in American High Schools, 1965–1975." *Journal of American History* 91 (2004): 522–43.

———. *Young Activists: American High School Students in the Age of Protest.* DeKalb: Northern Illinois University Press, 2006.

Grimsley, Wayne. *James B. Hunt, a North Carolina Progressive.* Jefferson, N.C.: McFarland, 2003.

Hill, Lance. *The Deacons for Defense: Armed Resistance and the Civil Rights Movement.* Chapel Hill: University of North Carolina Press, 2004.

Horne, Gerald. *Black and Red: W. E. B. Du Bois and the Afro-American Response to the Cold War, 1944–1963.* Albany: State University of New York Press, 1986.

Hossfeld, Leslie H. *Narrative, Political Unconscious and Racial Violence in Wilmington, North Carolina.* New York: Routledge, 2005.

Janken, Kenneth Robert. *Rayford W. Logan and the Dilemma of the African-American Intellectual.* Amherst: University of Massachusetts Press, 1993.

———. *Walter White: Mr. NAACP.* Chapel Hill: University of North Carolina Press, 2006.

Johnson, Cedric. *Revolutionaries to Race Leaders: Black Power and the Making of African American Politics.* Minneapolis: University of Minnesota Press, 2007.

Jones, Charles E., ed. *The Black Panther Party Reconsidered*. Baltimore: Black Classic Press, 1998.

Jones, Patrick D. *The Selma of the North: Civil Rights Insurgency in Milwaukee*. Cambridge, Mass.: Harvard University Press, 2009.

Jordan, Milton C. "Black Legislators: From Political Novelty to Political Force." *North Carolina Insight*, December 1989, http://www.nccppr.org/drupal/content/insightarticle/599/black-legislators-from-political-novelty-to-political-force, accessed 5 June 2013.

Joseph, Peniel. *Stokely: A Life*. New York: Basic Books, 2014.

Kelley, Robin D. G., and Betsy Esch. "Black Like Mao: Red China and Black Revolution." *Souls* 1 (1999): 6–41.

Korstad, Robert R., and James L. Leloudis. *To Right These Wrongs*. Chapel Hill: University of North Carolina Press, 2010.

Lahav, Pnina. "Theater in the Courtroom: The Chicago Conspiracy Trial." *Law and Literature* 16 (Fall 2004): 381–474.

Lang, Clarence. *Grassroots at the Gateway: Class Politics and Black Freedom Struggle in St. Louis, 1936–75*. Ann Arbor: University of Michigan Press, 2009.

Lewis, David Levering Lewis. *King: A Biography*. 2nd ed. Urbana: University of Illinois Press, 1978.

Marable, Manning. *Race, Reform, and Rebellion: The Second Reconstruction and Beyond in Black America, 1945–2006*. 3rd ed. Jackson: University Press of Mississippi, 2007.

McGeehan, Charles. "Getting to the Hospital: An Overview of the Winston-Salem Black Panther Party." Honors thesis, University of North Carolina, 2009.

McGuire, Danielle L. *At the Dark End of the Street*. New York: Vintage, 2010.

McNeil, Genna Rae. "'Joanne Is You and Joanne Is Me': A Consideration of African American Women and the 'Free Joan Little' Movement, 1974–1975." In *Sisters in the Struggle: African American Women in the Civil Rights–Black Power Movement*, edited by Bettye Collier-Thomas and V. P. Franklin, 259–79. New York: NYU Press, 2001.

Meier, August, and Elliott Rudwick. "The Origins of Nonviolent Direct Action in Afro-American Protest: A Note on Historical Discontinuities." In *Along the Color Line: Explorations in the Black Experience*, 314–22. Champaign: University of Illinois Press, 2002.

Moore, Wayne. *Triumphant Warrior: A Soul Survivor of the Wilmington Ten*. Ann Arbor: Warrior Press, 2014.

Myerson, Michael. *Nothing Could Be Finer*. New York: International Publishers, 1978.

Nash, June. "The Cost of Violence." *Journal of Black Studies* 4 (1973): 153–83.

O'Reilly, Kenneth. *"Racial Matters": The FBI's Secret File on Black America, 1960–1972*. New York: Free Press, 1989.

Poinsett, Alex. *Walking with Presidents: Louis Martin and the Rise of Black Political Power*. Lanham, Md.: Madison Books, 1997.

Reed, Adolph, Jr. *Stirrings in the Jug: Black Politics in the Post-Segregation Era*. Minneapolis: University of Minnesota Press, 1999.

Rosenbaum, Herbert D., and Alexej Urginsky, eds. *The Presidency and Domestic Policies of Jimmy Carter*. Westport, Conn.: Greenwood Press, 1994.

Sanders, Randy. "'The Sad Duty of Politics': Jimmy Carter and the Issue of Race in His 1970 Gubernatorial Campaign." *Georgia Historical Quarterly* 76 (1992): 612–38. Westport, Conn.: Greenwood Press, 1994.

Schutz, J. Christopher. "'Going to Hell to Get the Devil': The 'Charlotte Three' Case and the Decline of Grassroots Activism in Charlotte, North Carolina." Ph.D. diss., University of Georgia, 1999.

Sellers, Cleveland, with Robert Terrell. *The River of No Return: The Autobiography of a Black Militant and the Life and Death of SNCC*. New York: Morrow, 1973. Reprint, Jackson: University Press of Mississippi, 1990.

Smith, Robert C. *We Have No Leaders: African Americans in the Post–Civil Rights Era*. Albany: State University of New York Press, 1996.

Thomas, Larry Reni. *Rabbit! Rabbit! Rabbit! A Fictional Account of the Wilmington Ten Incident of 1971*. Charlotte, N.C.: KHA Books, 2006.

Tyson, Timothy B. *Blood Done Sign My Name*. New York: Crown, 2004.

———. *Radio Free Dixie: Robert F. Williams and the Roots of Black Power*. Chapel Hill: University of North Carolina Press, 1999.

Umfleet, LaRae. *1898 Wilmington Race Riot Report*. Raleigh: North Carolina Department of Cultural Resources Office of Archives and History, 2006.

Umoja, Akinyele Omowale. *We Will Shoot Back: Armed Resistance in the Mississippi Freedom Movement*. New York: New York University Press, 2013.

Von Eschen, Penny M. *Race against Empire: Black Americans and Anticolonialism, 1937–1957*. Ithaca: Cornell University Press, 1997.

Waller, Signe. *Love and Revolution: A Political Memoir*. Lanham, Md.: Rowman-Littlefield, 2002.

Williams, Rhonda Y. "'Something's Wrong Down Here': Poor Black Women and Urban Struggles for Democracy." In *African American Urban History since World War II*, edited by Kenneth L. Kusmer and Joe W. Trotter, 316–36. Chicago: University of Chicago Press, 2009.

Acknowledgments

I began this book more than a decade ago. And over this time, I have amassed a great debt to archives and archivists, scholars, participants in the multiple facets of the history of Wilmington Ten, and friends and family. I am deeply grateful for all of the help I received.

The members of the Wilmington Ten are profoundly inspiring. Along with their fellow students, they took action in 1971 to obtain a meaningful and relevant education for themselves and their peers, they stood up to the local authorities who tried to bully them into submission, and they tried to ride the wave of Black Power politics that washed over North Carolina and the nation in the late 1960s and 1970s. The Wilmington Ten were chosen seemingly at random in an attempt to exact a price for the uprising that shook the city and in particular to punish Ben Chavis, who was one of North Carolina's most effective black radical political organizers. Authorities tried to get the Wilmington Ten to turn on Chavis, but heedless of the consequences to their freedom, they refused and instead stood in solidarity with him and the movement in which they participated. It was my good fortune to meet and listen to Ben Chavis, Wayne Moore, Connie Tindall, and Willie Earl Vereen; I regret not being able to connect with Joe Wright and Jerry Jacobs, who both died before I came to the project, or with Reginald Epps, James McKoy, Marvin Patrick, and Ann Shepard. Reading about and hearing how the Wilmington Ten tried to put their lives together after their incarceration and after their convictions were overturned was both angering and humbling. It was also a lesson in how to live truthfully and honorably.

David Perry, at the time the editor-in-chief of the University of North Carolina Press, saw promise in a project whose research was not completed and whose first chapter was barely through a first draft. Nevertheless, he offered an advance contract, which was greatly comforting. When he retired in early 2013—perhaps he wearied of waiting for the finished product—Brandon Proia became this book's editor. His attention to language and detail and his knowing when to apply pressure, when to leave matters to brew, and when to supply an encouraging word made him ideal to work with.

This is the first book-length scholarly history of the Wilmington Ten, and one of the first challenges was identifying and gaining access to the appropriate archives and manuscript collections. The United Church of Christ Southern Conference Papers, which are deposited at Elon University's Belk Library Archives and Special Collections, are vital for understanding the denominational dimensions to the fight to free the Wilmington Ten, but they were at the time unprocessed and stacked in a satellite warehouse. Archivist Katie Nash gladly made the collection available to me and answered my many questions. Bridgette Kelly, the archivist at the United Church of Christ headquarters, whose Commission for Racial Justice Collection was also unprocessed, graciously responded to my many e-mails and made research space for me in her building's cramped quarters. At the Moorland-Spingarn Research Center at Howard University, Joellen ElBashir leads a staff that was most helpful in guiding me through the archive's rich collections. Much of the research for this book was conducted at large public institutions that have, sadly, been operating for years with diminished resources. Their archivists and librarians have assisted me with good spirits and efficiency and often suggested collections other than the ones I had initially identified. To Tim West (and now Bryan Giemza) of the Southern Historical Collection of the University of North Carolina at Chapel Hill; Jerry Parnell of the William M. Randall Library Special Collections at the University of North Carolina at Wilmington; and the staffs of the J. Murrey Atkins Library Special Collections at the University of North Carolina at Charlotte, the State Archives of North Carolina, the Schomburg Center for Research in Black Culture of the New York Public Library, and the Gerald R. Ford and Jimmy Carter presidential libraries, I offer my deep thanks.

James Mathis at the National Archives II in College Park, Maryland, is a wizard. He kept track of my considerable number of requests under the Freedom of Information/ Privacy Act and declassified them at a rate that was faster than I had expected. He made navigating the labyrinthine rules shrouding FOI/PA requests easier. Given the reductions in the staff whose job was processing FOI/PA requests, I still felt that my requests received his full and fair attention, and without his sleuthing ability, various federal agencies' misconduct, detailed in this book, would have remained opaque. The same cannot be said for the Department of Justice, which in 2008 denied my request to interview a career attorney in the department who had worked on the Wilmington Ten case in the Carter administration. The Justice Department also took two years to fulfill a 2008 FOI/PA request to make publicly available transcripts of the Wilmington Ten proceedings in its possession. The arrogance of secrecy about a nearly forty-year-old case that took place six presidents before is still stunning.

Signe Waller Foxworth, a survivor of the Greensboro Massacre of 1979 and a prominent figure in radical and social justice struggles in North Carolina, lent me her archive of Wilmington Ten material, which was invaluable to my understanding of the later phases of the campaign to free them and of the developing Marxist-led movement. The late Dan Pollitt, Graham Kenan Professor of Law emeritus of the UNC–Chapel Hill School of Law and outstanding fighter for civil rights and civil liberties, gave me his Wilmington Ten collection, too, which was critical to my comprehension of the legal phases of the movement.

After working through the voluminous research base contained in the above-named archives and libraries, no reasonable person could doubt the enormity of the injustice suffered by the Wilmington Ten. But in Perry Mason fashion, in 2012 Timothy Tyson produced the smoking gun proving the illegal conduct of the State of North Carolina in trying the Wilmington Ten: prosecutor Jay Stroud's handwritten jury selection notes in which he stated his preference for seating members of the Ku Klux Klan and excluding African Americans. How Tim came into possession of the notes is a story worthy of his keen storytelling skills. I thank him for making them available to me and for allowing me to reproduce some of the documents for the readers of this book.

More than any project I've taken up, this history of the Wilmington Ten relies on oral histories with all manner of participants. The nearly three dozen persons who talked with me are listed in the bibliography and have my deepest admiration and thanks. Other people with firsthand knowledge of the case spoke with me only informally or chose not to speak with me at all; I respect and appreciate their decision and thank them for their time and consideration. I learned enormously from them all; collectively and individually, they revealed connections among events and new ways of understanding this important history. Wilmington native Larry Reni Thomas is a scholar of the 1898 Wilmington riot and a tireless public advocate for its victims. He performed an invaluable service to the historical profession by conducting dozens of interviews with participants in the uprising of 1971. They are deposited in the Southern Oral History Program Collection at the University of North Carolina and in the David M. Rubenstein Rare Book and Manuscript Library at Duke University. These interviews enrich our understanding of the events in Wilmington and of the development of radical African American politics in the 1960s and 1970s, as well as give us a deeper understanding of the judicial minds that so warped the legal process for the Wilmington Ten and the attainment of justice for leaders and participants in the black freedom struggle. The Southern Oral History Program at the University of North Carolina is nonpareil in its collections and is a regional, national, and international treasure.

This project was facilitated by two research and study leaves granted by the UNC College of Arts and Sciences and by the award of a Spray-Randleigh Fellowship. Along the way, I was given several opportunities to work out and test my ideas in public. The students in my undergraduate course on the Civil Rights Movement were often the first to encounter my ideas, and colleagues in the Department of African, African American, and Diaspora Studies invited me to be a guest speaker in their classes as well. Also at UNC, the Program in the Humanities and Human Values and the Center for the Study of the American South sponsored lectures on the Wilmington Ten. The Sonja Haynes Stone Center for Black Culture and History, the Institute of African American Research, the Center for the Study of the American South, and the Department of African, African American, and Diaspora Studies additionally sponsored events marking the thirty-fifth and fortieth anniversaries of the Wilmington Ten events, at which participants in the struggle shared their lives and histories. Larry Thomas was instrumental to the organizing of the anniversary events. On the fortieth anniversary, UNC–Wilmington sponsored (with Wayne Moore as a central organizer) an evening event and panel discussion with many participants in the events of February 1971; I am grateful to have been given the opportunity to be a panelist. I also thank Shelia Bumgarner of the Spangler-Robinson Carolina Room of the Charlotte-Mecklenburg Public Library, Katie Knight of the Wake County Public Library, and Tim Tyson and Mary D. Williams, who taught the YWCA of the Lower Cape Fear's course on Wilmington in Black and White, for inviting me to talk.

I have been fortunate to be connected with a community of scholars who offered criticism, provided research leads, lent support, or just listened. Over the course of my career as a professional historian, David Levering Lewis has been an outstanding mentor and friend: generous with his time, honest with his opinions, and ever the exemplar of thorough research and clear thinking. I want to thank colleagues in the

UNC Department of African, African American, and Diaspora Studies and especially Eunice Sahle, Reginald Hildebrand, and Tim McMillan, who let me talk at length about this project. UNC also has a large number of scholars under the rubric of African American and southern studies who have lent assistance and support: William L. Andrews, Al Brophy, Ken Broun, Fitz Brundage, Fatimah Jackson, Jerma Jackson, Joseph Jordan, Genna Rae McNeil, Jocelyn Neal, Richard Rosen, Harry Watson, and the staff of that gem of a place, the Center for the Study of the American South. Beyond UNC, I express my profound thanks to David Cecelski, Matthew Countryman, Kevin Gaines, Matthew Guterl, Gerald Horne, John Inscoe, Clarence Lang, Waldo Martin, Khalil Gibran Muhammad, Donna Murch, Adolph Reed, Tim Tyson, and Patricia Sullivan. Anne Miller, the editor of the *North Carolina Historical Review*, which published my overview of the Wilmington Ten, found many of the riveting photographs that are included herein. Elizabeth Hines, a geography professor at UNC–Wilmington, allowed me to use her maps of Wilmington, which form the basis for the ones in this book.

Family and friends have sustained me during the many years of this project. The Janken, Hankin, and Puglisi families created no-pressure/judgment zones to rest, eat, drink, and/or talk. Ron Ashford, Penny Chin, Tom Clark, Dr. James Evans, Signe Waller Foxworth, Glen Janken, Rhonda Klevansky, Roy Levine, Lucy Lewis, Allan Miller, and Neil Prose also took an interest in the project. Much to my sadness, several persons who played important roles in my life passed away while I was working on this book. A. Harold Janken, Harold Hankin, Ann Toma, Vince Toma, Roy Levine, Helen Klein, and Norma Marks enriched my life and the lives of other people they knew.

Pat Puglisi has been a deep source of love since we met more than thirty years ago. I don't know what I did to deserve her. On this project, as on others, she has listened to me, argued with me, and offered alternative explanations for phases in the history of the Wilmington Ten; she helped me examine my preconceptions and offered ways to make my views clearer. More important, I cannot imagine a life in which she was not at the center. Together with our children, Eric and Sophia, we four have lived, grown, and been on a terrific adventure. Every day I am thankful for it and eagerly look forward to new chapters.

Index

Page numbers in italics refer to figures.